HISTORY FOR YOU

Britain since 1700

Robert Unwin

HUTCHINSON

London Melbourne Sydney Auckland Johannesburg

For Patrick and Tessa

Acknowledgements

The Publishers' thanks are due to the following for permission to use copyright photographs:

AUEW: page 138; Austin Rover Group Ltd: page 162(I); BBC Enterprises: page 175; BBC Hulton Picture Library: pages 14(C), 31, 46, 62, 67, 84, 87, 88, 94, 106, 110, 129, 141, 146(G and H), 167, 172, 178, 179, 183(J), 185, 208, 220(D, E, F, G, H); British Airways: page 169(G and H); British Library: page 209; The Trustees of the British Museum: pages 18(A), 48, 71(left), 131; British Rail: page 154; Cambridge University Library: pages 28(G), 112; Camera Press: pages 121(foot), 220(C); CEGB: page 134(E and F); Farmers Weekly: pages 120(O), 121(top); Ford Motor Company Ltd: page 162(H); The Fotomas Index: pages 35, 68, 69, 74, 93, 108, 211; The Greater London Council Photograph Library: pages 180, 196; Hoverspeed Ltd: page 130; The Illustrated London News Picture Library: pages 151(B), 152(C), 194(B); Imperial War Museum: pages 117, 119(L and M), 165, 215(N); Ironbridge Gorge Museum: page 33; The Labour Party: page 143; London Express News and Feature Services: pages 188, 190, 220(I), 221(K and L); London Regional Transport: page 151(A); The Mansell Collection: pages 11, 18(B), 22, 28(E and I), 41, 47, 57, 60, 64, 76(D), 99, 109, 123, 156, 166(D), 204; The Marconi Company: page 173; Mary Evans Picture Library: pages 114, 152(D), 159, 164, 166(C), 182(H), 194(A), 214; Hugh McKnight Photography: page 44; Milk Marketing Board of England and Wales: page 120(N); Mirror Group Newspapers: pages 187, 189(C); The Museum of London: page 215(M); National Dairy Council: page 118; The National Maritime Museum, London: page 126; The National Maritime Museum, London and Mr David Cobb: page 128; The National Motor Museum, Beaulieu: page 157; National Museum of Labour History: page 142; The Post Office: pages 49, 219; Punch: pages 102(I), 181, 182(G), 189(D), 212, 220(J); The Royal Institution: page 132; Trustees of the Science Museum: pages 14(D), 27, 54, 55, 171; St James's University Hospital, Leeds Eastern Health Authority: page 203; Topham: page 198; Trades Union Congress Library: page 140; University of Reading, Institute of Agricultural History and Museum of English Rural Life: pages 6(E), 113; Wayland Picture Library: page 91; Josiah Wedgwood & Sons Ltd: page 42; Wellcome Institute Library, London: pages 70, 202.

The Publishers would be pleased to hear from the copyright holders of the following illustrations, whom regretfully they have been unable either to trace or to make contact with: pages 4, 6(D), 9, 16, 71(right), 76(F), 82, 100, 102(H), 127, 133, 216, 145, 191.

I wish to acknowledge the invaluable contribution made by Pat, my wife, in the preparation of this work.

Cover:
'Mr and Mrs Andrews', Thomas Gainsborough. Courtesy of the National Gallery, London and 'Shipbuilding on the Clyde: Riveters' (detail) by Stanley Spencer. Courtesy of the Trustees of the Imperial War Museum.

Hutchinson Education

An imprint of Century Hutchinson Ltd
62–65 Chandos Place, London WC2N 4NW

Century Hutchinson South Africa (Pty) Ltd
PO Box 337, Bergvlei 2012, South Africa

Century Hutchinson Australia Pty Ltd
PO Box 496, 16–22 Church Street, Hawthorn, Victoria 3122, Australia

Century Hutchinson New Zealand Ltd
PO Box 40–086, Glenfield, Auckland 10, New Zealand

First published 1986
Reprinted 1986, 1987 (twice)

© Robert Unwin 1986

Designed by Robert Wheeler

Typeset in Plantin in Helvetica

Printed and bound by Acford Ltd., Chichester

British Library Cataloguing in Publication Data

Unwin, Robert
    History for you; Britain since 1700
    I. Great Britain – History
    I. Title
    941.07 DA470

ISBN 0-09 160-921-6

Contents

During the period 1700–1850 important changes occurred in farming. The open-field system gradually gave way to enclosure of the land. Production of food and raw materials such as wool and leather was increased. Improved methods of stock-breeding produced larger animals of better quality and new kinds of farming machinery were introduced. These changes enabled farmers to produce the food needed by the rapidly growing population. By the mid-nineteenth century English farming had become the most efficient in Europe.

A *A series of pictures which summarize the main features of British farming around 1700*

■ What was the open-field system of farming?

Under the open-field system of farming which had existed for many centuries, the land in each village was divided into three or four large open (unfenced) fields. These fields were sub-divided into strips. Both the freeholders (who owned their land) and the tenants (who rented their land from a landlord) held a number of strips scattered in the open fields. The common and wasteland around each village was of great value to the village people. It was used for grazing animals and as a source of food, timber and fuel.

Q (a) Each picture has been given a number. Copy the table below and identify each picture by linking the numbers with the correct descriptions.

Main features of British farming around 1700	
Description	Number of picture
Ploughing the land	7
Sowing the seed broadcast (scattering by hand)	
Harrowing the land (levelling ploughed land and covering seed)	
Tree planting	
Bee-keeping	
Haymaking with a scythe	
Binding the sheaves after harvesting	
Carting	
Ringing a bull	
Making a fence or fold for sheep	

(b) List all the farming implements (tools) being used.
(c) In what ways do you think broadcast sowing might be wasteful?

What were the disadvantages of the open-field system?

Banks or *balks* of unploughed land separated each strip in the open fields, which was very wasteful of land. Because the fields were divided into strips the system of drainage was often in-efficient. Lack of knowledge about fertilizers meant that a system of crop rotation had to be practised to restore goodness to the land, with one of the three or four fields lying *fallow* (left unsown after ploughing) each year (**B**). This system was wasteful. It meant that there was little winter fodder (food) available for cattle, so many animals had to be slaughtered in the autumn. There were no hedges around the open fields, so much crop damage was caused by straying animals.

The villagers could not develop special breeds of animals and animal diseases spread rapidly, especially after harvest when the fields were laid open for grazing.

B *An example of the crop rotation system which left one-third of the land fallow every year.*

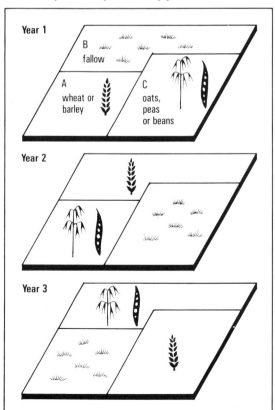

■ Early improvements in farming

Enterprising landowners

A growing number of landowners and farmers, particularly in East Anglia, experimented with new methods and introduced some of the superior techniques already practised in Holland. One such technique was the growing of clover and turnips as field crops, both of which provided extra food for the farm animals. In addition, growing turnips or clover between years of crops meant that fields no longer had to lie fallow. Clover actually enriched the soil. Turnips, because they take their nourishment from the soil at a deeper level than grain crops, allowed the top soil to refresh itself ready for the next year's corn.

Another helpful technique was to improve the soil by adding manure and marl (a mixture of clay and lime).

The Norfolk four-course rotation system

By the early eighteenth century, the Norfolk four-course rotation system was being practised on many farms, especially in East Anglia. The most important feature of this system was that instead of leaving one-third of the land fallow, *all* the fields were cultivated. Each year a different crop was grown in each field.

In the *first* year turnips or some other root crop were grown.

In the *second* year barley was sown and harvested for sale (a cash crop).

In the *third* year clover or a grass crop was grown.

In the *fourth* year wheat was grown as another cash crop.

The Norfolk system was popularized by Viscount 'Turnip' Townshend. In 1730, after a career in politics, Townshend retired to his family estate at Raynham in Norfolk, where he became known as an agricultural improver.

Changes in farming machinery

A number of improved or new machines were developed in the eighteenth century including the Rotherham plough. Jethro Tull, a Berkshire farmer, wrote a book called *Horse-Hoeing Husbandry* (1733) in which he described the development of two farming tools, the horse-drawn seed drill for sowing seed and the horse-drawn hoe for weeding the fields (**C** and **D**). However, many of his ideas, such as his opposition to manuring the land, were old-fashioned.

C *An Extract from* Horse Hoeing Husbandry

It was very difficult to find a man that could sow clover tolerably; they had a habit to throw it once with the hand to two large strides and go twice in each cast; thus with 9 or 10 lb of seed to an acre, two thirds of the ground was unplanted. To remedy this I made a hopper, to be drawn by a boy, that planted an acre sufficiently with 6 lb of seed; but when I added to this hopper an exceeding light plough that made 6 channels eight inches assunder, into which 2 lb to an acre being drilled, the ground was well planted.

Q (a) Why did Tull criticize the broadcast (scattering by hand) method of sowing seed?
(b) What did Tull invent so that seed could be sown more efficiently?
(c) What advantages did Tull claim for his method?

E *Woburn sheep-shearing festival, 1811*

his four Wheel Drill Plow with a Seed and a Manure Hopper was first Invented in the Year 174
d is now in Use with Wᵐ Ellis at Little Gaddesden near Kempstead in Hertfordshire, where any per
a light that a man may Draw it, but Generally drawn by a pony or little Hors

D *Drill plough and hopper*

Q (a) Copy out the caption on the illustration.   (b) How was the hopper of use?

Improvements in animal breeding

To improve the quality of stock, healthy male animals were mated with healthy female ones. Robert Bakewell (1725–95), who farmed at Dishley in Leicestershire, encouraged the system of controlled breeding of horses and Dishley Longhorn cattle. He chose pedigree stock selected for a particular purpose, fed and housed his animals with care, and kept elaborate tables of his results. Bakewell was most famous for his success in breeding high-quality New Leicester sheep, the average weight of which doubled within a few years. Two brothers, Charles and Robert Colling of Ketton near Darlington, developed the Durham Shorthorn breed of cattle.

■ The spread of new farming methods

One of the most effective ways of spreading the new ideas was through farming fairs and festivals. At Woburn, the estate of the Duke of Bedford, an annual sheep-shearing festival at-tracted thousands of visitors (**E**). Even better known were the Holkham gatherings held by Thomas Coke (1754–1842) at his estate at Holkham in Norfolk. Coke, later Earl of Leicester, became known for his Southdown sheep and Devon cattle. He granted long leases to his tenant farmers and this encouraged them to develop new farming methods. Local Agricultural Societies also helped to spread the new farming ideas.

King George III, who was known as 'Farmer George', set up a model farm at Windsor and wrote articles about farming methods. A successful farming journalist was Arthur Young. Although Young failed as a farmer he became a famous writer on agriculture and published detailed descriptions of farming methods. He strongly attacked the open-field system and wrote in favour of enclosure, large farms and the new farming methods, in particular the Norfolk four-course crop rotation. Young was appointed the first Secretary of the newly established Board of Agriculture in 1793.

■ Enclosure

These improvements in farming techniques usually required the enclosure of farmland. Enclosure may be described as re-organizing the land into compact farms whose fields were enclosed by hedges. By the mid-eighteenth century most pasture land and over one-half of the arable land of England and Wales was enclosed. The farming changes were carried out almost entirely by the wealthy landowners and tenant farmers.

How was enclosure carried out?

Enclosure was carried out partly by general agreement but mainly by Acts of Parliament. Between 1750 and 1850 more than 4,000 Enclosure Acts of Parliament were passed. The years of greatest activity were during the years of war against France (1793–1815), when more than 2,000 Enclosure Acts were passed.

The enclosure of the open fields, common and waste lands was usually promoted by the leading landowners. If the owners of three-quarters of the land (not, it must be noted, three-quarters of the inhabitants) agreed that enclosure was worthwhile then a Bill could be promoted in Parliament. The promoters had to tell the other farmers in the village of their proposals. To do this it was necessary to put a notice on the church door on three consecutive Sundays. Sometimes there was opposition from those who feared change and the notice might be pulled down. In more extreme cases riots might occur.

How was an Enclosure Bill passed through Parliament?

The proposals for enclosure were presented to Parliament in the form of a petition (a written request) and a Bill (the proposed details set down in legal language). In the House of Commons a committee of MPs would consider the details of the proposal. If Parliament agreed with the Bill, it would become law as an Act. Parliament then appointed a number of commissioners to go to the village in question, map out the land, check all claims and re-allocate it. The commissioners had to settle any differences about such matters as fencing, pasture and the ownership of the woodland, common and waste land.

Who gained as a result of enclosure?

The large landowners and large tenant farmers benefited from enclosure, especially during the years 1793–1815 when wheat prices and land rents were high. The profits from farming provided money for investment both in agriculture and in other areas of the economy, for example transport.

How did enclosure affect the smaller farmers?

The effects of enclosure on the smaller landowners and poorer tenant farmers varied. Although many profited during the war years, when food prices were high, they suffered hardship after 1815 when food prices fell. During the years of post-war depression many smaller landowners and tenants were forced to leave the land.

How did enclosure affect the poorer villagers?

The cottagers and squatters, those villagers who had the least right to land, suffered most from the enclosure of fields and the break-up of waste and common land. Enclosure resulted in the use of more efficient farming methods and machinery which brought unemployment and hardship to many farm labourers.

The worst poverty existed among farm labourers in the south, and hardship increased with the widespread use of the threshing machine from the 1820s. This machine, invented by Andrew Meikle in 1786, separated the wheat from the chaff, a task previously performed by hand and providing work in the winter. Severe poverty and the fear of unemployment led to the Swing Riots (1830) in a number of counties (**F**). The labourers demanded higher wages and the destruction of the threshing machine. The riots were harshly put down; nine rioters were hanged and 450 transported to Australia. By that time, many farm labourers had moved to the growing towns or had emigrated (gone to live in another country).

■ Results of the changes in farming

1 Changes in agriculture enabled British farmers to produce more food for the growing population.

2 More winter food for cattle meant that fewer animals had to be killed off in the autumn. A greater supply of fresh meat was therefore available throughout the year and this greatly benefited the diet of the people.
3 The enclosure of land and the end of the open-field system enabled improved farming methods to spread more rapidly and more land to be cultivated.
4 The social effects were less favourable and the divisions between the social classes in the countryside widened.

■ **Was there an agricultural revolution?**
By the early nineteenth century farming was becoming larger in scale with greater investment of money as enclosures and the new scientific methods became more widespread. However, the changes took place gradually and new ideas and methods spread only slowly. It is therefore probably more accurate to say that the period was one of 'agricultural *evolution*' rather than one of 'agricultural *revolution*'.

Sir
This is to acquaint you that if your thrashing Machines are not destroyed by you directly we shall commence our labours signed on behalf of the whole
Swing

F *A letter sent during the Swing Riots*

Q (a) Copy the letter into your book.
(b) Who do you think would send such a letter?
(c) To whom would it be sent?
(d) What was the writer of the letter asking for?

QUESTIONS

1 (a) Why was it necessary to increase the amount of food produced during the period 1700–1850?
(b) How did farmers try to increase the yield of the land?
(c) What was enclosure and how did it affect village life?
2 Look at diagram **B**, then answer the following questions.
(a) Why was one-third of the land left fallow each year?
(b) What was the reason for the different use of the fields each year?
(c) What were the main disadvantages of the fallow system?
(d) How did the Norfolk four-course rotation differ from the fallow system?
3 (a) When did the threshing machine come into general use?
(b) Why did some labourers oppose the introduction of threshing machines?

4 Study picture **E**, then write a description of how a visiting farmer might have spent a day at the Woburn sheep-shearing festival. Here are some topics you might like to mention:
annual festival; Duke of Bedford; tenant farmers; Woburn Abbey; visitors from England and abroad; country people of all classes.
5 Copy the chart below. Fill in details of all the agricultural improvements during the period 1700–1850 which are mentioned in the chapter.

Agricultural improvements, 1700–1850		
Date	Improvement	Person associated with improvement
Late 17th century	Four-course rotation introduced from Holland	
	(to be completed)	

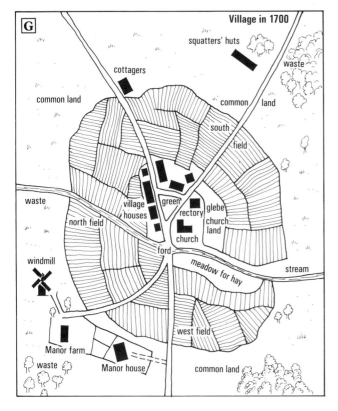

G Village in 1700

squatters' huts

waste

cottagers

common land

common land

south field

waste

village houses

green

glebe

rectory

church land

north field

church

ford

windmill

meadow for hay

stream

west field

Manor farm

waste

Manor house

common land

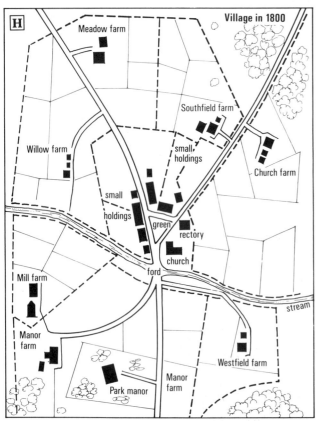

H Village in 1800

Meadow farm

Willow farm

Southfield farm

small holdings

Church farm

small holdings

green

rectory

Mill farm

church

ford

Manor farm

stream

Manor farm

Westfield farm

Park manor

-------- boundaries of new holding

6 Write a short paragraph on each of the following questions.
   (a) Why were new farming methods essential in the period 1700–1850?
   (b) Was there, in your opinion, an 'agricultural revolution'? Explain your answer.

7 Study illustration **G** carefully, then answer the following questions using the text also.
   (a) How many arable fields were there in this village?
   (b) How were the strips separated from each other?
   (c) Where did the lord of the manor live?
   (d) How did part of his land appear different from that held by the majority of the villagers?
   (e) The parish church often had land which the local vicar farmed. This was called church land or . . . .
   (f) What benefits would come from having a river running through the village?
   (g) Where were the meadows situated and what was grown on them?
   (h) How was arable and meadow land distributed between the people of the village?
   (i) What were the main disadvantages of this system of farming?
   (j) Why was the common land important to the villagers and squatters? List the main uses of the common land.
   (k) Why might the waste land have been important to the poor of the village?
   (l) Were there any advantages in this system of farming?

8 Now study illustration **H**.
   (a) List the main changes that can be observed in the village by 1800.
   (b) What had happened to the strips?
   (c) How many new compact farms were there?
   (d) Suggest how *four* of the farms got their names.
   (e) How did the changes affect the lord of the manor and the church?
   (f) What had happened to the common and waste land?
   (g) Who appears to have gained most from the changes?
   (h) Who appears to have suffered most from the changes?
   (i) In a maximum of *ten* words state what had happened to the village between 1700 and 1800.

2 Textiles

In 1700 the making of woollen cloth was the most important British industry. In contrast, the amount of cotton manufactured was small. However, between 1750 and 1850 cotton took over from wool as Britain's most important industry, and developments in the manufacture of cotton textiles were largely responsible for the change from cottage industry to the factory system. Unlike the cotton industry, which developed rapidly with the introduction of new machinery, the woollen industry changed more slowly and was also less willing to adopt new inventions.

■ The woollen industry

Where and how was woollen cloth produced in the early eighteenth century?

In 1700 there were three important regions for woollen manufacture, namely East Anglia, the West Country and the West Riding of Yorkshire.

In East Anglia and the West Country, the industry was organized by wealthy clothiers who bought raw wool and distributed it to the cottages of the spinners (usually women) and weavers (usually men). These merchant clothiers arranged for the sale of the finished cloth. This system of producing woollen cloth in the homes of the country people was called the *domestic system* (**A**).

In the West Riding woollen industry, the situation was different. Here the clothier was usually a farmer-weaver who employed a few assistants in a workshop and a team of spinners in the village. The raw wool was thoroughly washed or *scoured*, combed or *carded* (in which the fibres were untangled or straightened) and spun (in which the fibres were twisted together using a spinning wheel to make a continuous thread) under the domestic system. The cloth was then woven either in the cottages or workshops. When the pieces of cloth were ready, the weavers took them to large cloth halls in towns such as Leeds, Halifax and Wakefield (**B**), to sell to the merchants. The merchants usually controlled the finishing processes which were: 1 *fulling* (thickening by beating the cloth in a water-powered mill with water and a chemical called *fuller's earth*); 2 *stretching* (on frames called *tenter frames*); 3 *cropping* (raising the cloth fibres and trimming with shears to improve the quality); 4 *dyeing*.

Q Write two paragraphs, drawing out the most important points of information in picture **A**. You should include details of the processes being carried out, the people carrying out the activities, and living conditions in the cottage.

A *The 'domestic system'*

B *An extract from* A Tour through the Whole Island of Great Britain *by Daniel Defoe*

. . . the nearer we came to Hallifax, we found the Houses thicker and the Villages greater. . . . the People were generally employ'd in . . . the Clothing Trade, . . . two Things essential to the Business . . . are found here . . . Coals and running Water . . . almost at every House there was a Tenter, and almost on every Tenter a Piece of Cloth . . . at every considerable House was a Manufactory or Work-House, and as they could not do their Business without Water, the little Streams were so parted and guided by Gutters or Pipes . . . that none of those Houses were without a River, if I may call it so, running into and through their Work-Houses. . . . Dying-Houses, Scouring-Shops and Places where they used this Water . . .

Every Clothier must keep a Horse, perhaps two, to fetch and carry for the use of his Manufacture . . . to fetch home his Wooll and his Provisions from the Market, to carry his yarn to the Spinners, his Manufacture to the Fulling Mill, and, when finished, to the Market to be sold . . . Among the Manufacturers Houses are . . . scattered an infinite Number of Cottages or small Dwellings, in which dwell the Workmen which are employed, the Women and Children of whom, are always busy Carding, Spinning . . . so that no Hands being unemploy'd all can gain their Bread, even from the youngest to the antient. . . . This brought me from the Villages where this Manufacture is wrought, to the Market where it is sold, which is at Leeds. These Goods, as well here as at Wakefield and at Hallifax, are . . . disposed of . . . for the home Consumption . . . also very great quantities . . . for exportation.

On account of this trade . . . an Act of Parliament was obtained for making the Rivers Aire and Calder navigable from Leeds and Wakefield to Hull.

Q (a) Which woollen-cloth-producing region is described in extract **B**?
(b) Which two things were essential to cloth manufacture?
(c) How had the local streams been adapted for the use of the industry?
(d) Why did the Halifax clothiers find it necessary to keep at least one horse?
(e) Which processes were carried out by the women and children in the cottages?
(f) Can you explain the phrase 'all can gain their Bread'?
(g) Which towns in Yorkshire were noted for the marketing of woollen cloth?
(h) How would the improvement of river navigation assist the growth of the Yorkshire woollen industry?

Why did the woollen industry become concentrated in the West Riding of Yorkshire?

The advantages of concentrating the woollen industry in the West Riding included water power, cheap labour, plentiful supplies of coal, and water transport. By the end of the eighteenth century the West Riding had become the most important woollen and worsted (high quality woollen cloth) manufacturing region, while East Anglia and the West Country had declined in importance.

Why was the woollen industry slow to adopt mechanization?

1   Machinery was useful for the manufacture of textiles on a large scale and required larger amounts of raw material. There were difficulties in increasing the supply of raw wool and the situation did not greatly improve until sheep farming developed in Australia in the nineteenth century.

2   Wool is a softer fibre than cotton and often broke on the early textile machines.

3   Some woollen manufacturers were reluctant to change their ways. Some groups of workers, fearing unemployment, blocked attempts to introduce new machinery. Some textile machines were smashed by displaced hand-workers called the Luddites (see page 97).

The domestic system survived for many years and the manufacture of woollens did not become a complete factory industry until the 1870s.

■ The cotton industry

The rise of the Lancashire cotton industry

The cotton industry was founded in Lancashire in the seventeenth century and produced yarn or thread which was usually mixed with either linen or wool to produce a cloth known as *fustian*.

Raw cotton from the East Indies and the West Indies was imported through the Lancashire port of Liverpool. Linen yarn was imported from Ireland and flax for linen was grown in Lancashire.

How was cotton manufactured?

The merchant clothiers had the raw cotton and linen distributed to domestic cottage workers. In the cottages, women and children carried out the processes of carding and spinning. The climate of Lancashire was suitable for the cotton spinning process because the damp atmosphere reduced the likelihood of the thread breaking.

The spun yarn was then woven on a machine called a loom. Two kinds of thread, called warp and weft, were needed for this process. The warp threads were stretched vertically across the frame of the loom. The weaver then crossed the weft threads horizontally over the warp threads by passing a shuttle by hand across the frame of the loom. The fact that the shuttle was passed over by hand meant that the width of cloth a man could weave was limited by the length of his arms.

After weaving, the cloth was returned to the merchant clothier who usually owned dye and bleaching houses where the finishing processes were carried out. Many of these processes required soft, lime-free water, water power and coal for heating purposes. Lancashire had excellent resources for all these industrial activities.

Why did the demand for cotton increase?

1　To protect the English woollen industry, Parliament banned the import or the wearing of pure cotton fabrics. However, this ban did not prevent the wearing of cotton mixtures such as fustians, and so the Lancashire cotton industry was unharmed. It was also able to operate without foreign competition.

2　Cotton was an attractive alternative to wool because it was lighter, could be washed more easily, and produced more cheaply. The public were therefore eager for cotton textiles.

■ The textile inventions

The work of John Kay

In 1733 John Kay of Bury in Lancashire made a 'flying shuttle' for weaving. The shuttle could be moved from side to side by pulling on a cord. This meant that broadcloth (cloth made to a wide measure) could be woven by one weaver without the help of an assistant. There was much opposition among weavers who feared unemployment and the use of the flying shuttle did not become widespread until the 1760s.

The use of the flying shuttle made it difficult for the spinners to keep the weavers supplied with enough yarn. An invention to speed up spinning was therefore desperately needed.

The supply of raw cotton

Another invention which helped in the development of the cotton industry was Eli Whitney's 'gin'. This American machine speeded up the cleaning of raw cotton on the plantations and so Britain was able to import increased amounts.

Hargreaves' Spinning Jenny

The world's first successful spinning machine was patented in 1770 by James Hargreaves, a weaver and carpenter of Blackburn in Lancashire (**C–F**). Hargreaves' first Spinning Jenny could spin eight threads at a time instead of just the one on a traditional spinning wheel. This number was soon increased to 120. The machine was not expensive and it could be worked by hand. The Spinning Jenny fitted easily into a cottage. Fearing that the new Jenny might take their work away, a number of workers broke into Hargreaves' house in Blackburn and destroyed his machines.

Gradually the machines came into general use. The main disadvantage of the Spinning Jenny was that the yarn it produced was not strong enough to be used as warp thread. Some way of producing stronger yarn was needed.

C *Spinning on one-thread wheels*

E *from Ree's* (Cyclopaedia) (1808)

A number of young people were one day . . . at play in Hargreaves' house . . . and the wheel at which he or some of his family were spinning, was by accident overturned. The thread still remained in the hand of the spinner, and . . . the spindle continued to revolve as before. Hargreaves . . . continued again and again to turn round the wheel as it lay on the floor . . . He had before attempted to spin with two or three spindles affixed to the ordinary wheel, holding the several threads between the fingers of his left hand, but the horizontal position of the spindles rendered this attempt ineffectual; it is not therefore improbable that he derived from the circumstances above-mentioned the first idea of that machine which paved the way for subsequent improvement.

F

HARGREAVES' PATENT (No. 962), 1770
I had, after . . . many trials . . . at last invented and brought to perfection a method of making a wheel . . . of an entire new construction (and never before made use of), in order for spinning, drawing and twisting of cotton, and to be managed by one person only . . . the wheel . . . will spin, draw and twist sixteen or more threads at one time . . . .

D *Hargreaves' Spinning Jenny*

Q Consider the story about James Hargreaves' invention of the Spinning Jenny (Source **E**). Using *all* the sources **C**–**F** do you agree:
  (a) that Hargreaves got the idea of the Jenny from this event?
OR (b) that it is highly unlikely that an accident in the home would lead to a successful invention?
OR (c) that there is insufficient evidence to make a judgement?
Give reasons for your answer.

The water frame

In the 1760s Richard Arkwright, a barber and wig-maker of Preston in Lancashire hired a skilled mechanic, Thomas Highs, to construct a machine, and in 1769 Arkwright patented the water frame. Like most of the inventions he patented, the water frame was not Arkwright's own discovery but, as a successful businessman, he saw the advantages of developing an effective spinning machine which could produce a strong yarn suitable for warp thread as well as for weft. Although the yarn produced by Arkwright's water frame was coarse and uneven at first, its introduction had important effects on the organization of the cotton industry.

Water power and the early cotton factories

Arkwright's water frame was large and needed a fast-flowing stream to drive it. Arkwright, who is often regarded as the founder of the factory system, built a water-powered mill at Cromford in Derbyshire in 1771, in partnership with a wealthy stocking manufacturer, Jedediah Strutt (**G**). He also built a village to house his workers.

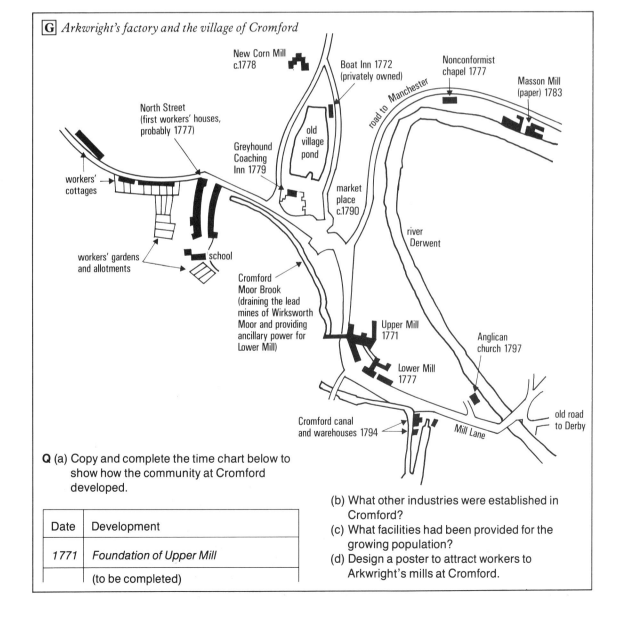

G *Arkwright's factory and the village of Cromford*

Q (a) Copy and complete the time chart below to show how the community at Cromford developed.

Date	Development
1771	*Foundation of Upper Mill*
	(to be completed)

(b) What other industries were established in Cromford?
(c) What facilities had been provided for the growing population?
(d) Design a poster to attract workers to Arkwright's mills at Cromford.

H *Advertisement which appeared in Bolton, Lancashire in the early nineteenth century*

Q What did the mill owners offer to persuade spinners to apply for jobs?

Between 1770 and 1785 a number of new cotton-spinning mills were established. They were sited near fast-flowing streams and depended on water power. They were often located in remote river valleys in Lancashire, Derbyshire, Nottinghamshire, North Wales and Scotland. Such places were a long way from the ports where the raw cotton was landed; far from the towns which could provide the labour force for spinning; and far from the main marketing centres, where cloth could be sold.

Changing location of the cotton industry

In 1785 steam power was used at a cotton-spinning mill at Papplewick in Nottinghamshire. The industry was no longer dependent on water power, so many of the later cotton factories were built in or near towns. The cotton industry became increasingly concentrated in south Lancashire and the rapidly growing towns of Liverpool and Manchester became major marketing centres. Further north, Clydeside and the area around Glasgow became noted for cotton manufacture.

The development of fine cotton spinning

In 1779 another spinning machine, the mule, was invented by a Bolton weaver, Samuel Crompton. The mule combined the best features of the Spinning Jenny and the water frame. It produced a strong, fine, even yarn, suitable for both warp and weft, and capable of producing material of a very high quality. At first the mule was worked by hand in the cottages, but soon water power and later steam power were applied and the machine was used in factories (**H**).

The mechanization of other textile processes

The improvement of the spinning process forced changes in the other stages of cotton manufacture. In 1775 Arkwright patented a carding machine using rollers.

In 1783 Thomas Bell patented a device for printing using revolving cylinders, instead of by hand. Dyes manufactured from minerals gradually replaced vegetable dyes. In the 1790s the industry began to use chlorine bleaching powders.

The introduction of the power loom

The increased supply of spun yarn from the new spinning machinery meant that, for a time at least, the handloom weavers were kept busy and earned high wages. Improvements in the weaving process were slow, partly because the loom was a complex machine. Edmund Cartwright, a clergyman, patented a power loom for weaving in 1785. However, this had to be improved before it was suitable for use in factories. The power loom was not widely used by manufacturers until after 1825.

■ Cotton: 'The Wonder of the Age'

1 Between 1750 and 1850 cotton became the most important British manufacturing industry.

2 New machinery greatly improved the efficiency of the cotton industry which was quicker than the woollen industry to adopt new methods.

3 Cotton goods replaced woollens as the most valuable export.

4 By 1850 nine-tenths of all cotton mills were steam-powered and the handloom weaver had almost ceased to exist.

QUESTIONS

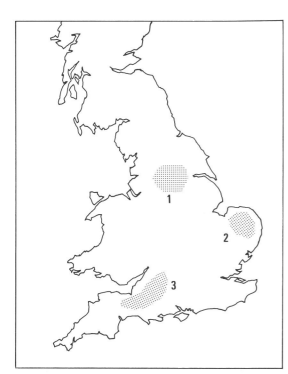

1 The outline map of England and Wales above indicates three areas. Name each one and state what they have in common.

2 What name was given to the system of producing woollen cloth in people's homes?

3 (a) How was the woollen cloth industry organized in East Anglia and the West Country?

(b) Copy and complete this diagram about the woollen industry.

Merchant clothier

bought	distributed	sold
?	?	?
from	to	to
?	?	?

4 (a) How did the woollen industry of the West Riding of Yorkshire differ from that of East Anglia and the West Country?

(b) For what reasons did the West Riding become the most important woollen manufacturing region by the end of the eighteenth century?

5 Explain in your own words why the woollen industry was slow to introduce changes.

6 Match up the names on the left with the correct phrase from the right.

Carding   crossing of warp and weft
Spinning   fulling, stretching, cropping, dyeing
Finishing   twisting fibres to form a continuous
processes   yarn
Weaving   straightening the fibres

7 (a) Copy and complete this chart to show the principal textile inventions and developments.

The development of the textile industry		
Date	1733	
Invention	Flying shuttle	
Inventor	John Kay	
First used or patented	1733	
Location	Bury, Lancs	
Process	Weaving	
Advantages	(to be completed)	
Disadvantages		

(b) Which of the inventions do you think was the most important? Explain your answer.

8

Value of textile products (in £ million)		
	1770s	1830s
Woollens	8	17
Linen	2	5
Silk	1	6
Cotton	1	22
	12	50

Write a short essay comparing and contrasting the growth of the woollen and cotton industries (see table above). Here are some topics you might like to mention:
shortage of raw wool; woollen manufacturers reluctant to change their ways; the public eager for cotton textiles; Eli Whitney's gin; textile inventions.

3 Reform of factory conditions

Working conditions under the domestic system were bad, but under the factory system they were even worse. Conditions varied from area to area, and from industry to industry. Long hours were worked, often in poor or dangerous conditions, and the employment of women and children was common (**A** and **B**). It took many years to bring about reform in factory conditions, for Parliament and the Government were reluctant to place restrictions on factory owners. Eventually, in the face of strong opposition, Parliament passed a number of Acts to regulate conditions in the factories.

A *The domestic system – working at home*

B *A cotton factory in the 1840s*

Q (a) What do illustrations **A** and **B** show?
   (b) Make a list of all the differences in the working conditions which you can find in the illustrations.
   (c) How do you account for the differences?
   (d) Are there any similarities in the two scenes?
   (e) How might the picture sources assist an historian trying to reconstruct what working conditions were like in the Industrial Revolution?
   (f) What problems does the evidence pose for the historian?

■ The development of the factory system

The early factories

The introduction of machines worked by water-power and later by steam-power led to the concentration of workers in mills and factories. As early as 1717 Thomas Lombe set up a water-powered silk factory on an island in the river Derwent at Derby. In 1771 Richard Arkwright set up his cotton-spinning mill at Cromford, and after 1780 many large water-driven factories for spinning cotton were built.

Each factory employed several hundred people, many of them children. Because these early factories were often built in isolated places, some mill owners had pauper (poor) children sent from the workhouses (see page 79) in London and the south-east of England, to work for them.

The introduction of steam power for cotton spinning made it possible to build factories in the towns, since they were no longer dependent upon fast flowing streams.

The employment of children continued in the town factories. By the early 1830s nearly 250,000 workers were employed in cotton factories, of whom one in eight were aged under 13 years and three out of ten were aged between 13 and 18 years.

What were working conditions like in the factories?

Factories were usually planned to make use of the new machines with little regard for the health or safety of the workers. Bad ventilation and the damp atmosphere of spinning mills led to diseases, such as factory fever which was similar to typhus. Many factories had working days of fifteen hours or more. The long hours, often worked in cramped positions and with unguarded machinery, sometimes led to permanent deformities.

Mill owners sometimes made agreements with the head of a family for the employment of the whole family. The majority of parents were easily persuaded to send their children to the mills, because they needed their earnings. Discipline was largely imposed on the children by their own parents which made the harshness of the factory system more acceptable.

Why was factory reform necessary?

Sometimes, mill owners put overseers in charge of the workers. Overseers were paid according to the amount of work produced by the women and children employed under them. Thus hours were long and children – especially paupers – were often cruelly exploited (taken advantage of). Even well-meaning employers regularly made children aged seven and upwards work from 6 a.m. to 7 p.m. with only one hour off for meals. Although wages were usually higher in factories than under the domestic system, many workers disliked the discipline of factory working and the loss of independence. The factory owners imposed fines for lateness, talking at work, or even opening a window. Some factory owners operated a 'truck' system whereby workers were paid in goods or tokens instead of money. The tokens could be exchanged for goods only in the employer's own 'truck' or 'tommy' shop, where prices were high.

A factory reformer: Robert Owen

Robert Owen was born in Wales in 1771. He attended a local school and later served as pupil-teacher at Newtown. At the age of ten he left home to seek his fortune, but spent the next eight years as an assistant in drapery shops.

In 1799 Owen became general manager and part owner of David Dale's New Lanark Mills in Scotland. Dale had built the New Lanark cotton-spinning Mills and had apprenticed 500 children from the workhouses of Edinburgh. To accommodate the children he had built a settlement at New Lanark and provided low-rent houses to attract adults.

At the New Lanark Mills, Robert Owen demonstrated how manufacturers should look after the welfare of their workers. Working hours were reduced to ten-and-a-half hours per day, wages were raised and were paid even when workers were sick. He also stopped children under the age of ten from working. Owen's intention was not just to provide better working conditions but also to create a favourable living environment for his workers. Out of the surplus profits made at New Lanark, Owen improved sanitation in the existing houses and built new rows of dwellings for his workers. Schools were provided for the younger children, a grocery store was opened to sell essential goods at cost price and a communal wash-house was built.

The beginning of factory reform
Robert Owen was one of the first to publicize the evils of the factory system. Together with Sir Robert Peel the elder, another enlightened cotton manufacturer, Owen promoted Acts of Parliament in 1802 and 1819 which were designed to limit the working hours of children, especially pauper apprentices. However, there was to be no inspection of the factories and therefore the Acts were not effective.

Many manufacturers argued that factory reform would ruin trade and put them at a disadvantage with foreign competitors. Thus, although some people admired Owen and the enlightened factory owners, only a few manufacturers were prepared to follow their lead.

The changing nature of factory employment
The introduction of automatic spinning mules and effective power looms in the later 1820s broke the tradition of family employment. When discipline and standards of work were imposed by foremen and managers, rather than by family groups, working conditions became intolerable. It was argued that factories disrupted family life and led to the loss of independence. Factory discipline and insistence on punctuality, were disliked by workers who were used to the relative freedom of the domestic system. For some workers the factories represented the final break of their links with the land.

■ The Ten-Hour Movement
From the 1830s the demand for factory reform came increasingly from the workers themselves. Meetings were organized to press for the reduction of the working day.

Outside of Parliament, the movement for a shorter working day, the so-called Ten-Hour Movement (C, D and E), was led by Richard Oastler, a Yorkshire land agent. In 1830 Oastler published a series of letters in a newspaper, the *Leeds Mercury*, under the title of 'Yorkshire Slavery', which shocked the public. Oastler argued that the child workers in the textile mills of Yorkshire were treated worse than West Indian slaves, and that if it was right to cam-

paign against slavery then it was also right to campaign for factory reform. In the cotton areas of Lancashire, the factory reform movement was encouraged by John Fielden.

The Factory Act, 1833
In Parliament, the reformers had the support of a number of Tory MPs, especially Michael Sadler and Anthony Ashley Cooper (later Lord Shaftesbury). Ashley Cooper was concerned with improving the conditions of life for working children, including 'climbing boys' (sweeps who were sent up chimneys). He also encouraged 'Ragged Schools' (schools for poor children).

In 1832 a Select Committee was appointed to examine factory conditions. Its published Report aroused public opinion in favour of some regulation of factory labour, although there was strong opposition from those who wanted factory owners to be left alone to get on with their own business. However, the Whig government decided to introduce a Bill in Parliament. After a major Parliamentary battle, the Althorp Act (taking its name from the Home Secretary at the time) was passed in 1833.

Under its terms (which applied to all textile mills except silk) no children under 9 years of age were to be employed; children between 9 and 13 years were to work a maximum of nine hours per day and to attend school for two hours daily; and young persons between 13 and 18 years were not to be employed for more than twelve hours per day. Young persons under 18 years of age were not to be employed in night work. In an attempt to ensure that the terms of the Act were obeyed, four factory inspectors were appointed.

How successful was the 1833 Factory Act?
It is sometimes claimed that Althorp's Act of 1833 was the first effective factory reform, enforced by government inspectors. However, the provisions were often evaded and the Act was a disappointment to those reformers who wanted a ten-hour day. The number of inspectors appointed at first was very small and the lack of compulsory registration of births and deaths made it very difficult to tell the ages of the child workers.

C *Richard Oastler to editor of* Leeds Mercury, *16 October 1830*

Let the truth speak out . . . . Thousands of our fellow-creatures and fellow-subjects, both male and female, the inhabitants of a Yorkshire town . . . are at this very moment existing in a state of slavery more horrid than are the victims of that hellish system – 'Colonial Slavery'. . . . The very streets which receive the droppings of an 'Anti-Slavery Society' are every morning wet by the tears of innocent victims at the accursed shrine of avarice, who are compelled, not by the cart-whip of the negro slave-driver, but by the dread of the equally appalling thong or strap of the overlooker, to hasten half-dressed, but not half-fed, to those magazines of British Infantile Slavery – the Worsted Mills in the town and neighbourhood of Bradford!

Thousands of little children both male and female, but principally female from seven to fourteen years, are daily compelled to labour, from six o'clock in the morning to seven in the evening with only – Britons, blush whilst you read it! – with only thirty minutes allowed for eating and recreation . . . .

D *From* The Philosophy of Manufacture *by A. Ure, MD (Doctor of Medicine) (1835)*

I have visited many factories, entering the spinning rooms, unexpectedly, and often alone, at different times of the day, and I never saw a single instance of corporal chastisement inflicted on a child, nor indeed did I ever see children in ill-humour. They seemed to be always cheerful and alert, taking pleasure in the light play of their muscles . . . . The work of these lively elves seemed to resemble a sport, in which habit gave them a pleasing dexterity. As to exhaustion by the day's work, they evinced no trace of it on emerging from the mill in the evening; for they immediately began to skip about any neighbouring playground and to commence their little amusements with the same alacrity as boys issuing from school.

E *From* An Economic and Social History of Britain since 1700 *by M. W. Flinn (1975)*

For the worker there were both bad and good features about factory employment. The factories were often able to offer more attractive wages than those earned by the workers in the competing domestic industries. But once inside the factory the worker became a slave to the machine. The result of long hours of work tending machinery in a mill was often deformity, disease or proneness to rheumatic or internal complaints. But perhaps the most serious indictment of the early factories was the excessive use they made of child labour.

Q (a) Of the three sources, **C**, **D** and **E**, which are primary and which are secondary? Give reasons for your answer.
  (b) How do you account for the differences between the sources concerning working conditions in the factories?
  (c) What would you look for in a 'balanced' piece of evidence?
  (d) Where could you find additional information to help you decide which of the sources was nearest to the truth?
  (e) Which source seems to be least biased? Explain your answer.

Q Look at picture **F** on page 22. Does the way the children are shown in the illustration support the views of Richard Oastler (source **C**) or of Dr Ure (source **D**)? Give reasons for your answer.

F *Factory children in the early nineteenth century*

However, the Registration Act (1836) which provided for the official recording of births and deaths greatly assisted the factory inspectors as they now could check on children's ages. The annual reports of the inspectors showed that manufacturers were not ruined when the terms of the Act were properly carried out.

The 1844 Factory Act

This Act was passed largely through the efforts of Lord Shaftesbury. Under its terms, children from 8 to 13 years were not to work more than six-and-a-half hours a day, with three hours' compulsory schooling. Women were to work a maximum of twelve hours per day. Machinery was to be fenced and was not to be cleaned while still in motion. However, the Act did not satisfy the reformers because a clause to include the ten-hour day was rejected by Parliament.

The ten-hour day established

In the 1840s John Fielden became the leader of the factory reform movement. In 1847 an Act was passed which limited the hours of work for women and young persons in textile factories to 58 per week, with a maximum of ten on any one day. It was impossible to run textile factories for long hours without the work of women and children. The mill owners got round this by organizing the work in relays or shifts. This meant that the men were still forced to work fifteen or sixteen hours per day.

Further Acts of 1850 and 1853 fixed the times at which the mills might remain open, and effectively established the ten-hour day.

■ The effects of factory reform on the textile industry

1 Despite the arguments of the manufacturers against reform, the Factory Acts and the improvement of working conditions did not ruin the textile industries.
2 The mid-nineteenth century was a period of remarkable industrial progress and the opposition of factory owners gradually faded.
3 Partly through mechanization, each reduction of working hours was followed by increased output.
4 However, until the mid-nineteenth century, the Factory Acts applied only to the textile mills.

QUESTIONS

A Multiple choice Choose the correct answer for each question and write it into your book.

1 In the early nineteenth century it became necessary to pass laws against the 'truck' system, which was a common feature in many factories, in order to:
(a) prohibit the use of ponies in coal mines;
(b) prohibit the payment of wages in tokens exchangeable only at the 'tommy shop';
(c) prevent the use of small mobile platforms to move goods round the factory;
(d) prevent workers being dismissed for unpunctuality.

2 What name was given to machine breakers in the early nineteenth century:
(a) Peelites; (b) Radicals; (c) Fabians; (d) Luddites; (e) Chartists?

3 The earliest factory legislation applied to:
(a) chimney sweepers;
(b) women in sweated trades;
(c) pauper apprentices; (d) married men.

4 Factory reforms were introduced at the New Lanark Mills by (a) Richard Arkwright; (b) Robert Peel; (c) Robert Owen; (d) William Wilberforce.

5 The Factory Act of 1833 was largely the work of Lord Althorp. The Act: (a) banned the employment of women in coal mines;
(b) insisted on improved safety standards in factories;
(c) prohibited the use of children under 9 years of age in textile mills;
(d) restricted the working hours of men to a ten-hour day.

6 The 1833 Factory Act was more effective than previous attempts to regulate factory conditions because it: (a) required the fencing of machinery;
(b) made provision for women as well as children;
(c) provided for government inspectors to enforce the Act; (d) applied to all textile factories.

7 A Tory MP who tried to introduce a ten-hour day for factory workers was (a) the Duke of Wellington; (b) Benjamin Disraeli; (c) Anthony Ashley Cooper.

8 The first effective legislation on textile factory conditions for *all* children was passed in: (a) 1802; (b) 1833; (c) 1844; (d) 1847.

9 The first Factory Act to make provision for adult workers was passed in: (a) 1819; (b) 1833; (c) 1844; (d) 1847.

B

1 In your own words, explain what the 'Ten-Hour Movement' was.

2 Copy and complete the chart below to show the progress of factory reform in the textile industries.

3 You are a newspaper reporter in 1830. Write a short article for your newspaper about the factory system, the employment of women and children, and working conditions. Suggest ways in which conditions might be improved by employers and by the Government.

Factories and factory reform				
Date of Act of Parliament	Reformers	Main terms	Benefits	Weaknesses
1802	Robert Peel (the elder) and Robert Owen	To limit the working hours of children		No inspectors to enforce it
	(to be	completed)		

4 The coal industry

By the early eighteenth century, a number of industries were beginning to use coal as fuel. Before that time, coal had been used mainly in the home. Surface mining was common, the pits were often small and about 2 million tons of coal was produced annually. By 1850 the output of coal had risen to more than 60 million tons per annum, the collieries were much larger and deeper, and many more industries were using coal. The rapid expansion of the British coal industry led to the employment of a large number of workers in the mines, many of whom were women and children. The conditions in which they worked were bad and often dangerous. Parliament eventually agreed to regulate (make rules for) working in the mines.

■ The demand for coal

Why did the demand for coal increase?

1 During the period 1700–1850 the non-ferrous metal industries (lead, tin and copper) began to use more coal.
2 A number of industries switched to coal as fuel. The iron industry, for example, used coke (a solid substance of nearly pure carbon, obtained from coal) in place of charcoal.
3 The development of the steam engine also required coal.
4 Following the invention of steam-driven machinery more coal was used in the textile industries.
5 More coal was also needed for domestic purposes in the rapidly growing towns.
6 By the mid-nineteenth century coal was being used to produce gas, which was mainly used for gas lighting in some towns.

This rise in domestic consumption and the development of industry and transport increased the demand for coal, and for improved methods of mining.

How was coal mined?

In the eighteenth century, the largest coalfield was situated in the North-East. Coal was sent by ships called 'colliers' from Newcastle to the London market. This was known as the 'sea-coal trade'.

The first surface coal mines were known as *drift* mines. Later, shafts were dug into the ground where coal was known to be. Some of these mines were called *bell pits*, because of their shape. Others were known as *adit* mines (an *adit* was a drainage channel dug from the coal face so that the water would flow away from where the miners were working) (**A**). Most of these early mines were very small and were often situated in remote areas.

Q Using the diagrams in **A**, explain the main differences between bell pits and the adit mining of coal.

A *A bell pit (left) and an adit mine (right)*

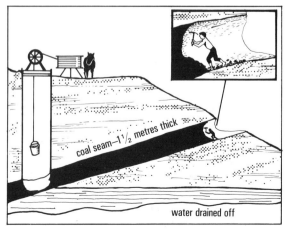

The coal industry 25

B 'Mining operations' from A Tour of England and Scotland in 1785

The principal riches . . . [of] Newcastle are from its coal-works . . . To a pit . . . the largest in the county. Arrived at the spot where our expedition was to commence, we found a large fire-engine at work, draining the water from the pit; and adjoining to it a circular hole . . . filled with smoak . . . We next prepared for our descent down this suffocating hole. A piece of board of about one foot and a half long, and of about the breadth and thickness of three inches, was fastened at each end to a rope reeved through it. This sling . . . was . . . the seat on which we were to repose ourselves till we got to the bottom. . . . each of us (for two went at a time) with a leg through it, and our arms twisted round the chain, we in that manner were . . . gently lowered by the operation of six horses, till we found ourselves at the end of about five minutes safely landed on solid ground, and with a huge fire burning on one side to keep the air in proper temperature. . . . The quantity of coal in these places is really wonderful. A good vein . . . generally runs seven feet high, and in depth ad infinitum. They do not, however, cut all down . . . pillars are left between every

apartment that is worked, to support the roof. That which surprised me the most were the horses I found living there . . . The coal . . . is wound up in baskets and these . . . emptied into carts, which are placed upon cylindrical wheels . . . carried along by sleepers to the warehouse or wharf, where it is . . . thrown into barges for exportation.

Q (a) What was the main industry in the Newcastle area (source B)?
(b) How was the coal mine or pit drained?
(c) How was the descent into the pit made?
(d) What was used to power the lowering mechanism?
(e) How long did it take to reach the bottom of the pit shaft?
(f) How might accidents occur when miners were going down or coming up the pit shaft?
(g) Why was a fire burning at the bottom of the pit shaft?
(h) Why were pillars of coal left unworked in the pit?
(i) Describe in your own words the way in which coal was carried from the coal face to the barges.

The problems of coal mining

Problems which arose during the course of mining included extraction of the coal; roof support; drainage; ventilation; lighting; carrying coal underground; raising it to the surface; and providing carriage to the main markets (B).

Extraction and roof support Two main methods were used to extract coal. In northern England the 'bord and pillar' method (sometimes called 'pillar and stall') was used. The bords or stalls (small areas) in which the miners hewed (cut) coal were separated by pillars of uncut coal. These also supported the roof after the coal had been taken away. This was a wasteful method because more than one-half of the coal might be left unworked.

In the Midlands, the longwall method of extracting coal was more common. As the coal was removed, wooden props and stone packs were used for support.

In some instances it became possible to use gunpowder for extraction.

Drainage By 1700 colliery shafts, particularly in the North-East coalfield, had reached depths of 60 metres and it was necessary to keep the shafts and underground galleries (tunnels or passageways) free from flooding.

The use of engines for pumping water from the mines, for example the steam engines of Thomas Savery and Thomas Newcomen (see page 37), enabled coal to be mined at deeper levels and so increased output. However, it was not until the development of James Watt's steam engine, first used in 1776, that really effective pumping equipment (see page 37) was available to drain deep coal mines.

Ventilation Ventilation of a mine means taking stale air out and replacing it with fresh air. The most important reasons for ventilating mines are to bring in oxygen so that the miners are able to breathe and work underground; and to take away dangerous gases which can cause explosions. Dangerous gases were often present in the coal mines. 'Choke damp' (carbon dioxide) could suffocate miners. It could be dispersed by dragging furze (a thorny evergreen shrub) along the underground galleries. A more serious problem, because of its high carbon monoxide content, was 'after damp'. Burning braziers placed at the bottom of pit shafts increased the circulation of air and improved ventilation.

The most serious problem was methane or 'fire-damp', an explosive gas which caused great loss of life to miners working by candlelight. Early attempts to solve this problem were primitive and dangerous – for example, a 'fire man' covered with wet sacks was sent along an underground gallery with a lighted candle on a long pole in order to burn the pockets of gas.

The most significant advance in ventilation was probably the use of triple shafts by John Buddle at the end of the eighteenth century. Later he installed the first air pump for ventilation and, from the 1830s, the Fourness exhaust fan was gradually introduced. The use of parallel underground galleries, which ran from the shaft to the coal face, also enabled air to circulate around the pit. Following a serious colliery disaster in Northumberland, the use of double or triple shafts was made compulsory in 1862.

Lighting In some pits, to avoid the use of lighted candles which might ignite gases, other methods – for example the flint and steel mill – were used to provide miners with light. However these were not completely safe and many accidents occurred. In 1813, following a series of disastrous explosions on the North-East coalfield (**C**), the Sunderland Society for preventing accidents was formed. Appeals from this Society led to the invention of a number of safety lamps, including one by George Stephenson and another by Sir Humphry Davy (**D**). In the safety lamp devised by Davy (1815), the naked flame – an oil-burning wick – was surrounded by gauze. At first, because the Davy lamp led to the working of even deeper coal seams, it increased the danger of explosions. However, in the long run, it helped to make mining safer.

C *A list of the persons killed by the explosion at Felling Colliery, 25 May 1812*

	Name	Day of Burial	Years old	Employment
	John Knox	May 27		Trapper
	Robert Harrison	27	14	Waggon Driver
	John Harrison	27	12	Waggon Driver
	George Ridley	27	11	Waggon Driver
	Robert Hutchinson	27	11	Trapper
	Thomas Robson	July 8	18	Putter
m*	John Pearson	8	58	Shifter
	Philip Allan	8	17	Putter
	Geo. Bainbridge, *unk.*	8	10	Putter
	Isaac Greener	9	24	Hewer
	James Craigs	13	13	Waggon Driver
	Edward Bell	15	12	Putter
m	Ralph Harrison	15	39	Horse-keeper
m	Matthew Brown	16	28	Hewer
	James Kay	16	18	Putter
	George Bell	16	14	Putter
	Thomas Richardson	16	17	Putter
	Henry Haswell	16	18	Putter
	Joseph Anderson	16	23	Putter
	Joseph Pringle	16	16	Putter
	—— Dobson, *unknown*	16	a boy	Trapper
	George Pearson	16	26	Hewer
	Robert Hall	16	13	Putter
	Gregory Galley	16	10	Trapper
	Benjamin Thompson	17	17	Craneman
	George Mitcheson	17	18	Putter
	Matthew Pringle	17	18	Putter
m	Nicholas Urwin	17	58	Braking inclined plane
m	John Wilson	17	32	Hewer
m	Thomas Young	17		Putter
	John Jacques, *unknown*	17	14	Putter
	Edward Pearson	17	14	Putter
	William Richardson	17	19	Putter
	Christopher Culley	17	20	Putter
	William Boutland	17	19	Crane On-setter
	Jacob Allan	17	14	Putter
m	Isaac Greener	17	65	Hewer
	Thos. Bainbridge, *unk.*	17	17	Putter
m	John Wilson	18	30	Hewer
	Matthew Bainbridge	18	19	Putter
	John Surtees	18	12	Trapper
	Ralph Hall	18	18	Putter
	Paul Fletcher	18	22	Hewer
	William Galley	18	22	Putter
	John Hunter	18	21	Hewer
m	Thomas Bainbridge	22	53	Hewer
m	John Wood	22	27	Hewer
m	Jeremiah Turnbull	22	43	Hewer
m	John Haswell	22	22	Hewer
	John Burnitt	22	21	Hewer
	George Culley	22	14	Trapper
m	Joseph Wilson	23	25	Hewer
m	John Boutland	23	46	Hewer
	George Reay	24	9	Trapper
	William Gardiner	24	10	Trapper
m	Thomas Craggs	24	36	Hewer
	Thomas Craggs	24	9	Trapper
	John Greener	24	21	Hewer
m	Edward Richardson	24	29	Hewer
	Robert Dobson	24	13	Trapper
m	William Dixon	25	35	Hewer
	George Robson	25	15	Putter
	Andrew Allan	25	11	Trapper
m	John Thompson	25	36	Hewer

Name	Day of Burial	Years old	Employment
m John Pearson	25	64	Hewer
m Thomas Bears	25	48	Hewer
Charles Wilson	25	20	Hewer
m Michael Gardiner	25	45	Hewer
m James Comby	25	28	Hewer
Joseph Gordon	25	10	Trapper
m Robert Haswell	25	42	Hewer
m Joseph Wood	27	39	Hewer
m John Wilkinson	27	35	Hewer
m John Turnbull	27	27	Hewer
m Matthew Sanderson	27	33	Hewer
m Robert Gordon	27	40	Hewer
Thomas Gordon	27	8	Trapper
m Christopher Mason	27	54	Hewer
Robert Gray Leck	28	16	Putter
m William Jacques	28	23	Putter
William Hunter	29	35	Deputy
Thomas Ridley	29	13	Putter
m William Sanderson	30	43	Hewer
George Lawton	30	14	Lamp-keeper
Michael Hunter	30	8	Trapper
William Dixon	31	10	Waggon Driver
Edward Haswell	Aug. 1	20	Hewer
Joseph Young	3	30	Trapper
George Kay	26	16	Putter
Robert Pearson	Sept. 1	10	Trapper
John Archibald Dobson	19	15	Trapper

*Those marked *m*, were married men: the rest single.

Two original Davy safety lamps

Glossary: *Trapper* – a young child who opened and closed trap doors underground; *putter* – youth or young person who pulled the baskets (corves); *shifter* – a shift worker; *hewer* – worked at coal face to cut coal; *brakeman* – controlled the inclined plane, more generally, the engine man who controlled the winding engine; *onsetter* – loaded corves at the bottom of the shaft.

Q (a) Make a chart like the one below to show what happened to particular workers at Felling Colliery following the disastrous explosion in 1812.

A mining disaster, 1812				
Nature of employ-ment	Number killed	Average age	Oldest	Young-est
Hewer	34	35 years	65	20
Putter	(to be	completed)		

(b) How many people were killed in the explosion?
(c) What was the age and employment of the youngest person killed?
(d) What was the age and employment of the oldest person killed?
(e) How many married men were killed?
(f) Which type of employment was carried out by the group with the youngest average age?
(g) Which type of employment was carried out by the group with the oldest average age?
(h) How many bodies were recovered in May, July, August, September? Why do you think there were gaps in the dates of burials?

Q How did the use of the lamps shown here affect safety in the mines?

E *A woman coal drawer at work around 1840*

F *Betty Harris, aged 37, drawer in a coal pit at Little Bolton*

I have a belt round my waist, and a chain passing between my legs, and I go on my hands and feet. The road is very steep and we have to hold by a rope; and when there is no rope, by anything we can catch hold of . . .
I am not as strong as I was and cannot stand the work so well as I used to. I have drawn till I have had the skin off me; the belt and chain are worse when we are in the family way . . .

G *A young trapper*

H *Evidence of Sarah Gooder, aged eight years*

I'm a trapper in the Gauber Pit. I have to trap without a light and I'm scared. I go at four and sometimes half-past three in the morning, and come out at five and half past (at night).
I never go to sleep. Sometimes I sing when I've a light but not in the dark; I dare not sing then. I don't like being in the pit.

I *Carriers with bags of coal*

Q Look again at sources **E–I**. Write a letter to a Member of Parliament demanding that women and children should not be employed to work underground in coal mines. Set out the reasons why you believe Parliament should pass an Act to prohibit such employment.

Transporting coal underground Sometimes women and children were employed to pull coal tubs underground (**E–I**). From the mid-eighteenth century ponies were used to pull tubs along cast iron rails. By the mid-nineteenth century steam haulage was becoming more common in the larger underground galleries, but in the smaller galleries ponies were still used.

How was coal raised to the surface? Coal was brought to the surface using a number of methods: windlasses, hoists, gins and ladders. (A windlass is a simple machine used for lifting materials up and down a well or mine shaft using a rope and a bucket; a gin is a shortened word for engine, and usually refers to an engine for winding.) As late as 1840 some women in Scotland were employed to carry coal in wicker baskets up a series of ladders from the shaft bottom to the pit top (**I**).

Many of the English coalfields began to use mechanical apparatus for winding or hoisting coal up the shaft, and also to lower and raise the underground miners. Horse gins or 'whimseys' (small cranes) were commonly used for these operations. However, in the West Riding, hand-winding girls were still at work in the 1840s. Winding by steam power had been introduced in a few areas.

The carriage of coal In order to transport coal more easily and cheaply, rivers were improved in the early eighteenth century and, after 1760, canals were constructed (see Chapter 7). Wealthy landowners, like the Duke of Bridgewater, who had coal reserves on their estates invested in the development of water transport.

River boats used for transporting coal were known as keels. Coasting coal vessels were known as colliers. The waggonways on the coalfields were built to carry coal the short distances from the pit heads to the navigable waterways. New forms of locomotion, especially steam engines, were pioneered. The coming of the railways, which used coal for steam power *and* provided better transport, made the nineteenth century the age of coal.

■ The regulation of the mines

Royal Commission on Conditions in the Mines

In 1840, under Lord Shaftesbury, a Royal Commission was set up to investigate working conditions in British coal mines. The Report of the Commission (1842) showed that the miners' lives were often dominated by powerful coal owners, many of them magistrates (JPs), who often also owned the miners' houses. In many districts, mining was sub-contracted to 'butties', who were paid on the amount of coal mined, and who worked the men they employed as hard as possible. In other districts, male hewers (coal cutters) employed children and women to push coal tubs through small underground passages, and to carry it to the surface. Children were also employed to look after the pit ponies. Cruelty was commmon, and children from five years of age upwards were employed for long hours underground in darkness and solitude. Some young children worked as 'trappers', minding the doors in the underground galleries which increased ventilation and the circulation of air. Sometimes children were left in charge of the engines which were used to haul miners up and down the shaft and, consequently, there were many accidents.

Although the wages of adult miners were often higher than those in other industries and agriculture, the truck system of payment was common (see page 19).

What was the importance of the 1842 Report?

The 1842 Report was one of the most sensational Government documents ever published. It was written in vivid language and was also illustrated. It shocked and horrified the British public.

In the same year, 1842, despite opposition from landowners who received much income from the mines, the Mines Act was passed. This forbade the employment, underground, of all women and girls, and of boys under ten years of age. Mine owners were also prohibited from placing boys under 15 years of age in charge of machinery. A further Act of 1850 appointed government inspectors of mines, to make sure that the new laws were carried out.

■ **Coal and the Industrial Revolution**

1   The increasing demand for coal, transport improvements and greater investment helped to overcome the problems of mining.
2   By the mid-nineteenth century the coal industry employed more than 200,000 people and shafts had been sunk to over 300 metres.
3   Other industries were increasingly sited on the coalfields.
4   About one-third of all coal mined annually in Britain was exported.
5   Despite the opposition of mine owners, by the mid-nineteenth century action had been taken to protect women and children working in the mines.

QUESTIONS

1 Copy the map into your book and indicate:
  (a) the most important coalfield in the eighteenth century;
  (b) how coal from Newcastle could be easily exported to London and the east coast ports.
2 (a) Why were rivers and the sea important in the development of the coalfields?
  (b) How did progress in the iron industry and in the use of steam power affect the coal industry?
  (c) In which other industries was coal used in large quantities?

3 (a) What dangers were there for those working in coal mines?
  (b) Copy and complete this chart to show problems of coal mining and the efforts made to overcome them.

Problem	Attempted solution	Effect
Gas in the mine	Miner, a 'fire man' in wet clothes with long pole and light – trying to find gas	Not effective and dangerous
	(to be completed)	

4 Study the figures for British coal production. When did the coal tonnage figures start to rise rapidly, and why?

Coal Production	
Year	Tons
1700	2 000 000
1770	6 090 000
1800	10 000 000
1850	65 000 000

5 Write a short essay on each of the following topics:
  (a) For what reasons did British coal output increase in the period 1700–1850? What factors encouraged that expansion?
  (b) What difficulties and dangers did coal miners face? How far were these difficulties overcome before 1850?

5 The iron and steel industries

An iron industry had existed in Britain for many centuries but its growth had been slow. However, during the period 1700–1850 the British iron industry underwent great changes. It contributed to the expansion of Britain's economy and was one of the leading industries in the Industrial Revolution. Compared with the rapid changes in the iron industry, the steel industry developed much more slowly.

■ The iron industry

How was iron produced in the early eighteenth century?

The making of iron involves a number of processes. Iron ore, a rock containing iron and other substances such as oxygen, sand and sulphur, is mined. It is then smelted (melted) in a blast furnace to free the iron from the ore. The molten (liquid) iron is then run off into moulds called 'pigs'. This is known as pig iron.

Cast iron is made by pouring the molten iron straight into a mould. Although cast iron is brittle, it was one of the most important metals of the industrial age. Wrought iron is produced by refining, that is, burning out more of the impurities until the metal is almost pure. Wrought iron is softer than cast iron, so it is supple and not so brittle.

The process of iron making required heating in furnaces and forges. The fuel used was charcoal. Charcoal is wood that has been dried and burned very slowly. It was made in clearings in the forests by charcoal burners who built special woodpiles covered with turf and soil which kept the air out while the wood was burning.

Where was iron produced?

Large quantities of charcoal were needed as fuel, and regions with plenty of woodlands were the original sites of the iron industry. The ironmasters also needed fast flowing streams to provide water power to work the bellows at the blast furnaces and the hammers at the forges.

Problems for the iron industry

In the early eighteenth century Britain's iron industry faced a serious shortage of charcoal. Ironmasters had to search for new centres where timber was still plentiful, for example in remote sites in Shropshire, South Wales, South Yorkshire, Cumberland and Scotland.

The high cost of producing British iron meant that it was cheaper to import iron of better quality from Sweden, Russia and Britain's colonies in North America.

The demand for iron

The development of other industries and transport increased the demand for iron. Iron was also required for the making of cannon and armaments to fight the frequent wars.

■ The ironmasters

Who were the most important ironmasters?

The Darbys of Coalbrookdale British ironmasters needed an alternative fuel to charcoal. Coal was used in other industries but could not be used for smelting iron ore because it contained sulphurous fumes and made the iron impure and brittle.

A *View of the Coalbrookdale works, 1758*

Q (a) What relation was the writer of Source **B** to Abraham Darby I?
  (b) What were the natural advantages of Coalbrookdale for setting up an ironworks?
  (c) How was the blast furnace fuelled when Darby first moved to Coalbrookdale?
  (d) What did Darby successfully achieve in 1709?
  (e) What evidence can you find that, in the long run, Darby's discovery helped to solve a crisis in the iron industry?
  (f) How did the second Abraham Darby improve on his father's work?
  (g) How was transport at Coalbrookdale improved?
  (h) Describe in detail the scene of Coalbrookdale (source **A**). The letter of Mrs Abiah Darby (**B**) may help you.

The first real breakthrough was made by Abraham Darby I, who set up as an ironmaster at Coalbrookdale, near the river Severn, in Shropshire (**A**). The site had the advantages of water carriage and water power, as well as local supplies of charcoal and iron ore. In 1709 Darby succeeded in producing pig and cast iron using coke, made from local 'clod' coal, as the fuel instead of charcoal (**B**). Shropshire 'clod' coal had a low sulphur content, and was particularly suitable for making coke (which burns smokelessly at intense heat).

Darby was a Quaker by religion and so refused to make cannons or any other weapons. Instead he made a variety of cooking utensils.

Darby's discovery was only useful for making cast iron (wrought iron still had to be made by using charcoal) but it meant that the industry could gradually be re-located on the coalfields where there were also supplies of iron ore. At first, the new method was only used at Coalbrookdale. Although Darby did not deliberately keep his discovery a close secret, he did not go out of his way to publicize it. His technique, which meant that the blast furnaces were no longer dependent upon charcoal, did not become widespread until the 1760s.

Abraham Darby's sons continued to expand the Coalbrookdale works which began to produce cast-iron rails for horse-drawn waggonways and cast-iron parts for steam engines. In 1779 the world's first iron bridge was built across the river Severn, south of Coalbrookdale (**C–G**). It was built by Abraham Darby III and another local ironmaster, John Wilkinson, from iron ribs cast at Coalbrookdale.

C *Shrewsbury Chronicle, 15 May 1776*
A bridge to be built

Any person willing ... to build a bridge of one arch over the Severn from Benthall ... to the opposite shore in Madeley Wood, of stone, brick, or timber ... Send proposals to ... Coalbrookdale.

D *The world's first iron bridge*

E *Ironbridge Sharelist 1777 – 64 shares of £50 per Share*

Rev. Mr Harris	10	John Morris	2
Abraham Darby	15	Charles Guest	2
John Wilkinson	12	Roger Kynnaston	1
Leonard Jennings	10	John Hartshorne	1
Samuel Darby	4	Sergeant Roden	1
Edward Blakeway	2	John Thursfield	1
Farnells Pritchard	2	John Nicholson	1

F *Minute Book of the Proprietors of the Ironbridge*

18 October 1776. . . . Abraham Darby agreed to erect an Iron Bridge of one Arch one hundred and twenty feet span and the superstructure not less than eighteen feet wide . . . to be completely finished with roads . . . to and from the same as described in the Act of Parliament, on or before the twenty fifth day of December 1778 . . .

Q (a) Was the river Severn navigable up to Coalbrookdale (source **D**)?

(b) How were people and goods carried across the river *before* the bridge was built (source **D**)?

(c) List as many reasons as you can why a bridge was necessary.

(d) How had the construction plans changed between May and October 1776 (sources **C** and **F**)?

(e) What part did Abraham Darby play in the building of the bridge (sources **E** and **F**)?

(f) How much capital had each shareholder invested in the bridge (source **E**)?

(g) Which other famous ironmaster was included in the list of shareholders?

(h) How long did it take to build the bridge?

(i) Write a newspaper report about Ironbridge on the occasion that it was opened.

G *From* Britannia *(1806)*

Coalbrookdale is one mile long . . . Over the Severn in this Dale was laid 1779, a bridge of cast iron . . . a large scaffold being previously erected, each part of the rib was elevated to a proper height by strong ropes and chains, and then lowered till the ends met in the centre. All the principal parts were erected in three months without any accident . . . or . . . obstruction to the navigation of the river. . . . On the largest and exterior rib is inscribed in capitals
THIS BRIDGE WAS CAST AT COALBROOKDALE AND ERECTED IN THE YEAR MDCCLXXIX.

John ('Iron-Mad') Wilkinson Having inherited a small iron-founding business in Shropshire, John Wilkinson set up his own iron works at Broseley. Wilkinson promoted the use of iron for a variety of purposes including iron drainage pipes to carry water (he cast the iron piping for the Paris waterworks) and cast-iron barges. He patented a new lathe (a machine for turning and shaping wood or metal) for accurately boring cannon and this process was soon adapted for use on the pistons and cylinders of the new steam engines of James Watt. Wilkinson was the first ironmaster to use a steam-engine to blow the blast of the furnace and to drive the forge hammers. He was known as 'Iron-mad' Wilkinson because of his keenness to use iron – he even made an iron coffin for himself!

John Roebuck Roebuck is best known as a pioneer in the Scottish iron industry. He set up the first iron works on the river Carron near Falkirk in Scotland in 1759, which soon became noted for the production of armaments (weapons) (**H**).

H *Instructions to an industrial spy employed by the Carron company to obtain information about John Wilkinson's iron works.*

What part of Lancashire or Cumberland does their Ore come from? Bring us a specimen of that and of their Clod Coal. Bring us an exact sketch of the machine for turning of their gunheads, also a description of their Wheel as we fear our Boring Wheel will not be strong enough to support the gun when the head is turning off. We also want a sketch of the cranes for hoisting their large Guns . . . and of the different movements about it with a drawing of their Iron Carriages for carrying the large Gun Boxes into the Stove and of the Carriage and method of conveying the Guns to and from the Boring Mill . . . .

Q (a) Where was the Carron iron works located and for what kind of products did it become noted?
  (b) For what purposes did the Carron iron works ask an industrial spy to provide information about Wilkinson's iron works?
  (c) Apart from written descriptions, what else was the spy instructed to provide, and why?

The work of Henry Cort To convert pig iron into wrought iron at the forge was a slow and costly process which required prolonged hammering and the use of charcoal and water power.

Henry Cort, who supplied the Navy with iron for anchors and guns, was one of a number of ironmasters who found it increasingly difficult to obtain wrought iron. He therefore set up a forge at Fontley near Portsmouth and in 1784 began to produce his own wrought iron. Pig iron was heated in a special 'reverberatory' furnace fed with coke (**I**). When it became molten, it was stirred with long rods that helped to burn off the impurities. This was known as *puddling* (**J**). The iron was then taken out of the furnace in a semi-molten state to be hammered and passed through grooved rollers, which produced bars or plates of wrought iron. This was known as *rolling*.

The puddling and rolling processes saved time and fuel and meant that cheap wrought iron could be produced in larger quantities. Cort's breakthrough allowed coal and steam power to be used for wrought iron manufacture and eliminated the need for the prolonged hammering of pig iron.

■ **The growing demand for iron**

The wars against France (1793–1815) increased the demand for iron to manufacture armaments. After the wars new uses were found for iron, for example gas pipes. With the use of coke there was a great increase in the size of the blast furnaces and iron works. The largest iron works were in South Wales. Richard Crawshay, who owned the iron works at Cyfarthfa, Merthyr Tydfil, became the 'iron king' of South Wales.

■ **What technical progress was made in the early nineteenth century?**

The continued growth in iron making was helped by the invention of the hot blast furnace by James Neilson in 1828. Neilson, who was the manager of the Glasgow Gas Works, realized that, if the blast of air was pre-heated before it entered the furnace, the cost of production could be reduced by cutting fuel consumption. Following Neilson's discovery iron output expanded rapidly.

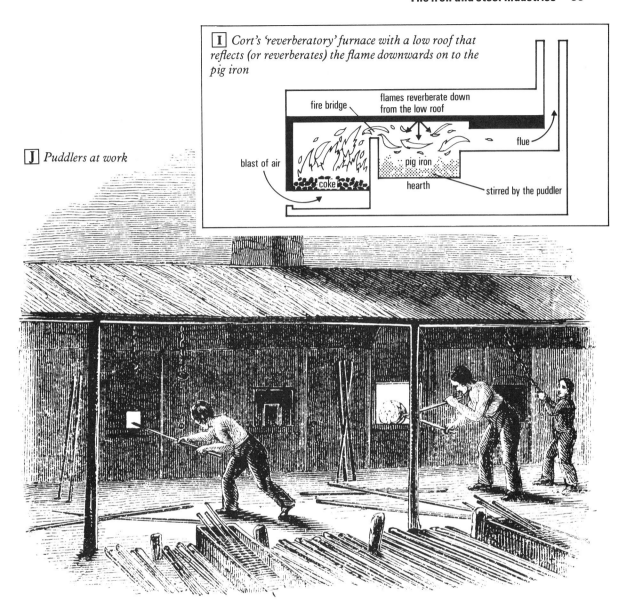

I Cort's 'reverberatory' furnace with a low roof that reflects (or reverberates) the flame downwards on to the pig iron

fire bridge

flames reverberate down from the low roof

flue

blast of air

coke

pig iron

hearth

stirred by the puddler

J Puddlers at work

After 1840 the large-scale manufacture of wrought iron was made possible by an invention of James Nasmyth, a Scottish engineer who had settled in Manchester. Nasmyth devised a steam hammer which made it possible to forge large iron plates and long bars of iron. The steam hammer enabled large quantities of iron to be produced for the railways and steamships.

■ The steel industry

The manufacture and use of steel

Steel is iron with a small amount of carbon in it (and sometimes other metals as well). It is as hard as cast iron, as supple as wrought iron, and stronger than both.

Compared with the rapid changes in the iron industry, the manufacture of steel remained a workshop trade dominated by skilled craftsmen, who worked as a 'domestic industry'.

In 1740 Benjamin Huntsman, a clockmaker from Doncaster, who moved to the Sheffield region, discovered a method of making better steel. Pieces of blister steel (which was obtained by packing bars of wrought iron with charcoal in clay boxes and heating them in a furnace for about ten days) were mixed with charcoal and limestone in small clay pots or 'crucibles'. This was then smelted in coke-fired furnaces to produce cast or 'crucible' steel. Crucible steel was of much better quality than the existing steel but it was expensive and was made only in small quantities.

Steel was used mainly for the fine products made in the Sheffield region, where the cutlery industry was already well established. Small-scale workshops predominated in the Sheffield steel industry where over 500 tiny furnaces were in operation by the mid-nineteenth century. By that time, total steel output in Britain was about 60,000 tons per annum and the amount of iron processed into steel was very small. The cost of manufacture limited the large-scale use of steel.

■ A new 'Iron Age'

1 Iron making was Britain's most important metal industry and it underwent major changes in the period 1700–1850.
2 The dependence of the iron industry on charcoal and water power had been ended by innovation and invention, and new large-scale iron works using steam power had been developed on the coalfields.
3 Many new uses were found for iron, including bridges, water and gas pipes, cables, railways and steamships.
4 Cheap iron in large quantities stimulated other industries and led to rapid industrial and social changes.

QUESTIONS

1 The following table is incorrectly arranged. Copy it into your book, rearranging it correctly in chronological order. Then write a sentence about each personality, using the information given.

Date	Personality	Place	Industrial Process/Event
1840	Benjamin Huntsman	Carron Works	used clay crucibles to produce cast steel
1779	Henry Cort	Manchester	helped to build the first iron bridge
1759	Abraham Darby I	Sheffield	hot-blast furnace
1828	John Wilkinson	Broseley	puddling and rolling
c.1737	James Neilson	Glasgow	smelting pig iron with 'clod coal'
1740	John Roebuck	Coalbrookdale	steam hammer
1784	James Nasmyth	Coalbrookdale	making bar iron from coke-smelted pig iron
1709	Abraham Darby II	Fontley	pioneer of Scottish iron industry

2 Copy and complete this sentence by choosing the correct word from each column.

One important result of ___(a)___ work was that the iron industry, which had previously been ___(b)___ moved to ___(c)___ to be within easy reach of ___(d)___ .

(a)	(b)	(c)	(d)
James Nasmyth's	small-scale	Scotland	railways and steamships
Abraham Darby's	located in Britain	Sweden	European markets
Henry Cort's	widely scattered around the country	the coalfields	the main source of fuel

3 **Essay topic:**
Why did the demand for iron grow in the period 1700–1850? How did technical improvements lead to an increase in output and changes in the location of the iron industry?

6　A new form of power

For many centuries, windmills, watermills and simple machinery using horse or human energy had been the sources of power available to agriculture and industry. In the eighteenth century water power became more efficient but it could not provide all the energy needed by industry and new forms of power were required. Steam power and, later, coal gas were developed, and by 1850 the supply of energy had greatly increased.

■ The use of water power

Throughout the period 1700–1850 water remained an important source of power for industry. By the early nineteenth century much larger iron water wheels were being constructed, but they could power large factories only where there were good streams of swiftly flowing water. The amount of energy required in the industrial revolution could not be supplied by water power alone. Very slowly, water power was replaced by steam power.

■ The development and use of steam power

The early pioneers of steam power

The principles of steam power had been known to the Ancient Greeks but they had not developed that knowledge in practical ways. It was the conditions of the eighteenth century that led to the development of steam power.

In 1698 Thomas Savery constructed an engine known as the 'Miners' Friend', to pump water out of the Cornish copper mines. However, Savery's engine was not powerful enough to drain the deeper mines.

The first practical steam pump was introduced in the early eighteenth century by Thomas Newcomen, a Devon blacksmith (**A**). Newcomen's engines were widely used to pump water out of tin, copper and coal mines and, by the mid-eighteenth century, about one hundred engines were working, mainly in Cornwall and the North-East. Newcomen engines were adapted for other purposes, for example blowing blast furnaces in the iron industry and pumping drinking water in towns. Some Newcomen engines were exported to Europe.

Because steam was condensed inside the cylinders, which had to be alternately heated and cooled, the Newcomen engine was inefficient and used large quantities of fuel.

The work of James Watt

James Watt, the son of a shipwright from Greenock in Scotland, was interested in mechanics and in mathematics. He set up as a scientific instrument maker to Glasgow University. In 1764 Watt was given a small-scale demonstration model of a Newcomen engine to repair. He succeeded in making a model for an engine which would be greatly superior to that of Newcomen. To overcome the problems of alternately heating and cooling the cylinder, Watt used a separate condenser where the steam was cooled. Watt's engine was cheaper to run, and more efficient than Newcomen's.

In order to produce a full size steam engine that could be widely used, Watt needed money, materials and skilled workmen. He therefore went into partnership with John Roebuck, owner of the Carron ironworks. However, Roebuck went bankrupt and Watt fell into debt.

The partnership of James Watt and Matthew Boulton

After his failure in Scotland, Watt was taken into partnership by the industrialist, Matthew Boulton, who owned the Soho metal works at Birmingham and was probably the most important iron manufacturer in Europe.

Boulton wanted an effective steam pump to provide extra water to drive the water wheels at his works. In 1776 Watt produced an engine which worked better than the Newcomen engine and used one-third less coal. The first Boulton and Watt steam engines were only an improved form of pump with a simple up and down action. They were first used at collieries near Birmingham, at iron mines in Shropshire and at the tin and copper mines in Cornwall.

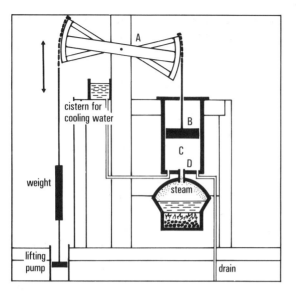 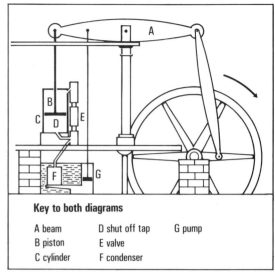

Key to both diagrams

A beam	D shut off tap	G pump
B piston	E valve	
C cylinder	F condenser	

A *Newcomen's steam engine (left); Watt's steam engine (right)*

Q (a) Examine the diagram of the Newcomen engine. The engine used expanding steam from the boiler. When the shut-off tap (D) was opened the steam rushed into the cylinder (C). As the steam filled the cylinder, what happened to the piston (B)? Did it move up or down? What happened to the pump in the shaft? Did it move up or down?

(b) What happened to the piston (B) when the steam in the cylinder (C) was condensed with cold water from the cistern? Did it move up or down? What happened to the pump in the shaft? Did it move up or down?

(c) Describe in your own words how the Newcomen engine worked. (The beam (A) vibrated up and down 12 times per minute and each stroke lifted 10 gallons of water from a mine from a depth of 150 yards.)

(d) Read source **B**. What was James Watt experimenting on in 1765?

(e) According to Watt's improvements, was steam to be cooled (a) in the cylinder or (b) in a separate condenser?

(f) How is the improvement shown in the diagram of Watt's steam engine?

To prevent the escape of steam, and to make the engine more efficient, Watt needed accurately bored cylinders. John 'Iron-mad' Wilkinson (see page 34), had invented a new lathe for boring cannon more accurately. This invention was exactly what was needed for boring the cylinders and the Boulton and Watt engines became much more reliable.

Watt's rotary engine
In 1781, with the help of the Soho works foreman, William Murdock, a new kind of engine was patented. Using a system of gear wheels called a 'sun and planet' motion, Watt's pumping engine was converted into a rotary engine, which could turn a wheel and drive

B *Improvements on Newcomen's engine*
One Sunday afternoon in 1765 . . . I had gone for a walk in . . . Glasgow . . . my thoughts turning naturally to the experiments I had been engaged in for saving heat in the cylinder, the idea occurred to me that, as steam was an elastic vapour, it would expand, and rush into a previously exhausted space; and that if I were to produce a vacuum in a separate vessel, and open a communication between this and the steam in the cylinder, such would be the result.

machinery (**C**). Later improvements helped to regulate the speed of the rotary engine and to secure a smoother movement.

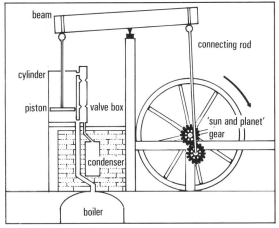

C *James Watt's rotary engine of 1781*

The growing use of steam power

After the 1780s, the rotary engine was used in a number of industries. The first cotton-spinning mill to be worked by steam power was erected at Papplewick in Nottinghamshire in 1785. After that time Boulton and Watt engines began, slowly, to replace water power in cotton-spinning mills. In the iron industry steam power was used by ironmasters to provide blast in their furnaces, to operate hammers at the forge and to work rollers. Other industries also began to introduce steam engines, for example pottery, brewing, distilling, flour milling, sugar-refining, paper-making, printing and coin-minting.

To begin with only the larger and more successful mines and factories could afford to use steam power. Steam engines were costly to buy, to install and to work. Therefore it took a long time for steam to replace other power sources. However, from the 1830s onwards, mass-produced steam engines were manufactured and their use became more widespread.

■ Benefits of steam power

1 Steam power, unlike water power, was not affected by weather conditions.
2 Steam engines, again unlike water power, were less restricted to the waterway systems and could be used wherever they were needed.
3 Steam power gave a boost to the coal, iron and engineering industries, and enabled industry to be located on the coalfields.

QUESTIONS

1 Copy and complete this table to show the development of steam power.

Date	Inventor	Description	Information
1698	Thomas Savery	'The Miner's Friend' – for pumping water out of Cornish copper mines (to be completed)	Not powerful enough to drain the deeper mines

2 Write a short essay on the benefits of steam power and on the change from water power to steam power during the Industrial Revolution.

3 Copy and complete the following passage by choosing (from the list provided below) the correct words. (There are more words than spaces.)

The _____ Engine and the _____ Engine had been used since the early eighteenth century for _____ in mines. Steam was condensed inside the _____ of the engine. _____ improved the steam engine by the invention of the separate _____. Later his _____ engine was applied to the driving of machinery. By the end of the eighteenth century the improved engines were being used in a number of industries including _____ and _____. Steam power enabled industry to be located on the _____.

windmills	textiles	boiler	piston	horse power	cylinder
James Watt	ironmaking	pumping	rotary	watermill	rivers
condenser	Thomas Newcomen	beam	revolutionary	Thomas Savery	coalfields

In the early eighteenth century the sea and rivers were important for the carriage of bulky goods, especially coal, grain and building materials. Between 1700 and 1850 the waterway system of England and Wales was extended from about 1,600 kilometres to about 6,500 kilometres, mainly by the building of canals. However, by the mid-nineteenth century, many of the waterways were in decline.

■ The need to improve waterways

The age of river improvement

Britain was fortunate in having many kilometres of navigable rivers which could be used for the carriage of goods by boat. In the later seventeenth and early eighteenth centuries many rivers were deepened, straightened and their navigable stretches extended; and new inland ports were developed. These improvements were encouraged by those who were likely to benefit – the Aire and Calder Navigation, for example, was promoted by the cloth merchants of Leeds and Wakefield.

Sometimes river improvement schemes were opposed by landowners who feared that their lands would be flooded or by mill owners who used the rivers as sources of water power. The use of rivers to carry goods had a number of drawbacks: seasonal variations in water levels; meanders (bends in the river); and the use of people and horses to haul vessels, which was slow. Rivers could only serve a limited area. As trade and industry grew, the improved rivers could no longer carry the increased amount of traffic.

Why were canals constructed?

Landowners, industrialists and merchants considered that the existing river and road transport systems were costly and inadequate. Water access was also needed for those regions of Britain not served by rivers. A major reason for the development of the canals was the need to carry large quantities of coal cheaply.

It was known that canals had already been successfully constructed and operated on the continent, especially in Holland and France. Many of the techniques needed for the construction of canals had been acquired by the engineers working on river improvements and water mills.

■ The canal network

The early canal age

In England, the demand for canals came first from the fastest growing industrial region, south Lancashire. The first modern British canal was the Sankey Brook Navigation, opened in 1757 to carry coal from the St Helens coalfield to the Mersey and the port of Liverpool, and to bring Cheshire salt to Lancashire.

Canals, like the earlier river navigations, were set up by private Acts of Parliament. These Acts gave powers to individuals or groups of promoters (sometimes called 'undertakers') to carry out, or undertake, the construction of canals. They imposed tolls (taxes) on those using the canal and paid farmers for the land they had lost.

James Brindley and the Bridgewater Canal

In 1759 the Duke of Bridgewater (**A**), who owned large coal mines at Worsley in Lancashire, obtained an Act of Parliament which allowed him to build a canal to Manchester, 11 km away. The Bridgewater Canal was built by James Brindley (1716–72), a Derbyshire millwright and self-taught engineer (**B**). Brindley included a number of important engineering features on the canal, such as a tunnel and an *aqueduct* (a bridge which carries water) which carried the canal over the river Irwell at Barton. To hold the water in the canal, Brindley lined the base and the banks with puddled clay (a mixture of clay and sand, wetted and kneaded until no water will seep through it) to make it watertight. The Bridgewater Canal was opened in 1761 and at once the price of coal in Manchester fell by half, which benefited coal consumers and industrialists.

A *A portrait of the Duke of Bridgewater*

Q (a) What is the background and setting for the portrait? Can you suggest why?

(b) The Duke is pointing to the principal engineering feature of the Bridgewater Canal. Can you name what it is?

(c) What evidence can you find from sources **A** and **B** that the early canals followed the contours of the land?

B *From the* Annual Register *1763*

Manchester 30 September 1763

Sir,

I have been viewing . . . the Duke of Bridgewater's navigation . . . the ingenious Mr Brindley has indeed made such improvements . . . as are truly astonishing. At Barton bridge he has erected a navigable canal in the air; for it is as high as the tops of the trees. Whilst I was surveying it . . . four barges passed me in the space of about three minutes, two of them being chained together, and dragged by two horses, who went on the terras of the canal, whereon, I must own, I durst hardly venture to walk, as I almost trembled to behold the large river Irwell underneath me across which this navigation is carried by a bridge . . . From Barton I steered my course towards this place and saw the navigation carried over public roads, in some places over bogs, but generally by the side of hills . . .

By 1767 the Bridgewater Canal had been extended from Manchester to Runcorn, which provided a water route that was an alternative to the Mersey and Irwell Navigation between Manchester and Liverpool. The success of the Bridgewater Canal encouraged other land-owners and industrialists to build canals.

The Grand Trunk Canal

Brindley was involved in the construction of the Grand Trunk Canal (1766–77), which included the Harecastle tunnel which was 2·6 km long. The Grand Trunk Canal was about 145 kilometres in length. It was financed by the Cheshire salt industry, the Severn valley iron industry and the Staffordshire pottery manu-facturers. Josiah Wedgwood, a famous pottery manufacturer, was the main shareholder in the canal. He built the 'Etruria' pottery works on the banks of the Grand Trunk Canal in North Staffordshire (**C** and **D**). The canal provided a cheap and reliable route for Wedgwood to import clay from Cornwall and to send the finished pottery to Liverpool for export. The Grand Trunk Canal linked the river Trent with the river Mersey, so that there was a direct water route between Liverpool on the west coast and Hull on the east. It became a main artery or 'trunk' to which many smaller canals were connected.

C *From* History of the Staffordshire Potteries *(1829)*

The Potteries . . . covering above twenty thousand acres with Towns, Villages, and Hamlets, and forming one of the most populous and industrious districts . . . about fifty thousand persons in the parishes of Stoke, Burslem, and Wolstanton, supported by the Manufacture, as operatives, colliers, and persons employed on the canal to bring the raw materials, and carry away the manufactured productions . . . The largest Potteries . . . being Wedgwood's, Etruria; Spode's, Stoke; Wood's, Burslem; Minton's, Stoke. . . .

Q (a) Identify the main features of illustration **D** by linking the numbers with the correct descriptions in the chart.

Feature	Number (1–5)
Etruria works Loading dock and crane Kiln or pottery oven Horse-drawn barge Towing path	

(b) Using sources **C** and **D**, and the text, write a short essay in answer to the following topic: How did the canals encourage the development of industry and the growth of towns in the Potteries?

D *The Etruria pottery works*

'The cross'

As the canal system developed, its central pivot lay between Birmingham, Coventry and Stafford. The area became known as 'the cross', from which the central industrial region and the Midland coalfield were opened up to the major ports. By 1790 Birmingham, the 'hub' of the canal system, was linked by water to Liverpool, Hull, London and Bristol.

The trans-Pennine canals

Three trans-Pennine canals provided waterway links across the industrial north, and made the carriage of coal and other goods much easier. They also helped the development of the foreign trade of south Lancashire and the West Riding, whose textile industries were gaining a position of world renown in the nineteenth century.

The Rochdale and the Huddersfield canals were completed before the Leeds and Liverpool Canal. A feature of the 204-kilometre Leeds and Liverpool Canal was the 'staircase', a system of several locks one after the other, which enabled the canal boats to climb or descend steep gradients in the Pennines.

What was canal mania?

There was a burst of canal activity in the years 1788–94, sometimes referred to as 'canal mania', when many over-ambitious projects were started.

The canals which were begun in the boom period include the Grand Junction Canal which ran from London to Birmingham; the Kennet and Avon Canal which linked the Severn and the Thames; and the Caledonian Canal in the Highlands of Scotland built by Thomas Telford, and financed by the Government for military purposes to save the long and exposed journey round the north of that country.

Unlike the earlier canals, which aimed to keep building costs low by following the contours of the land, the later canals tended to be straighter and involved expensive engineering works. Telford's first canal, the Ellesmere Canal in North Wales, for example, included two well-constructed but costly aqueducts.

By 1830 Britain had an extensive system of inland waterways, about £20 million having been spent on their construction and improvement.

■ The benefits of canals

1 Canals offered a cheaper and more reliable form of transport for bulky goods, including raw materials, fertilizers, foodstuffs and finished manufactured goods.
2 Canals opened up new lines of communication between industrial areas, and encouraged the development of industries. Canal transport was particularly important in the development of the inland coalfields.
3 The growth of coastal and inland ports was encouraged because food supplies, coal and other goods could be drawn from a wider area. A number of new canal towns were created, such as Runcorn, Stourport, Ellesmere Port and Goole. A few canals also ran passenger boats.
4 The building of the canals created work for a new group of mobile workers. These were the navigators, or 'navvies', who were later to work on the construction of the railways.

■ What were the disadvantages in the canal system?

1 Canals came into existence without an overall plan. Sometimes they were built too close together and were unprofitable.
2 There was little uniformity in the size of the numerous locks which were necessary on many canals to enable boats to climb and descend gradients (**E** and **F**).
3 A cross-country journey might involve the use of several different canals with different tolls and variations in the size of vessels. This made transhipment (moving goods from one boat to another) necessary.
4 The canals were subject to weather hazards such as water shortage, drought, flood and frost.
5 The narrowness of canals prevented the use of larger barges. The widening of waterways was expensive, partly because mills and factories had been built along canal banks.
6 Transport was slow (it took thirty-six hours to carry cotton from Liverpool to Manchester) and to use faster transport such as steam boats might wash away the banks of the canals.

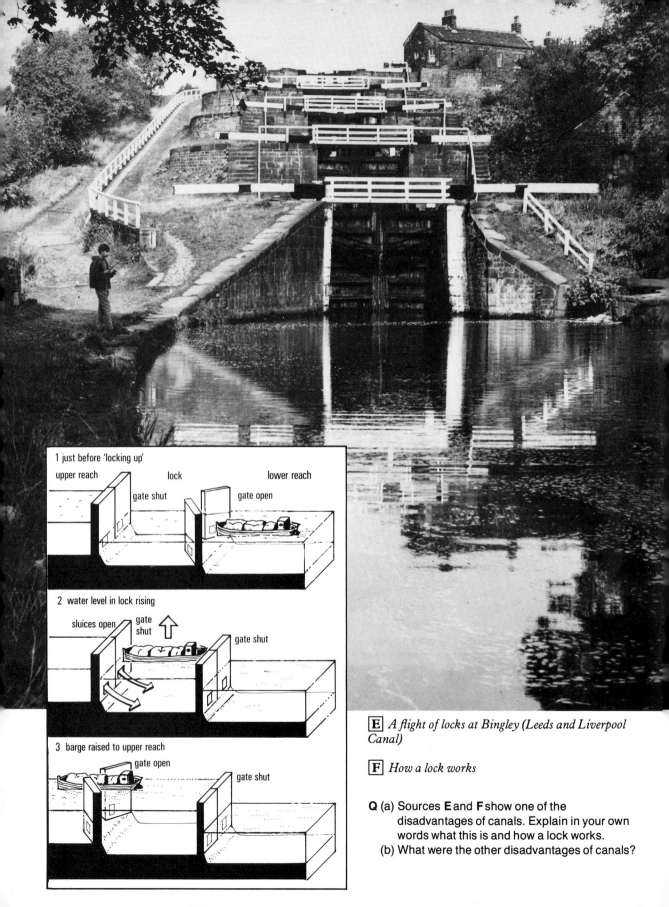

1 just before 'locking up'

upper reach   lock   lower reach

gate shut   gate open

2 water level in lock rising

sluices open   gate shut   gate shut

3 barge raised to upper reach

gate open   gate shut

E *A flight of locks at Bingley (Leeds and Liverpool Canal)*

F *How a lock works*

Q (a) Sources **E** and **F** show one of the disadvantages of canals. Explain in your own words what this is and how a lock works.

    (b) What were the other disadvantages of canals?

7   Canals were expensive to construct. Money was needed to obtain the Act of Parliament, to survey the routes, to buy the land, to pay the engineers and the navvies, and to buy the construction materials. A number of canals were badly managed, and by the early nineteenth century they were in financial difficulties.

■ Competition from the railways

With the development of the railways, the problems of the canal companies increased. Many canal users turned to the faster and more efficient railways for transport. Sometimes, railway companies bought up local canals and then deliberately let them fall into decay or imposed such high tolls that canal users turned to the railways. However, although some canal companies failed to compete with the railways, others continued to carry a declining proportion of traffic.

QUESTIONS

1 Using the map to help you, answer the following questions.

(a) Between which two places was canal A built?

(b) What was the main cargo carried on the canal?

(c) Who was the engineer responsible?

(d) Name one of the engineering features on canal A.

(e) Why was the canal extended to Runcorn?

(f) Which pottery manufacturer invested much money in canal B?

(g) Why was it known as the Grand Trunk Canal?

(h) Who was the engineer responsible for canal B?

(i) Which industry in Cheshire benefited from the building of canal B?

(j) Why was it particularly important to link the Stoke area to the canal network?

(k) Which raw material was carried along route C?

(l) Explain why canal D was of particular importance in the expansion of the textile industries of Lancashire and Yorkshire.

(m) What would be the advantages of building canal E?

(n) Which industrial area became the centre of the canal network?

2 Imagine that a company has been made responsible under an Act of Parliament for building and managing a canal. Describe the experiences of the canal company. Include: the reasons for promoting and building the canal; financing, planning and constructing the canal; details of the barges and goods carried; reasons for the eventual decline of the canal.

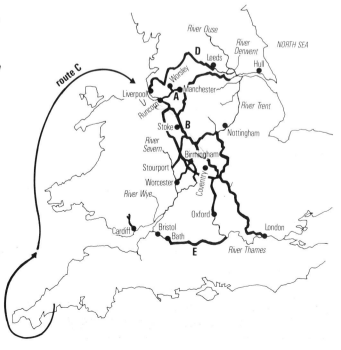

8 Roads and road transport

To travel as a passenger between London and Edinburgh in 1700 could take up to two weeks. By the mid-nineteenth century the time had been cut to two days. This remarkable increase in the speed of travel was due to better methods of road transport and to improvements in the construction of roads. Between 1660 and 1830 many turnpike trusts (see page 48) were set up to improve the roads between towns.

■ The need for better roads

Road travel in the early eighteenth century

In 1700 many of the roads in Britain were in a bad state of repair and some were no more than cart tracks. Many roads were narrow and wheeled traffic could be overturned in the deep potholes. The surfaces were often soft and muddy in winter and hard and dusty in summer.

In some parts of the country the pack horse and the mule train were still used to carry goods. The high cost of wheeled road carriage meant that bulky goods like coal could be carried only over short distances. Some goods were carried partly by road and partly by water. Wherever possible, heavy goods were sent by river or sea. Animals, such as sheep and cattle, were driven 'on the hoof' along the poor roads to distant markets.

For those who wished to travel quickly, post horses, which travelled at about 10 or 12 miles (16 or 19 kilometres) per hour, could be hired from certain inns along all the main roads. The horses could be changed as they grew tired. After 1660 stage coaches became more common for passenger travel (**A**, **B** and **C**). They usually covered about 30 to 40 miles (50 to 60 kilometres) a day. Travel by stage coach was expensive and poorer people either walked or travelled by the slow stage waggons.

How were roads kept in repair?

Under an Act of Parliament of 1555, each parish was responsible for the upkeep of its own roads.

YORK Four Days Stage-Coach.

Begins on Friday the 12th of April. 1706.

ALL that are desirous to pass from *London* to *York*, or from *York* to *London*, or any other Place on that Road; Let them Repair to the *Black Swan* in *Holbourn* in *London*, and to the *Black Swan* in *Coney* street in *York*.

At both which Places, they may be received in a Stage Coach every *Monday, Wednesday* and *Friday*, which performs the whole Journey in Four Days, (if God permits,) And sets forth at Five in the Morning.

And returns from *York* to *Stamford* in two days, and from *Stamford* by *Huntington* to *London* in two days more. And the like Stages on their return.

Allowing each Passenger 14l. weight, and all above 3d. a Pound.

Performed By { Benjamin Kingman, Henry Harrison, Walter Baynes

Also this gives Notice that Newcastle Stage Coach, sets out from *York*, every *Monday*, and *Friday*, and from *Newcastle* every *Monday* and *Friday*.

Rocd. in pt. 05:00. of Mr. Bodingfeld for 5 for Munday the 3 of June 1706.

A *Early stage coach advertisement*

However, many parish authorities were unwilling to force people to work on the roads and claimed that it was through traffic and not the local traffic that damaged the roads.

In order to minimize the damage to the road surface, further Acts of Parliament were passed. These controlled the weight of vehicles and regulated the size of their wheels. In the belief that broad wheels caused less damage to the road surface, the Broad Wheels Act (1753) compelled goods waggons to have wheels at least 23 cm wide (**D**). These Acts were not effective.

B *From* A Tour through the Whole Island of Great Britain *by Daniel Defoe*

Suppose we take the great northern post road from London to York . . . you have tolerable good ways and hard ground, 'till you reach Royston . . . from thence you enter . . . the clays which . . . holds on 'till we come almost to Bautree . . . in Yorkshire and there the country is hard and sound.

Suppose you take the other northern road [from London], namely, by St Albans . . . Nottingham . . . On this road, after you are pass'd Dunstable . . . you enter the deep clays . . . that it is perfectly frightful to travellers . . . great number of horses every year kill'd by the excess of labour in those heavy ways . . . To the very bank of Trent these terrible clays continue; at Nottingham you are pass'd them . . . the coach road . . . is a most frightful way . . . call'd Baldock Lane, famous for being so unpassable, that the coaches and travellers were oblig'd to break out of the way . . . rather than plunge into sloughs and holes, which no horse could wade through.

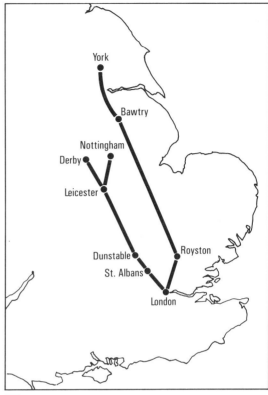

C *Routes between London and the North*

Q (a) How long did the journey from London to York take by stage coach in 1706 (**A**)?

(b) Why did coaches always start from, and travel to, inns?

(c) At what time of the morning did they set out?

(d) How much luggage weight could each passenger carry without extra charge?

(e) Why might passengers be reluctant to carry much luggage?

(f) The distance between London and York is approximately 322 kilometres. How many kilometres did the coach travel each day?

(g) What words in the advertisement (Source **A**) suggest that it might take longer to complete the journey?

(h) On which stretches of the London to York road was travelling most difficult (sources **B** and **C**)?

(i) What similar difficulties might be met with on the other northern route (source **B**)?

(j) Using the information in the sources **A**–**D**, write four entries as in a diary describing a journey in the early eighteenth century.

(k) Can you name the two modern roads which pass along or near the routes shown on the sketch map **C**?

D *An old English waggon*

■ The turnpike age

What were turnpike trusts?

Local parishes were unable to carry out effective road repair, especially on the through routes, and another method had to be found. From 1663 onwards, private Acts of Parliament were passed giving groups of local people, called turnpike trustees, permission to make or improve stretches of main road (about 16 to 32 km). These were known as turnpike roads. Toll bars or toll gates were erected at each end of the section of road and all road users had to pay a certain amount of money (known as a toll) to the trustees (**E** and **F**). The tolls varied according to the type of vehicle and the goods being carried. This meant that those who used the roads also paid for their upkeep. Sometimes there was local opposition to paying tolls, and even occasional turnpike riots.

How were the turnpike trusts financed?

The initiative for the setting up of a turnpike trust came from local people and was financed in part from the profits of farming. The treasurers (people who looked after the money) of the turnpike trusts were often local bankers. Some turnpike trusts were dishonest and concentrated on collecting the tolls rather than on repairing the roads. However, many trusts repaired and widened roads, built bridges and made steep gradients easier for traffic.

E *From* A Tour through the Whole Island of Great Britain *by Daniel Defoe*

. . . the consequence has been, that turnpikes or toll-bars have been set up on the . . . great roads of England, beginning at London, and proceeding thro' almost all those dirty deep roads, in the midland counties . . . at which turnpikes all carriages, droves of cattle, and travellers on horseback, are oblig'd to pay . . . toll; that is to say, a horse a penny, a coach three pence, a cart four pence, at some six pence to eight pence, a waggon six pence, in some a shilling, and the like; cattle pay by the score, or by the head, in some places more, in some less . . . the benefit of a good road abundantly making amends for that little charge the travellers are put to at the turnpikes . . . .

Q (a) On which roads were turnpikes first set up? Why do you think this was? (Look back to source **B**.)

(b) How was the money collected in tolls to be spent?

(c) Copy and complete this table of tolls for a turnpike by using the information in source **E**.

Table of tolls
A horse – *1 penny*
A coach – *3 pence*
(to be completed)

(d) If you could impose your own tolls, which types of traffic would you order to pay most; and which the least? Give reasons for your answer.

F *An unusual view of Oxford Street at the Tyburn turnpike at the western entrance*

THE *Original* BATH *Mail Coach of 1784* | AN *Attack on the* EXETER *Mail in 1816* | THE NORWICH *Mail in a Thunder Storm 1827* | THE HOLYHEAD & LIVERPOOL *Mails 1828* | THE EDINBURGH *Mail Snowbound in 1831*

The turnpike road system

The first turnpike trusts were set up for roads around London and in the south east of England.

Regional turnpike networks were built up in the later eighteenth century and by the 1830s there were about 1,100 separate turnpike trusts controlling about 35,400 kilometres of road. However, at no time did the number of turnpike roads outnumber the ordinary roads of the kingdom, and in some places turnpikes were unknown.

Carriage and travel in the turnpike age

Waggons on the repaired roads could carry nearly twice as much as before and the charges were almost halved. Freight costs fell greatly and a network of waggon services was run by individual carriers and by large companies like Pickford's.

The stage coaches were improved to make them more comfortable for passengers. Services expanded and became more reliable with faster vehicles.

The routes were divided into 'stages', each of about 24 kilometres, after which the horses were changed at the inns. By the early nineteenth century fares were approximately 3d (3 old pennies = 1½ new pence) per mile to ride on the outside of the stage coach, and nearly 6d (6 old pennies = 3 new pence) per mile to travel inside the coach.

Improvements on the roads and better forms of transport led to a great reduction in travel times.

Improvements in the postal service

In 1784 John Palmer, a theatrical manager in Bath and Bristol, suggested to the Government that the mail should be carried by coach to replace the system of post boys on horseback. The first service, organized by Palmer, ran between Bristol, Bath and London (**G**). Soon afterwards mail coaches were running on all the

G *Modern stamps*

> **Q** (a) What have all the coaches shown in source **G** in common?
> (b) What evidence can you find (source **H**) that there was an improvement in travelling times between 1801 and 1831?
> (c) Two of the stamps in source **G** show recorded events in the history of the Royal Mail – the attack by a lioness on the Exeter Mail; and a terrible storm in which the Norwich Mail was caught. Select *either* of these and write an imaginary story of the events which preceded and followed the scenes shown.

H *Advertisements from the* Shrewsbury Chronicle

April 3, 1801

The Royal Mail coach every morning at 6.0 clock, through Birmingham and Oxford to the Bull and Mouth Inn, London in 22 hours.

The Holyhead coach, at 4.0 clock on Monday, Wednesday and Friday mornings, the New Road which avoids Conway Ferry, lies at Conway and arrives at Mr Jared Jackson's, Holyhead, the next day.

July 1, 1831

Royal Mail every morning at half past 11 to the Swan with two Necks, Lad Lane, London, by 6 the following morning.

Holyhead . . . Royal Mail, every morning at 12, to Spencer's Royal Hotel by half past 10 the same night . . . .

main roads (**H**). The mail coaches also carried a small number of passengers and travelled, at first, at an average speed of about 12 kilometres per hour. Thus the period of road improvement was also the age of the mail coach.

In 1840 Rowland Hill proposed a change in the system of paying for postage. He suggested that a standard rate of a penny (½p) be charged for every letter up to half an ounce (14 grams), with additional charges for extra weight, and that the cost should be paid by the sender rather than by the receiver. His plan was accepted and the world's first postage stamps, the 'Penny Blacks', were produced. Gradually, a uniform system of postage was developed. However, with the coming of the railways, mail could be carried more quickly and safely by rail, and the mail-coach service declined.

■ The road engineers

The work of the road engineers

As a result of the increase in road traffic and the setting up of turnpike trusts, the work of the road engineer became important. In the later eighteenth and early nineteenth centuries a number of important road engineers worked out scientific principles of road construction.

John Metcalf (1717–1810)   Although blind from the age of six, John ('Blind Jack') Metcalf became engineer for the Harrogate-Boroughbridge turnpike trust in 1763. He built many roads across difficult land in the Pennine counties of Yorkshire, Lancashire, Derbyshire and Cheshire. Metcalf paid great attention to drainage and included ditches along his roads so that rainwater could run away easily. He laid firm foundations of large stones, and used bundles of heather as a foundation on roads which were constructed over soft or boggy ground. In all, Metcalf constructed almost 322 kilometres of road.

Thomas Telford (1757–1834)   Telford was a stone mason who became a famous civil engineer. He built roads and bridges, many of them in Scotland, and also canals. His greatest works were the reconstruction of the London to Holyhead road (1815–30) and the construction of the Menai Suspension Bridge which carried that road from the mainland to the island of Anglesey. Telford constructed the Ellesmere and Caledonian Canals, and many aqueducts and harbours.

Although Telford's road engineering work was often expensive, he was a better engineer than Metcalf. His road foundations were more solid and he laid drains under the foundations to carry off the rainwater. Other features of Telford's roads included accurate surveys, moderate cambers (see source **J**), gentle gradients and wide surfaces (**I**). Few turnpike trusts could afford such expensive methods.

John Macadam (1756–1836)   Macadam was a Scottish engineer. He built roads much more cheaply than the other road builders of the time. He concentrated on good drainage and the construction of a good surface by means of small broken stones which became bound together under the pressure from the traffic. This process came to be known, after Macadam himself, as 'macadamised' roads (**J**). More than 1,000 miles (1,600 kilometres) of road were constructed under Macadam's supervision.

Macadam became Surveyor General of the Metropolitan Turnpike Trust (formed from all the small turnpike trusts in the London area) and, partly under his influence, the General Highways Act was passed in 1835. This Act finally repealed the old Act of 1555. Local rates were now to be raised by the parishes for the upkeep of the roads.

What was the importance of the road engineers?

The more scientific road-making techniques of Metcalf, Telford and Macadam meant that a greater volume of wheeled traffic could use the roads.

I *From* Journal of a Tour in Scotland in 1819 *by Robert Southey*

The Plan upon which he [Thomas Telford] proceeds in road-making is . . . first to level then, like the Romans, to lay a solid pavement of large stones . . . as close as they can be set; the points are then broken off, and a layer of stones broken to about the size of walnuts, laid over them, so that the whole are bound together; over all a little gravel if it be at hand, but this is not essential . . . .

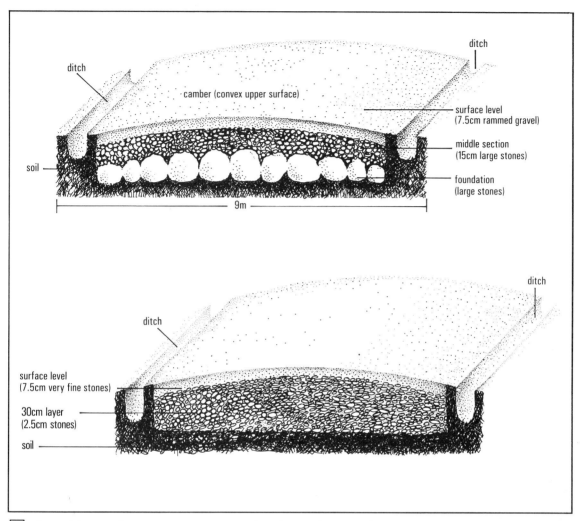

J *above: A section of road built by Thomas Telford below: A section of road built by John Macadam*

Q (a) What purpose did the large stones, shown in the cross-section of Telford's road, serve?

(b) What was different about the way Telford laid the foundation stones for his roads?

(c) What was the main purpose of the middle section of Telford's roads and what kind of stones were used?

(d) What material did Telford use for the surface level?

(e) Why was the surface given a camber?

(f) What purpose was served by the ditches?

(g) Name *one* similarity and *one* important difference between Telford's and Macadam's method of road building.

(h) Name *one* advantage of Telford's method and *one* advantage of Macadam's method of road building.

■ The end of the turnpike age

1 Not every road was looked after by a turnpike trust and so there were many gaps and poor stretches of road in the network.

2 The method of setting up turnpikes was expensive and it was not until the 1820s that the roads were in reasonable condition.

3 Just as the roads had reached a reasonable standard, construction of the railways began.

4 With growing competition from the railways from the 1830s onwards, the roads were increasingly neglected until the coming of the motor car in the twentieth century.

QUESTIONS

1 (a) What benefits did the turnpike roads bring?
  (b) Why were turnpikes sometimes opposed?

2 The graph shows the approximate number of daily departures of Royal Mail and stage coaches from leading provincial towns in Britain between 1770 and 1850.
  (a) Why were there relatively few stage-coach services before 1790?
  (b) Account for the decline in stage-coach services after 1830.
  (c) At which time did the stage-coach services reach their peak?
  (d) In what ways were stage-coach services improved between 1790 and 1830?

3 (a) Why was the turnpike age an important period for road engineers?
  (b) Why was the use of more scientific road-making techniques important?

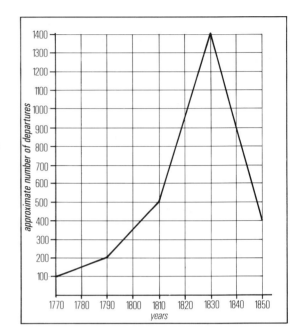

4 Rearrange this chart correctly.

Name of person	Problems they faced	Solution
John Metcalf	Speeding up the carrying of the mail	Using large stones as a foundation with smaller stones above
Thomas Telford	Road building through marshy moorland	Improving the London–Bath–Bristol route
John Macadam	To build an all-weather road between London and Holyhead	Using bundles of heather as a foundation
John Palmer	To ensure good drainage and a hard surface at low cost	Using fine stones laid over slightly larger material

5 Complete the following passage, using a word from the list below. (NB: there are more words than spaces.)

Under an Act of _____ the responsibility for road repair lay with each_____ . Urgent improvements were necessary in the eighteenth century and _____ were developed. Travellers had to pay at _____ built along the roads. Some roads in the Pennines were improved by _____ . The most famous improved road was built by _____ between Holyhead and _____ .

county council; parish; turnpike trusts; motorways; toll gates; coaching; 1555; 1662; 1760; customs houses; Metcalf; Telford; Macadam; London; Edinburgh; Swansea; twelve; eight; two

9 Railways

In the early eighteenth century, a few wooden tracks were used to carry horse-drawn waggons of coal on the main coalfields of Britain. By 1850 about 8,000 kilometres of iron track had been constructed for steam locomotives. The development of a national railway network to carry both goods and passengers had a great effect on industry, social life and on other forms of transport.

■ The track

Origins and early development of railways
The movement of heavy or bulky goods along a regular route between two points often led to the development of a 'track'. The earliest tracks were built on the coalfields and were simply lines of wooden blocks along which horses could pull coal waggons. They were laid down over short distances and acted as 'feeder' routes to rivers, ports and, later, to the canals.

After 1760 the use of cast-iron rails for waggonways became more common. Iron rails could carry heavier loads than wooden rails. In 1767 Richard Reynolds built a cast-iron track from Coalbrookdale to the river Severn. The rail had a *flange* (a raised edge) which held the wheel on the line. Later, the flange was moved from the rail to the wheel. In 1820, stronger wrought-iron rails were patented by John Birkinshaw, of Bedlington in Northumberland.

■ Locomotion
Before the coming of the locomotive horses were widely used to move waggons along the tracks. Sometimes full waggons were allowed to roll down hills, pulled by gravity. The empty waggons were then pulled back up again by the weight of the full waggons going down. This was known as a self-acting incline. In at least one instance, wind power and sails were used.

What factors led to the development of steam locomotion?
During the long wars against France horse power became more expensive because horses were in demand by the army. It was therefore important to find a cheaper way of moving coal and other bulky goods along the tracks. In 1800, the patent on Watt's steam engine ended, which meant that other people could copy it. Watt believed that steam locomotion had no future.

The work of Richard Trevithick
In 1801 Richard Trevithick (1771–1833), a Cornish engineer and one of the most brilliant inventors of the age, built a steam carriage to carry passengers on the roads. In 1804 he built the first locomotive to run on rails for the carriage of coal and iron in Merthyr Tydfil, South Wales. Four years later, in 1808, Trevithick demonstrated an engine, 'Catch Me Who Can' which ran on a circular track in London (**A** and **B**).

The work of George Stephenson
George Stephenson (1781–1848), the son of a colliery fireman (someone who looked after the steam-pumping engines) in Northumberland, became the most famous of British railway engineers. He had no formal education but gained expert practical knowledge of engineering from working with the Boulton and Watt steam engines which were used to pump water from the collieries.

In 1812 he was put in charge of the engines at the Killingworth Colliery near Newcastle and became so skilled with steam engines that other collieries employed him too. He became fascinated with steam locomotives and built his first one, called 'Blucher', at Killingworth in 1814. At neighbouring Wylam Colliery, William Hedley had constructed the famous early locomotive 'Puffing Billy'.

The Stockton and Darlington Railway
The colliery owners around Darlington, and coal traders such as the Quaker businessman Edward Pease, wanted a cheaper and quicker means of sending coal to the port of Stockton for shipment. They received permission from Parliament to build a railway and Stephenson was appointed the engineer. The 43-kilometre

A *Richard Trevithick's railroad in London (1808)*

Stockton to Darlington railway was opened in 1825 and, at first, used both horses and steam engines. The gauge (the width) of the line was 4 feet 8½ inches (1·44 m). The high costs of construction were recovered partly by charging for the carriage of goods, and by imposing tolls.

The Liverpool and Manchester Railway

This railway was promoted by a number of Liverpool merchants who were dissatisfied with local canal and river facilities. They wanted a better and cheaper means of carrying cotton, sugar and foodstuffs to Manchester.

An Act of Parliament, supported by William Huskisson MP, was obtained to build the 55 kilometres of double-track line and Stephenson was appointed the engineer.

There were construction difficulties to be overcome. At Chat Moss the railway had to cross boggy land and the track was floated on rafts of brushwood and heather. It also crossed the Sankey Brook Navigation, over which Stephenson built a large viaduct (a bridge with several arches). Near Liverpool a tunnel had to be bored and a deep cut made through the rock.

B *Letter to Mechanics' Magazine, 27 March 1847*

Sir,

. . . about the year 1808 he [Richard Trevithick] laid down a circular railway in a field adjoining the New Road . . . he placed a locomotive engine, weighing about 10 tons, on that railway . . . at the rate of twelve miles an hour [19 kph] . . . Mr Trevithick then gave his opinion that it would go twenty miles an hour [32 kph], or more, on a straight railway . . . the engine was exhibited at one shilling [5p] admittance, including a ride for the few who were not too timid . . . it ran for some weeks, when a rail broke and occasioned the engine to fly off in a tangent and overturn, the ground being very soft at the time.

Mr Trevithick having expended all his means in erecting the works and enclosure, and shillings not having come in fast enough to pay current expenses, the engine was not again set on the rail.

I am, Sir, your obedient servant,
John Isaac Hawkins,
Civil Engineer, London

The Rainhill Trials

In order to decide whether stationary engines (which would work a winch pulling the waggons) or locomotive engines (which would move along under their own power) should be used on the Liverpool and Manchester railway, a competition was held, with a prize of £500 for the winner. The trials held at Rainhill just outside Liverpool were an important testing ground for locomotives (**C** and **D**). The 'Rocket', a steam engine designed by George Stephenson and his son, Robert, was the winner and reached a speed of 30 miles per hour (48 kph).

The success of the Stephensons at the Rainhill Trials greatly helped their careers as engineers. Their locomotives, in addition to the 'Rocket', included 'Locomotion' and 'Northumbrian'.

A great occasion

The opening of the Liverpool and Manchester railway in 1830 was a great occasion attended by about 50,000 people, including the Prime Minister, the Duke of Wellington. Tragically, William Huskisson, the politician who had done much to promote the railway, was knocked down and killed by a locomotive during the opening ceremony.

C *Grand Competition of Locomotives on the Liverpool and Manchester Railway (1829)*

THE "ROCKET" OF MR ROBT STEPHENSON OF NEWCASTLE,
WHICH DRAWING A LOAD EQUIVALENT TO THREE TIMES ITS WEIGHT TRAVELLED AT THE RATE OF 12½ MILES AN HOUR. AND WITH A CARRIAGE & PASSENGERS AT THE RATE OF 24 MILES.
COST PER MILE FOR FUEL ABOUT THREE HALFPENCE.

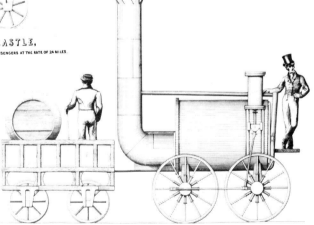

THE "SANSPAREIL" OF MR HACKWORTH OF DARLINGTON,
WHICH DRAWING A LOAD EQUIVALENT TO THREE TIMES ITS WEIGHT TRAVELLED AT THE RATE OF 12½ MILES AN HOUR. COST FOR FUEL PER MILE ABOUT TWO PENC

THE "NOVELTY" OF MESSR BRAITHWAITE & ERRICSSON OF LONDON,
WHICH DRAWING A LOAD EQUIVALENT TO THREE TIMES ITS WEIGHT TRAVELLED AT THE RATE OF 20½ MILES AN HOUR. AND WITH A CARRIAGE & PASSENGERS AT THE RATE OF 32 MILES.
COST PER MILE FOR FUEL ABOUT ONE HALFPENNY.

D *John Dixon (assistant to George Stephenson) in a letter to his brother, Dr James Dixon*

Patricroft 16 October 1829

Dear James,

We have finished the grand experiments on the Engines and G.S. and R.S. has come off triumphant . . . none of the others being able to come near them. The Rocket is by far the best Engine I have ever seen for Blood and Bone united . . . .

Timothy [Hackworth] . . . openly accused all G.S.'s people of conspiring to hinder him . . . however he got many trials but never got half of his 70 miles [112 km] done without stopping . . . burns nearly double the quantity of coke that the Rocket does . . . and moreover weighs about four and one-half tons . . . She is very ugly and the Boiler runs out [leaks] very much, he had to feed her with more Meal and Malt Sprouts than would fatten a Pig . . . .

The London engine of Braithwaite and Erickson . . . was a light one . . . but every trial he had some mishap, first an explosion of inflammable gas which Burst his Bellows then his feed pipe blew up . . . so that it was no go . . .

Report as to Fixed and permanent Engines stated that the whole power of the Loco. Engines would be absorbed in taking their own bodies up Rainhill Incline . . . consequently they could take no load, now the first thing old George did was to bring a Coach with about 20 people up at a galop and every day since he has run up and down to let them see what they could do up such an ascent and has taken 40 folks up at 20 miles an hour [32 kph].

Q (a) The letter (source **D**) states that G.S. and R.S. had won 'the grand experiments'. Who were G.S. and R.S.?

(b) Why do you think John Dixon was pleased with the outcome of the experiments?

(c) How is his evidence likely to be biased?

(d) How might other engineers and competitors explain why they were less successful than the 'Rocket'?

■ Problems and progress

Railway mania and 'The Railway King'

In the years 1834–7, and again in 1844–7, numerous railway companies promoted Acts of Parliament. During these periods of railway 'mania', there was heavy speculation (investing money, with a risk of loss) in railway shares and many fortunes were made or lost.

One of the leading speculators was George Hudson, a linen draper in York, who became known as 'The Railway King'. Hudson made a fortune in the railway mania of the 1840s and by 1847 was director of many railway companies, based mainly on York. However, Hudson had been concealing his losses and the financial crisis of the late 1840s ruined him.

Opposition to the building of some railways

There was opposition to some railway schemes from canal companies, coaching firms and turnpike trusts who feared competition (**E**). Sometimes landowners wanted to keep railways away from their estates. In one or two instances town traders and officials opposed the railways.

Costs of construction

The high cost of British railway construction was due partly to the cost of buying land and partly to the cost of building the lines over difficult ground. Tunnels, cuttings and viaducts to eliminate steep gradients were all expensive engineering activities.

What was 'the battle of the gauges'?

The use of Stephenson's gauge (the width between the rails) of 4 feet 8½ inches (1·44 m) was not universal in the early years of railway development. Isambard Kingdom Brunel (see pages 126–7) builder of the Clifton Suspension Bridge in Bristol and the Albert Bridge across the river Tamar, was the engineer for the Great Western Railway. This was constructed using the broad gauge of 7 feet (2·13 m). A possibility of conflict between the different railways was settled by the Gauge Regulating Act of 1846 which made Stephenson's narrow gauge the standard.

E *Cartoon by George Cruickshank*

F *From the Presidential address of Robert Stephenson at the Institution of Civil Engineers Meeting (January 1856)*

British railways . . . spreading like a network to the extent of 8054 miles (12886 km) completed . . . the companies employ 90,400 officers and servants . . . the engines consume annually 20 million tons of coal . . . 20,000 tons of iron required to be replaced annually . . . 26 million sleepers annually perished.

Q (a) Write out the captions in cartoon **E**.
(b) What are the men wearing and carrying which show that they are coachmen?
(c) How do they account for their distress and poverty?
(d) What is the cartoonist trying to show?
(e) Which other people felt that their livelihood was threatened by the coming of the railways?
(f) In what ways was the author of source **F** involved in the development of the railways?
(g) How does he suggest that railways created employment?
(h) Which other industries would need to employ more people as a result of railway development?

■ What were the effects of railway development?

1 By the mid-nineteenth century most important towns had been linked by rail with London, and a national railway network had been established.
2 The actual construction of the railways provided employment for more than 50,000 navvies.
3 The development of the railways led to a greatly increased demand for coal and iron, and provided a further stimulus for engineering (**F**).
4 A number of new towns were developed as railway centres, for example Crewe (which was built by a railway company) and Swindon.
5 The coming of the railways led to further reductions in transport costs and wider markets were created for goods of all kinds, including perishable agricultural produce.

■ Social effects

1 Travelling times between most major cities were reduced, and passengers were transported more cheaply.
2 Mobility increased for workers and for the public.
3 Popular travel was further encouraged by the passing of the Railways Act (1844), which stated that each railway company had to run at least one train, in each direction, every day. The so-called 'Parliamentary train' was to travel at a minimum speed of 12 miles per hour (19 kph), was to stop at every station and to charge no more than one penny per mile.
4 The remoter country areas became less isolated, postal systems improved and national newspapers appeared.
5 A new social habit, the taking of holidays, became possible for a growing number of people.

QUESTIONS

1 Give two reasons why there was a growing interest in steam locomotion in the early years of the nineteenth century.

2 Copy and complete the following sentences by filling in the gaps.

The S_____ and D_____ railway was opened in 1825 to speed up the transport of coal. G_____ S_____ built the railway.

The L_____ and M_____ railway was opened in 1830 to carry _____ , _____ and _____ . To decide between the various locomotives the R_____ T_____ were held.

The G_____ W_____ railway between London and Bristol was built by I. K. Brunel, using the broad gauge of _____ . The new town of S_____ became an important railway centre on this line.

One of the leading speculators in railway shares was G_____ H_____ of York who became known as the 'R_____ K_____'.

3 (a) Using map **G**, account for the greater number of lines in the following areas: the North-East; South Wales; London; Manchester.
 (b) Why were there very few lines in the South-West and North Wales?

4 (a) Look at the table on page 59. Can you explain why, in most years, the number of miles of railway approved in the Railway Acts was greater than the mileage of railways opened?
 (b) Can you explain the high mileage of railways authorized in 1835–6 and 1844–6?
 (c) In which two consecutive years were the most miles of railway opened?

5 Copy and complete the chart below to show the benefits and drawbacks of railways.

Railways: a balance sheet	
Good news	Bad news
A more rapid means of transport than anything else available at the time	*Serious accidents sometimes occurred*
(to be	completed)

6 Using the tables and the map to help you, describe the development of the railways in the first half of the nineteenth century.

7

Inland spa towns	Decline of turnpikes	The invention of steam locomotives
Growth of suburbs	Demand for iron and steel	Control of railways by Parliament

 (a) Choose *two* of the items from the above table which were important *results* of the railway boom of the 1840s. Give reasons for your choice.
 (b) Add *one* more *result* of the 1840s railway boom *not* shown in the table. Explain why the feature you have chosen was a *result*.

8 Using sources **C** and **D**, write out a judges' report on each of the following: the 'Rocket'; the 'Novelty'; the 'Sanspareil'. Describe the engines as seen in the illustrations, give an account of their performance in the trials (include details of the maker and where he came from) and conclude with the results of the experiments and why you have selected one of the engines as the winner.

9 *Either:*

Write an account for a nineteenth-century newspaper of the opening of Richard Trevithick's railroad in London in 1808 (see sources **A** and **B**, page 54);

or:

Design a poster to attract visitors to see the engine 'Catch Me Who Can'. Include details of date, place, price of admission, speeds, the engineer, and details of the engine, carriages and the circular track (see sources **A** and **B**, page 54).

Year	Mileage authorized by Parliament	Mileage opened each year
1825	14	27
1826	65	11
1830	61	47
1831	31	43
1835	201	40
1836	956	66
1839	55	227
1840	0	528
1844	811	192
1845	2816	288
1846	4541	634
1849	17	812
1850	7	621

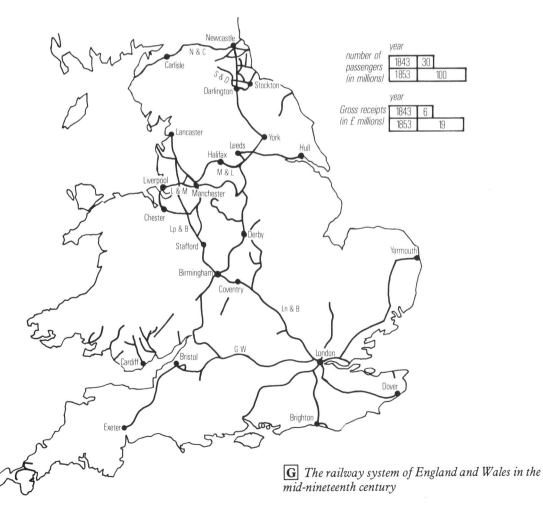

number of passengers (in millions)	year	
	1843	30
	1853	100

Gross receipts (in £ millions)	year	
	1843	6
	1853	19

G *The railway system of England and Wales in the mid-nineteenth century*

10 Trade unions

The history of trade unions between 1700 and 1850 was not one of continuous steady progress. For much of the period the Government was strongly opposed to the development of trade unions. However, by the mid-nineteenth century, and after many bitter struggles, workers had gained the right to unite together to protect their interests and to bargain with employers over wages and hours.

■ Trade and factory societies

The earliest trade unions

Trade societies were formed, at first, among the skilled craft workers such as printers, papermakers, hatters and cutlers (**A**). Most trade societies were small and local, but a few were nationwide – for example, the National Society of Brushmakers formed in 1747.

Q (a) Using the information on the border of illustration **A** (beginning on the left-hand side), copy and complete this chart.

Event/Activity	Date
Hats were first invented	*1456*
(to be completed)	

(b) What animals are shown in the room?
(c) Can you suggest any connection between the animals, the pictures on the wall and the work of felt makers?
(d) Can you say in which city the scene is set?
(e) Can you explain the connection between the motto ('We Assist Each Other in Time of Need'), the standing man showing his membership card, and the man at the table?

A *The emblem of the Association of Felt Makers*

The trade societies met regularly, often at local public houses. Each member would put a penny or twopence a week into a fund, to help any of their number in need. They tried to restrict the number of apprentices entering particular trades and crafts, so as to make themselves more valuable to their masters. Members also imposed work discipline, with a system of fines for rule breaking such as fighting, drinking and swearing.

Friendly Societies

By the later eighteenth century many craftsmen and workers belonged to Friendly Societies. These aimed to provide benefits in times of sickness and unemployment, and for widows and orphans. Respectable workers feared the social disgrace of having to depend on the poor rates or on the workhouse. At first the Friendly Societies were not protected by law and if someone ran off with a Society's funds the members could do nothing about it. In 1793, the Friendly Societies were recognized in law and this enabled them to protect their funds.

Trade unions at the end of the eighteenth century

The growing number of workers concentrated in the towns enabled them to combine (join together) to discuss their common grievances.

By the 1790s factory societies like the Stockport and Manchester Spinning Society had begun to develop. These local combinations or 'unions' of spinners existed in most of the Lancashire cotton towns. These societies, like the early trade societies, also tried to enforce the apprenticeship laws and attempted to establish a closed shop (prevent the employment of workers who were not members of the society). They also wanted to prevent blacklegging (strike-breaking) when strikes occurred.

The societies were successful in years of good trade but in periods of trade depression membership fell. The societies also had to face the hostility of the Government.

■ Trade unions and the law

What were the Combination Acts 1799–1800?

The British Government feared that workers might attempt to disrupt or overturn society, as had happened in France during the revolution. Disorder was harshly put down and the Government tried to suppress all working-class movements.

One way in which the Government showed its opposition to trade unions or combinations was by the passing of the Combination Acts in 1799 and 1800. The Acts banned all combinations or unions of both masters and workers. The Acts also prohibited strikes, union meetings and the collection of union subscriptions.

How effective were the Combination Acts?

The Combination Acts (**B**, and **C**) were not widely enforced in practice. Masters were rarely prosecuted but proceedings were sometimes taken against workers who combined to negotiate over wages and hours worked.

B *From* **General View of the Agriculture of the County of Essex** *(1793)*

. . . benefit clubs, holden at public houses, increase the number of those houses, and naturally lead to idleness and drunkenness . . . they afford numerous opportunities to form illegal combinations, which they have sometimes actually done, and that as far as I have . . . observed there is not the smallest probability in their general extensive application, that they ever have, or ever will diminish our poor rates but just the contrary.

C *A quote from the Duke of Portland, 1799*

If nothing injurious to the safety of the government is actually in contemplation, Associations so formed contain within themselves the means of being converted at any time into a most dangerous instrument to disturb the public tranquility.

Q (a) What arguments were raised against friendly societies and the early trade unions (source **B**)?
(b) Does source **C** support or contradict source **B**? Give reasons for your answer.
(c) When and why were the Combination Acts passed?

The real effect of the Combination Acts was to drive organized workers' groups underground and thus many societies survived. An investigation in 1806 revealed the existence of a widespread organization in the woollen manufacturing areas of Yorkshire. In Lancashire, despite the Combination Acts, strikes of cotton spinners occurred in 1810 and 1818.

Many older societies continued to exist as friendly societies collecting weekly subscriptions from members and making payments to workers at times of illness, or to the widows and children of deceased (dead) members.

Why were the Combination Acts repealed in 1824?

By the 1820s economic and social conditions in Britain were improving and there was less fear of disruption and revolution. A movement to repeal the Combination Acts was organized by Francis Place, a former strike leader and London tailor. He was assisted by his friend Joseph Hume, a Radical MP. A Parliamentary committee was set up to investigate the Combination Acts. In evidence to the Committee, many employers admitted that the Combination Acts were ineffective and hindered industrial relations. Place, Hume and their supporters persuaded Parliament to pass an Act which repealed the Combination Acts in 1824.

However, a wave of strikes swept the country and in 1825 the laws concerning trade unions were tightened up. Although trade unions (**D**) could now be formed legally, and could bargain with the employers for the regulation of wages and hours, they could not, at times of strikes, either obstruct (hinder) or intimidate (frighten)

Q (a) Which kinds of people does the cartoonist suggest might attend a meeting of trade unionists?

(b) Can you find evidence of any of their occupations?

(c) Were they rich or poor?

(d) Write out the 'speech' of the speaker. In what ways does the cartoonist try to ridicule trade unions?

D *A meeting of the trades unions*

fellow workers or employers. If trade union funds were stolen, the officials could only be prosecuted if the union was registered as a friendly society.

National unions and the Grand National

There were several attempts by local societies to form national associations. In 1829, John Doherty formed a Grand General Union of Operative Spinners in the United Kingdom for all spinning societies.

In 1830 Doherty attempted to include a number of trades in the National Association for the Protection of Labour. Although this collapsed, it became the model for the Grand National Consolidated Trades Union of 1834. Formed originally to support trade unionists in Derby against their employers, the Grand National quickly recruited several hundred thousand workers from many different trades, including farm labourers and women. It was greatly influenced by Robert Owen (see page 19). However, the Grand National soon failed.

Why did the Grand National fail?

1 The Grand National lacked the backing of many organized workers.
2 The four most important trade unions – the builders, the potters, the spinners and the clothiers – did not join.
3 The limited funds of the Grand National were spent in local disputes, and some of the Union's officials were dishonest.
4 The Grand National had to face the opposition of both the employers and the Government.
5 Many employers forced their workers to sign a 'document' stating that they neither belonged to, nor intended to join, a union.
6 Some employers locked out workers if they formed a branch of the Grand National.
7 Sometimes blacklegs or non-Union workers were brought in, by employers, to do the work of Union members locked out.

The Tolpuddle Martyrs

In the early 1830s the wages of farm workers were reduced from 40p a week to 35p and then further reduced to 30p. Some farm labourers from the village of Tolpuddle in Dorset attempted to form a local branch of the Grand National, despite the warnings of the local magistrates (**E**, **F** and **G**). The leader of the labourers was George Lovelace, a local preacher, who wrote to the Grand National for advice. Following this, the Tolpuddle labourers formed the Friendly Society of Agricultural Labourers. When it became known that the farm labourers were seeking to form a local union attempts were made to stop people from joining. These attempts failed, and in February 1834 Lovelace and five other labourers were arrested and imprisoned.

The trial of the Tolpuddle labourers at Dorchester was one of the most famous legal cases of the nineteenth century. They were found guilty, not of forming a union branch (for that was not illegal), but of asking new recruits to take a secret oath. This was illegal under a conspiracy Act passed in the 1790s. The six labourers, the so-called Tolpuddle Martyrs, were each sentenced to seven years transportation to Australia. There was a public outcry against the sentence and a campaign was organized in which Robert Owen was involved. In 1836 the Tolpuddle Martyrs were pardoned and allowed to come home.

Trade Unions in the 1840s

After the failure of the National Unions, many workers turned their attention to Chartism, factory reform and the Co-operative Movement. In the 1840s, more respectable unions, based on the traditional pattern of skilled workers, began to emerge. The first permanently successful workers' organizations began with the formation of the new model craft unions, led by the Amalgamated Society of Engineers in 1851.

E *Extract from a letter of George Lovelace, one of the Tolpuddle Martyrs*

About . . . 1832–3 the labouring men in the parish where we lived . . . asked the employers to give them more wages . . . We learnt that men in nearby areas were getting 10 shillings but we were only getting 9 shillings a week. After some months our wages were reduced to 8 shillings a week . . . Then a few weeks later our wages were reduced to 7 shillings and later there was talk of putting them down to 6 shillings. The labouring men consulted together about what had better be done, as they knew it was impossible to live on such scanty means . . . they willingly consented to form a trade society . . . So we formed our society. On the 9th of December, 1833, in the evening Edward Legge [a labourer] was admitted . . . he gave evidence against us at the trial . . . .

Nothing happened to us after Legge had first joined us. Then placards were put up cautioning any man from joining the union. This was the first time that I had heard of any law being in existence to forbid such societies . . . We were arrested on the 24th of February and were taken for our trial . . . .

As to the trial it was unfair and unjust . . . the cruel judge Williams sentenced the six of us who had been taken, to seven years transportation.

F *A warning to trade unionists*

CAUTION.

WHEREAS it has been represented to us from several quarters, that mischievous and designing Persons have been for some time past, endeavouring to induce, and have induced, many Labourers in various Parishes in this County, to attend Meetings, and to enter into Illegal Societies or Unions, to which they bind themselves by unlawful oaths, administered secretly by Persons concealed, who artfully deceive the ignorant and unwary,—WE, the undersigned Justices think it our duty to give this PUBLIC NOTICE and CAUTION, that all Persons may know the danger they incur by entering into such Societies.

ANY PERSON who shall become a Member of such a Society, or take any Oath, or assent to any Test or Declaration not authorized by Law—

Any Person who shall administer, or be present at, or consenting to the administering or taking any Unlawful Oath, or who shall cause such Oath to be administered, although not actually present at the time—

Any Person who shall not reveal or discover any Illegal Oath which may have been administered, or any Illegal Act done or to be done—

Any Person who shall induce, or endeavour to persuade any other Person to become a Member of such Societies,

WILL BECOME

Guilty of Felony,
AND BE LIABLE TO BE
Transported for Seven Years.

ANY PERSON who shall be compelled to take such an Oath, unless he shall declare the same within four days, together with the whole of what he shall know touching the same, will be liable to a Penalty of the like nature.

Any Person who shall directly or indirectly maintain correspondence or intercourse with such Society, will be deemed Guilty of an Unlawful Combination and Confederacy, and on Conviction before one Justice, on the Oath of one Witness, be liable to a Penalty of TWENTY POUNDS, or to be committed to the Common Gaol or House of Correction, for THREE CALENDAR MONTHS ; or if proceeded against by Indictment, may be CONVICTED OF FELONY, and be TRANSPORTED FOR SEVEN YEARS.

Any Person who shall knowingly permit any Meeting of any such Society to be held in any House, Building, or other Place, shall for the first offence be liable to the Penalty of FIVE POUNDS ; and for every other offence committed after Conviction, be deemed Guilty of such Unlawful Combination and Confederacy, and on Conviction before one Justice, on the Oath of one Witness, be liable to a Penalty of TWENTY POUNDS, or to be committed to the Common Gaol or House of Correction, FOR THREE CALENDAR MONTHS ; or if proceeded against by Indictment may be

CONVICTED OF FELONY,
And Transported for SEVEN YEARS.

COUNTY OF DORSET,
Dorchester Division.

February 22d. 1834.

C. B. WOLLASTON,
JAMES FRAMPTON,
WILLIAM ENGLAND,
THOS. DADE,
JNO. MORTON COLSON,

HENRY FRAMPTON,
RICHD. TUCKER STEWARD,
WILLIAM R. CHURCHILL,
AUGUSTUS FOSTER.

G. CLARK, PRINTER, CORNHILL, DORCHESTER.

G *From* The Times, *20 March 1834*

Spring Assizes, Western Circuit, Dorchester Monday, 17 March. Crown Court
Evidence of John Lock
I live at Half Puddle. I went to Toll Puddle a fortnight before Christmas. I know the prisoner, James Brine. He asked me if I would go to Toll Puddle with him. I agreed to do so. James Hammet was then with him. Edward Legge, Richard Peary, Henry Courtney, and Elias Riggs were with us . . . One of them asked if there would not be something to pay, and one said there would be 1s [5p] to pay on entering, and 1d [½p] a week after. We all went into Thomas Stanfield's house into a room upstairs. John Stansfield came to the door of the room. I saw James Lovelace and George Lovelace go along the passage. One of the men asked if we were ready. We said, yes. One of them said, 'Then bind your eyes', and we took out handkerchiefs and bound them over our eyes. They then led us into another room on the same floor. Someone then read a paper, but I don't know what the meaning of it was. After that we were asked to kneel down, which we did. Then there was some more reading; I don't know what it was about. It seemed to be out of some part of the Bible. Then we got up and took off the bandages from our eyes.

QUESTIONS

1 Complete the following passage by choosing (from the list provided below) the correct words or initials and writing them in the spaces. (NB: there are more words and initials than spaces.)

The ideas spread by the French Revolution and the disturbed economic and political conditions of the 1790s alarmed the British Government. In 1799 and 1800 a series of measures known as the _____ made it illegal for either masters or workers to form union-like organizations. A campaign to have these laws changed was led by Joseph Hume and _____ and in 1824 a _____ committee recommended that trade unions should be made legal. In 1830 the _____ was set up by John Doherty. This was popular at first but then faded. In 1833–4 it was largely replaced by the Grand National Consolidated Trades Union, which was greatly influenced by _____ . This was strongly opposed by some employers who made their workers sign a _____ stating that they neither belonged to, nor intended to join a trade union. During the following year, 1834, a number of _____ from the Dorset village of _____ were prosecuted for their activities and the taking of secret _____ . At Dorchester they were found guilty and were sentenced to _____ for seven years. They were pardoned in 1836.

Six Acts	Robert Owen
Combination Acts	petition
Master and Servant Acts	document
Robert Peel	coal miners
Francis Place	farm labourers
House of Lords	Tolpuddle
Parliamentary	Totnes
National Society of Brushmakers	codes
	oaths
National Association for the Protection of Labour	exportation
	transportation
	hard labour
Richard Oastler	

2 There are a number of errors in the following passage. Identify as many as you can, then rewrite the passage correctly.

In 1833 nine farm labourers from Tollgate in Durham came together to form a local branch of the Friendly Society of Agricultural Labourers. They were led by John Doherty. Their Society was part of the Grand National Consolidated Trades Union which was at this time led by Francis Place. Their actions alarmed the authorities and the secret oaths taken gave an excuse to try them for slander. Found guilty, all the men were sentenced to be transported for life to the penal colonies of Australia.

3 (a) Why did labouring men in the Dorset village of Tolpuddle form a trade society (source **E**)?
  (b) Describe in your own words what happened before a labourer could become a member of the society (source **G**).
  (c) Would labourers be guilty of an illegal action: if they attended meetings *or* if they formed societies or unions *or* if they took secret oaths? Which do you consider nearest to the truth? Give reasons for your answer.
  (d) Why, in *December 1833* had George Lovelace not 'heard of any law being in existence to forbid such societies'?
  (e) Why were the men of Tolpuddle brought to trial? Of what crime were they accused?
  (f) If Edward Legge and John Lock had not given evidence against the Tolpuddle Society, of what crime could they have been convicted?
  (g) What was the punishment for those found guilty of felony (source **F**)?
  (h) Can you suggest why John Lock had his eyes bound with a handkerchief at Tolpuddle (source **G**)?

11 Population

In the early eighteenth century the estimated population of England and Wales was five and a half millions and most people lived in the countryside. The life expectancy for people (that is, the average number of years from birth to death) was 38 years. By 1851, the population had risen to 18 millions and a larger proportion of people were living in the towns and in the industrial areas. The length of time people could expect to live ('life expectancy') had risen to 55 years.

Factors to consider in studying population

In any study of population, three factors must be considered. These are: changes in the birth rate; changes in the death rate; and immigration (see page 72) and emigration (see page 72). The birth rate and death rate (number of live births or deaths per thousand people in a given year) varied from year to year. It differed between one region and another, between town and country, and between rich and poor.

Other factors which influenced population change were marriage age and custom, the standard of living and health. Historians of population have made extensive use of the parish registers which recorded baptisms, marriages and burials. However, these sources are not complete. Births, marriages and deaths were not officially registered until 1837.

■ Population changes

Population in the early eighteenth century

In 1695 Gregory King estimated that the population of England and Wales was about five and a half millions. He based his estimate on information given by the collectors of the hearth tax. This was a tax, paid by householders, on the numbers of chimneys in each house. However, it was impossible to know the exact number of people in the country because the first national census (an official count of a country's inhabitants) was not taken until 1801.

In 1700 most people lived in the countryside for Britain was still mainly a farming country. Many people worked in their own homes under the domestic system, and sometimes combined the simple manufacturing or craft processes with farming. The most densely populated region was south of a line from the Wash to the Bristol Channel. Although there were many small towns, there were very few cities of any size. The cities with the most people were London (500,000), Norwich (30,000) and Bristol (30,000).

Population changes in the first half of the eighteenth century

The growth of population in this period was slow. In many parts of the country, poor employment opportunities meant that the age of marriage was late and this limited the number of children born. Bad harvests and diseases, such as smallpox and consumption (TB), contributed to the high death rate, especially among infants. It was also an age of cheap gin, although its large-scale consumption was mainly confined to London and the few large towns (**A** and **B**).

The rate of population growth was probably more rapid in the developing industrial districts where employment opportunities were greater and therefore the age of marriage was probably earlier. People were also moving into these areas from the surrounding rural communities. The main ports of London, Bristol and Liverpool expanded because of the growth of trade. Spas and watering places, such as Bath, became fashionable centres for members of the nobility and for wealthy merchants and traders.

Population changes in the later eighteenth and early nineteenth centuries

After the mid-eighteenth century, population grew more rapidly, rising from about six and a half millions in 1750 to more than nine millions in 1801 when the first official national census was taken for England and Wales. From that time onwards, a national census has been taken every ten years (with the exception of 1941, due to the Second World War). By 1851 the population of England and Wales had risen to over 18 millions.

A *'Gin Lane', an engraving by William Hogarth*

Q (a) List the ways in which the artist shows that the district was in decay (the scene is a slum in St Giles' Parish, Westminster, London).

(b) Describe the evils Hogarth has illustrated in **A**.

(c) Can you see any people working in Gin Lane?

(d) Do you think the artist was biased in the way he presented this subject? Give your reasons.

(e) Can you find the signs of the following: the pawnbroker (1), the distiller or gin maker (2), and the undertaker (3)? How does Hogarth show that these businesses were making money in Gin Lane? Can you suggest any connection between a pawnbroker, a distiller and an undertaker? How do their shops differ from the others?

(f) Can you find the sign for a barber (4)? Why had the barber in Gin Lane failed in business and hanged himself?

(g) Looking at (5), (6), (7) and (8) what do you think Hogarth is trying to tell people in his engraving?

B *'Beer Street'. The scene is London, possibly near St Martin's in the Fields*

Q Write down all the ways in which life in Beer Street (**B**) differed from life in Gin Lane (**A**).

■ Population explosion

Changes in the marriage and birth rates

With the growth of trade and the industrial revolution, employment prospects improved. This factor, and the decline of the apprenticeship system, led to earlier marriages which meant a rise in the birth rate. At the same time, improved standards of midwifery (a midwife is someone who assists at the birth of a baby) reduced the numbers of mothers and babies who died in child-birth. The fall in infant mortality meant that there were more future parents.

Why did the death rate fall in the later eighteenth century?

There were a number of reasons for the decline in the death rate:

Decline in gin drinking The extent of the gin-drinking craze was probably exaggerated, but in 1751 the Government took action to reduce the drinking of cheap gin by placing a high tax on spirits. The decline in gin drinking helped to reduce the death rate.

Improved and more varied diet Progress in farming provided more wheaten bread, meat and fresh vegetables. A better diet gave added resistance to disease. Improvements in transport meant that food supplies could be sent more easily to districts that were experiencing shortages. The growth of overseas trade meant that more food could be imported if necessary.

Living conditions With better employment opportunities there was some rise in living standards. Improvements in housing included the replacement of timber and thatch with brick and slate. The increasing use of coal for domestic fuel led to a reduction of dampness in many houses. Standards of hygiene improved with the production of more soap and with the greater use of cotton garments, which could be washed more easily than wool.

Advances in medicine The methods of surgery were improved by John and William Hunter. There were also improvements in medicine (**C**). Inoculation against smallpox was popularized by Lady Mary Wortley Montagu in the 1720s and, later, the technique of vaccination was developed by Edward Jenner (1749–1823) (**D–H**).

Other important advances occurred in the prevention of disease. For example, Captain Cook's voyage of 1772–5 gave clear proof that a lack of vitamin C found in fresh fruit and vegetables was the cause of the disease of scurvy. By 1800, scurvy, which had particularly affected British seamen, had almost been eliminated as a killer disease.

C *An operation 1793*

Q List all the differences you can between a hospital in the early nineteenth century and a modern hospital.

D *Extracts from* The Gentleman's Magazine, *1799–1807*

Jenner's publication of 1798: An Inquiry into . . . Variolae Vaccinae, a Disease known by the name of The Cow Pox. By Edward Jenner, M.D., F.R.S. . . . Dr J . . . is of opinion that this disease . . . prevents the constitution from being infected with the small pox.

E

The Medical Controversy: To inoculate with Small Pox or to Inoculate/Vaccinate with Cow-pox . . . The inoculation of the Cow-pock being . . . the introduction of a bestial disease into the human body . . . some other very different diseases . . . may arise in consequence . . . let it be remembered that the transfusion of blood from various animals into the blood-vessels of men, after having been most warmly taken up . . . in this as well as other countries, was found to produce serious . . . consequences, such as madness, and other diseases . . . (Letter signed) T.A.

F

Reply (Letter signed) G.C.J.
. . . T.A. took up the discussion of . . . Cow-pox . . . I will endeavour to set him right upon the subject. His principal fear is, that the introduction of the *bestial* humour may produce permanent ill effects . . . Let me assure him . . . that there is not a finer race of people . . . than the farmers and the farmers' wives in our Western dairy counties, many of whom had the Cow-pox when they were boys and girls . . . it does not injure the constitution in the least . . .

G

1807, July 29.
In the Commons . . . the Chancellor of the Exchequer moved that a further . . . £10,000 be granted to Dr Jenner for his discovery of the Cow Pox . . . He observed that the calculation of deaths . . . had been made in the three following classes, *viz*, in the Small Pox, the deaths were one in six; in Inoculation for the Small Pox one in 300; and in Inoculation under the present discovery of the Vaccine Pox, out of the immense number of 164,381, the deaths were only 3, which was only one in 54,761 . . . .

Q (a) What did Edward Jenner claim was the main benefit of cow-pox (source **D**)?

(b) What is the difference between inoculation with small pox and inoculation with cow-pox (vaccination)?

(c) Using all the sources, copy and complete this chart to show the arguments which were used *for* and *against* vaccination.

(d) Which case do you consider the most convincing? Explain your answer.

(e) What contribution did Edward Jenner make in assisting the fall in the death rate (source **G**)?

(f) If you had been living in the early nineteenth century would you: agree to be vaccinated/refuse to be vaccinated/wait for further evidence? Give reasons.

Vaccination (inoculation with Cow-Pox): A medical controversy	
Case for	Case against
Cow-pox: a mild disease which had never harmed farmers and other country people	(to be completed)

H *Jenner vaccinating a young child*

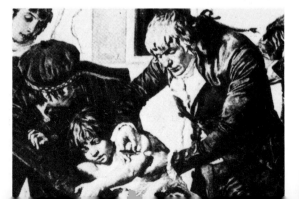

I *Families: Plenty and Want*

Q List all the differences between the two homes. In which of the families would you expect people to live the longest? Explain your answer.

Thomas Malthus

The rise in population growth encouraged a number of people to inquire into its causes.

In 1798 a clergyman, the Rev. Thomas Malthus, wrote a famous essay called *An Essay on the Principle of Population*. Malthus argued that, without certain checks, such as poverty, famine, disease, war and birth limitation, the population would grow faster than the country's ability to feed it. He believed that the more people there were, the poorer each would become (**I**). It was therefore argued that the poor must have smaller families and that the best method of population control was to pay workers such low wages that they could not afford to have children, and to give little or no poor relief to the unemployed.

Under the influence of Malthus, the system of giving parish relief to the poor – particularly the Speenhamland system (see page 79) – came to be regarded as a main reason for the increase in population.

How and why did people migrate?

Many people moved from one region of the country to another (migration). Farm labourers, attracted by the prospect of employment and higher wages, left the agricultural areas for the towns, the seaports and the industrial communities on the coalfields. The movement was usually over short distances. Occasionally, manufacturers moved and took their workers with them. Sometimes workhouse pauper children were sent from the towns to work in the textile factories and mills.

Many people migrated from Ireland to the industrial towns of England, especially south Lancashire and London. The greatest numbers came in the 1840s when many were seeking to escape the famine conditions in Ireland. Although the population of the British Isles as a whole increased considerably during the first half of the nineteenth century, Ireland lost about one-quarter of its population between 1840 and 1850. In the late eighteenth and early nineteenth centuries, many Irish workers were employed on the new turnpike roads, canals and railways, while others became handloom weavers.

Unlike the Irish, many of the Scots who moved into England were skilled workers, and a few became leading manufacturers.

(**Note:** During the nineteenth century many of the ideas of Malthus were shown to be wrong. Malthus was not correct in arguing that the system of poor relief in England caused the rise in population, for increases occurred in many countries at this time which did not have such systems of assisting the poor. Although population increased, Britain became a wealthier country. The development of towns and changes in farming, industry, transport and trade meant that Britain was able to support a rapidly growing population and, eventually, to increase the standard of living. However, in Ireland the warnings of Malthus proved more correct with the disastrous famine of the 1840s which resulted in heavy loss of life.)

Immigration

Immigrants, that is those who came from other countries to settle permanently in Britain, generally came to escape religious or political persecution or to make a better life. Immigrants came from many parts of the world. The Jewish community in Britain totalled about 35,000 by the mid-nineteenth century. By that time, many mainland Europeans, Africans, West Indians and Chinese were also living in Britain.

Emigration

The number of emigrants, that is people leaving Britain to live permanently abroad, was far greater than the number of immigrants. Emigrants went to North America, Australia and other parts of the world, where they helped to build up the British Empire. With the discoveries of gold in the mid-nineteenth century, there was a great increase in emigration to California and Australia. A number of Welsh people developed a new settlement in Patagonia in South America.

What were the effects of the changes in the size and distribution of population?

The rapid population growth meant that there was a larger workforce to fill the new jobs created by the industrial revolution. More people earning wages meant a greater demand for houses, and manufactured goods. This demand further stimulated industry, trade and transport. Feeding the population of the growing towns put pressure on agriculture and hastened farming improvements.

■ A historical debate: the standard of living question

Whether the standard of living rose or fell between the 1780s and 1850s is still a matter of debate among historians. What seems certain is that the combination of a rapidly growing population and the long years of war against France (1793–1815), and their aftermath, increased social problems, especially in the towns. The rapid growth of towns created health, housing, transport, poverty, law and order, and education problems. To help solve these a succession of reforms were passed.

If the population had increased without industrial change, living standards would have fallen, as occurred in Ireland. It is also clear that the expansion of industry in Britain did not cause the rise in population, for population also increased throughout most of Europe in the eighteenth century where no such rapid industrial growth took place.

QUESTIONS

Growth of Population   (E = estimate)

Date	England and Wales	Britain
1700	5,500,000 *(E)*	
1750	6,500,000 *(E)*	8,000,000 *(E)*
1780	8,000,000 *(E)*	
1800	9,000,000 *(E)*	
1801	8,893,000	10,500,000
1811	10,164,000	
1821	12,000,000	
1831	13,897,000	
1841	15,914,000	
1851	17,928,000	21,000,000

1 (a) Why are the population figures for the eighteenth century given as estimates?
(b) What sources can be used to make this guess-work more accurate?
(c) On whose work is the estimate for 1700 based?
(d) When and why did population figures become more accurate?
(e) What is a census and how often is it taken?
(f) Between which dates did population increase most rapidly?

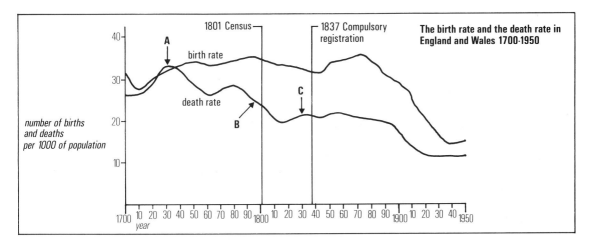

1801 Census

1837 Compulsory registration

The birth rate and the death rate in England and Wales 1700-1950

number of births and deaths per 1000 of population

2 (a) Look at the graph above. What is meant by birth rate and death rate?

(b) Why do the figures for birth rate and death rate become more accurate after 1837?

(c) Can you explain the increase in the death rate marked at A? What action was taken by the Government to overcome this?

(d) For what reasons did the death rate decline in the period marked B?

(e) Why did the death rate rise in the period marked C?

3 (a) What did Malthus believe would happen if the growth of population was not checked?

(b) What did Malthus believe would happen if population grew faster than the food supply?

(c) How do you think food shortages might lead to a fall in the rate of population growth?

(d) How were Malthus' ideas shown to be wrong in the nineteenth century? In which country were his ideas proved correct?

4 (a) Explain why the areas shaded ▨ and ▦ on the map had a high population per acre in 1801. Why were the areas shaded ▨ the most densely populated?

(b) In the early eighteenth century the most densely populated areas were south of the line marked between the Severn and the Wash. How had the distribution of population changed by 1801, and why did these changes occur?

(c) In 1700 the three largest towns were London, Bristol and Norwich. List in descending order the towns marked on the 1801 map, and their population in each case.

5 Write a short essay on either of the following two topics:

(a) Describe and explain the reasons for the increase in population 1801–51.

(b) What changes took place in birth and death rates in the period 1700–1850, and what were the effects upon the size of population?

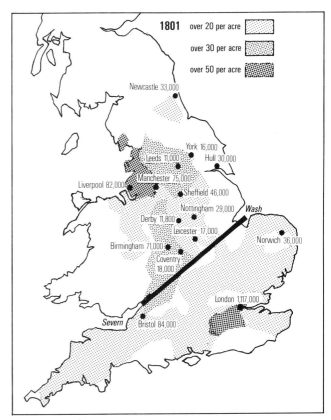

6 Copy and complete this chart to show the advances in surgery and medicine in the period 1700–1850.

Medical progress 1700–1850		
Date	Improvement	Effect
c.1720	*Inoculation spread to Britain*	*Some effect in checking smallpox*
	(to be completed)	

12 Town conditions and public health

Public facilities in towns, such as water supply, drainage, sewerage, paving and lighting, were often neglected or, in some cases, non-existent. Many towns were controlled by corrupt corporations (councils) and some had no town authority at all. Public health in towns became a cause for concern but Parliament was reluctant to introduce reforms. However, by the mid-nineteenth century, the poor standard of public health made it necessary for the Government to take action.

■ The need for reform

The rapid growth of towns

The standard of public health was poor in the eighteenth and early nineteenth centuries. Apart from London, most of the large and rapidly growing towns were located where industry had developed. Houses had to be built quickly in towns like Manchester, Leeds, Liverpool, Birmingham and Nottingham, to cope with the numbers of people flocking there to look for work.

The new town dwellers were often factory workers and could only afford to pay a small amount in house rent, so the building companies constructed housing as cheaply as possible. Insanitary dwellings were built without secure foundations, often back-to-back, with no through ventilation, along narrow streets or around airless courts.

What were living conditions like in the towns?

Dirt, squalor, misery and disease were common features in towns. Demand for houses was far greater than the supply, so millions of families had to share a room with others, and dwellings were desperately overcrowded (**A**). Water often had to be fetched from wells and streams. Sometimes private water companies piped water from the local rivers, despite the fact that such sources were often contaminated.

Drainage, sewerage, paving and lighting were inadequate and the graveyards in many towns were severely overcrowded and a health hazard. There were no parks or gardens in the industrial quarters (**B** and **C**).

Few authorities took any action, partly because the wealthy rarely saw the homes of the poorer workers and partly because of the cost of improvements.

What were the effects of insanitary town conditions?

The result of such conditions was a high death rate and low average life expectancy in the growing industrial towns. Infant mortality was very high, and about one-half of working-class children died before they were one year old.

A *Overpopulation*

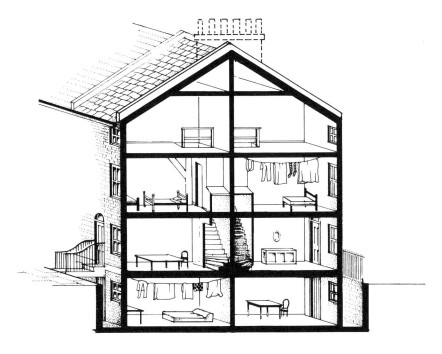

B

Q (a) Copy and complete the following diagram to show what the housing in **B** consisted of:

Type of accommodation	Number shown	Number of rooms in each	Number of doors	Number of windows	Stairs
cellar dwelling	2	1			*outside*
back to back	2	3			

(b) Was any toilet provision available in this type of housing?

(c) 'I attended a family of thirteen, twelve of whom had typhus fever, without a bed in the cellar, without straw . . . They lay on the floor, and so crowded that I could scarcely pass between them.' (A doctor's statement, 1842)

'The room was very dirty; it contained four beds, in which slept two men, four women, and thirteen children. I found in one of the beds two children very ill with scarlet fever; in another a child ill of the measles; in another the body of a child who had died of measles the day before; and in the fourth a woman and her infant born two days before.' (Newcastle, 1844)

Why did people live in such conditions?

> **C** *Report on the State of Large Towns (1844)*
>
> Many of these ranges of houses are built back to back, fronting one way into a narrow court, across which the inmates of the opposite houses may shake hands without stepping out of their own doors; and the other way into a back street, unpaved and unsewered. Most of these houses have cellars beneath them, occupied – if it is possible to find a lower class – by a still lower class than those living above them.

Babies were easy victims for disease and large numbers of the population died during epidemics of cholera or typhoid (**D, E** and **F**).

The wealthy factory owners and town traders lived either in the better quarters of the towns or some distance outside. Their houses were much better built. These wealthier town dwellers, and the people living in the countryside, had a longer life expectancy than did the poorer inhabitants of the industrial towns.

E *Charles Kingsley to his sister*
I was yesterday . . . over the cholera districts of Bermondsey, and, oh God! What I saw! People having no water to drink – hundreds of them – but the water of the common sewer which stagnates, full of . . . dead fish, cats and dogs, under their windows.

D *London, a court for 'King Cholera'*

F *Cholera at Dudley*

CHOLERA.

DUDLEY BOARD OF HEALTH,
HEREBY GIVE NOTICE, THAT IN CONSEQUENCE OF THE

Church-yards at Dudley

Being so full, no one who has died of the CHOLERA will be permitted to be buried after *SUNDAY* next, (To-morrow) in either of the Burial Grounds of *St. Thomas's*, or *St. Edmund's*, in this Town.

All Persons who die from CHOLERA, must for the future be buried in the Church-yard at Netherton.

BOARD of HEALTH, DUDLEY.
September 1st, 1832.

W. MAURICE, PRINTER, HIGH STREET, DUDLEY.

Q (a) How might conditions shown in illustration **D** lead to the spread of epidemic disease?

(b) Explain how the conditions described by Charles Kingsley (**E**) allowed disease to spread more quickly.

■ Stages in reform

Growing public concern

Parliament was strongly influenced by the ideas of *laissez-faire* (meaning to leave alone) and thought that the provision of essential services should be left to private enterprise.

Poor housing, overcrowding, a suspect water supply and inefficient methods of rubbish disposal contributed to epidemics of cholera and typhoid. The epidemics hit hardest in the slums of the industrial towns. These outbreaks encouraged investigations into living conditions and public health. Public opinion was much aroused by the outbreak of cholera in the 1830s but efforts at reform faded with the end of the epidemic.

Surveys and Parliamentary reports

In the 1830s and 1840s there were a number of surveys and reports on public health and living conditions.

Edwin Chadwick, in his work as a Poor Law Commissioner, recognized the connection between poverty and disease. He used the evidence of the registrations of births, marriages and deaths to show the appalling mortality of the labouring classes in the towns. Prompted by Chadwick, a survey was conducted which produced the *Report on the Sanitary Condition of the Labouring Population* (1842). The descriptions and the statistics in the *Report* shocked public opinion. It also showed that the bad conditions could not be blamed on the people themselves. In 1843 Chadwick produced another report, this time on the unhealthy state of many of the graveyards.

A Royal Commission on the Health of Towns published a report in 1844 (**G** and **H**). Of fifty towns investigated, only six were found to have satisfactory water supplies and only one had adequate drainage. However, in 1845 a Bill to set up a Government department to supervise water supply and street cleansing was defeated in Parliament.

Why and how did the British Government take action concerning public health?

Following another serious outbreak of cholera in 1847–8 in which 53,000 people died, there was a widespread campaign for Government action. In 1848 the Public Health Act was passed. This set up a central Board of Health in London whose members included Edwin Chadwick and Lord Shaftesbury. Local Boards were to be set up in towns where the death rate was above the national average. Boards could also be set up in towns if the ratepayers requested one. The Act increased the power of local authorities to deal with public health, and tried to prevent the re-occurrence of cholera. During the epidemic, a number of towns set about improving water supplies, drainage, street cleansing and refuse disposal.

G *Report on the State of Large Towns (1844)*

From some recent inquiries . . . it would appear that upwards of 20,000 individuals live in cellars in Manchester . . . These are generally Irish families – handloom weavers, bricklayers, labourers whose children are beggars or matchsellers . . . The Irish cottier has brought with him his disgusting domestic companion the pig; for whenever he can scrape together a sufficient sum for the purchase of one of these animals, it becomes an inmate of his cellar.

H *Report on the Sanitary Condition of Bradford*

In most of the inferior streets, chiefly inhabited by the working classes, few are paved at all; none of them properly. The dung heaps are found in several parts of the streets, and open privies are seen in many directions. The chief sewage is in open channels . . . Taking the general conditions, I am obliged to pronounce it to be the most filthy town I visited.

Q (a) Using the sources **G** and **H**, describe the living conditions of the poor classes in an industrial town in the first half of the nineteenth century.

A period of slow progress

With the ending of the cholera epidemic interest in reform faded. Only a few local boards were set up. The central Board of Health had no minister to represent it in Parliament. Its ideas were strongly opposed by slum owners and others whose financial interests were threatened by reform. Edwin Chadwick annoyed many people by his impatience and stubborn determination to get reforms carried out. In 1854 Chadwick was dismissed, and the central Board was abolished in 1858. For some years afterwards, progress in public health reform was slow.

QUESTIONS

Average age of death in 1842						
Type of People	Leeds	Liverpool	Manchester	Bolton	Wiltshire	Rutland
Professional persons, gentry and their families	44	35	38	34	50	52
Farmers, tradesmen and their families	27	22	20	23	48	41
Mechanics, labourers and their families	19	15	17	18	33	38

From Report of the Sanitary Conditions of the Labouring Population (1842)

1 (a) The six areas listed above show four urban and two rural places. The four towns are _____ ; the two rural areas are _____ .

(b) What was the *average* life expectancy within each of the three grouped types of people? Give the answer to the nearest whole number.

(c) The average length of life varied in different areas of the country. In which areas was life expectancy highest? In which areas was life expectancy lowest?

(d) Which types of people had the highest life expectancy? Can you explain why? Which types of people had the lowest life expectancy? Can you explain why?

(e) Why was there such a low expectation of life for mechanics and labourers in the towns in comparison with agricultural labourers and their families?

(f) Comment on the figures for Wiltshire and Rutland. What different health problems were there in rural areas as compared to the towns?

2 (a) Which town shown in the table below had the greatest increase in population between 1801 and 1851? Which industries were carried on in the growing towns?

(b) Which town shows the smallest increase in population between 1801 and 1851? Give *one* reason why this increase was so small.

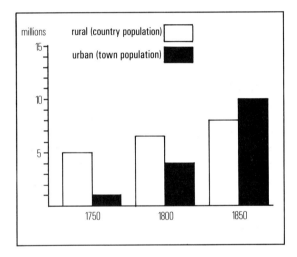

3 (a) What does the bar graph above tell you about the size of the urban (town) population in 1750?

(b) How many people lived in the countryside in 1750? Express this as a percentage of the total population.

(c) How many people lived in towns in 1850? Express this as a percentage of the total population.

(d) For what reasons did population distribution change during the period 1750 to 1850?

4 Draw up a petition to present either to the local Board of Health or to Parliament complaining about local health dangers. Prepare and design protest posters on the same theme.

5 **Essay topic:** Why did many towns increase so rapidly in the late eighteenth and nineteenth centuries? What were the main consequences that rapid growth had for life in the towns?

Town	Population 1801	Population 1851
Manchester/Salford	100,000	367,000
Leicester	17,000	61,000
Norwich	36,000	68,000
Bradford	13,000	104,000
Blackburn	12,000	47,000
Stoke on Trent	23,000	84,000
Bath	33,000	54,000

13 The Poor Law

In the eighteenth century, many people in Britain were very poor. Under Acts of Parliament which are sometimes given the term the 'old poor law', the parish authorities had the power to give assistance to those who had no money at all. By the mid-nineteenth century, a number of additional Acts had been passed by Parliament to deal with the problem of the poor. The Act of 1834 introduced the 'new poor law'.

■ The old poor law

The Poor Law Act, 1601

This Act divided the poor into groups: the old and the sick were to be provided with shelter; the unemployed were to be given work; and orphans were to be educated. The local magistrates were given the power to levy a poor rate (collect a sum of money in the form of a tax from most of the population). This money (known as poor relief) was then distributed to those most in need. The 'old poor law' was the basis of giving help to the poor until 1834.

The early workhouses

In the early eighteenth century almost one-half of the total population were unable to live on their income and were therefore dependent upon poor relief. In many towns, workhouses were built. The idea was that able-bodied (fit) poor people could be brought into the workhouses to live, and made to earn their keep. These workhouses were to be places of hard labour, and conditions were often harsh. In 1782 an Act of Parliament allowed parishes to join together to set up a workhouse.

What was the Speenhamland system?

During the wars against France, which broke out in 1793, food prices rose rapidly but the wages of farm labourers rose only slowly (**A**). This led to unrest, and even riots, in some industrial areas.

In 1795 the magistrates of Berkshire met at the Pelican Inn in Speen. As a way of helping the poor labourers in their own part of the country, they fixed a system of allowances. These allowances depended on the price of bread and the size of the labourer's family. If, for example, the price of a loaf was 1s (5p), each labourer was to have 3s (15p) for himself, and 1s 6d (8p) for each of his family. If the man's wages did not total this amount, the difference would be made up out of the poor rate. If the price of bread went up or down, so would the allowances. This was known as the 'Speenhamland system' and was soon copied in other counties where farming was the main occupation, especially in the south.

As an emergency means of coping with the crisis of low wages and high wartime prices, the Speenhamland system helped to remove much of the danger of serious unrest. But in the longer term, the Speenhamland system failed to deal with the problems of poverty.

What were the defects of the Speenhamland system?

First, so many labourers applied for help, that the amount of money people had to pay towards the poor rate increased greatly. Many could not afford it. Second, it discouraged farmers from raising labourers' wages because they knew that those on low wages would be assisted out of the poor rates. Third, some labourers felt that there was no need to work hard, because they would get poor relief anyway.

Critics of the Speenhamland system were influenced by the writings of Thomas Malthus (see page 71). They argued that changes in the poor relief system encouraged larger families, which in turn contributed to the rapid growth of population and an increase in the number of poor people. (*Note: Although the views of Malthus received support at the time, he was proved incorrect in the long term, for population continued to grow after the Speenhamland system had been brought to an end.*)

The amount paid out in poor relief increased from about £750,000 in the mid-eighteenth century, to £5,300,000 in 1803, and to over £8 millions in 1813, and it continued at that high level for many years.

A *Weekly budget of a labourer's family, 1795*

Income

	*s	d
Man, carter	12	0
Wife, roving cotton about	0	6
Girl 12, nursing for neighbour	2	6
Girl 9, nursing for neighbour	2	0
	17	0

Expenditure

	*s	d
Rent	2	0
Fuel	0	7
Oatmeal bread	5	0
Meat	1	6
Tea and Sugar	1	3
Potatoes	1	6
Milk	1	2
Butter	1	0
Soap, candles, groceries	1	0
Clothes and other expenses	2	0
Cheese	1	6
	18	6

Prices of provisions: 1795

			*s	d
Oatmeal	10 lb		1	11
Fresh butter	1 lb		1	0
Salt butter	1 lb	8d to 10d		
Beef	1 lb	3½d to 5d		
Mutton	1 lb			5
Veal	1 lb	5d to 6d		
Pork	1 lb			5
Bacon	1 lb			8
Potatoes	253 lb		6	6
Skimmed milk	quart			1½
New milk	quart			3
Coal	cwt	6d to 7d		
Candles	1 lb			8
Treacle	1 lb			5½
Soap	1 lb			10
Rent for two small rooms for a year				
£4 to £6				

*s = shillings (one shilling = 5 new pence)
d = old penny (one old penny = ½ a new pence)

Q (a) Look at **A**. What was the weekly income of the labourer's family?
  (b) What was the weekly expenditure of the family?
  (c) What did this difference mean?
  (d) Looking at the items of expenditure do you think there are any ways they could have spent less?
  (e) Why did the children work at such an early age?
  (f) Do you think the parents welcomed or objected to their children working? Explain your answer.
  (g) What would happen to the family income if the neighbours did not require the nursing services of the two girls?
  (h) At which times of the year would the family find life most difficult?

■ The new poor law

The Royal Commission

In 1832 a Royal Commission was set up to inquire into the administration of poor relief which had become expensive to run, and inefficient. The secretary of the Commission, Edwin Chadwick, wanted to abolish the Speenhamland system. In its report, the Commission recommended that the Speenhamland system and the payment of outdoor relief (payments to the poor not in a workhouse) should be brought to an end. Instead, poor relief should be given *only* in the workhouse where conditions should be so harsh that only those in real need would enter. The report was welcomed by many MPs and was followed, shortly afterwards, by the passing of an Act of Parliament.

The Poor Law Amendment Act, 1834

Under this Act, parishes were to be grouped into large Unions which were to provide workhouses. In each Union the poor law was to be administered by Boards of Guardians elected by the local ratepayers. A central Poor Law Commission, consisting of three members, was set up to ensure that the Guardians in each Union did their duty.

The Poor Law Amendment Act had serious weaknesses. The Act did not deal with the causes of poverty and unemployment. No allowance was made for the difference between farming areas, where poverty was often a long-term problem, and industrial areas where unemployment tended to be a short-term problem. It was wrongly assumed that if conditions inside the workhouses were worse than those existing outside, then the able-bodied would take work rather than enter the workhouse. However this was not the case when no work was available.

The operation of the new poor law

Outdoor relief was rapidly brought to an end in southern England, and Poor Law Unions were established in the agricultural areas. The new system was feared by the poorer classes but, despite some protests, there was little resistance from the demoralized farm labourers, particularly after the defeat of the last Labourers' Revolt in 1830.

Although many workhouses were clean and gave sufficient, if plain, food, individual personal circumstances were not given consideration. Families were often broken up, and strict rules separated men from women. Visitors were not allowed and the able-bodied were compelled to work at hard tasks such as stone-breaking (**B** and **C**).

The harshness of the new poor law was attacked by many reformers, for example by Charles Dickens in *Oliver Twist* (1838).

Opposition to the new poor law

The Act was not appropriate for the problems of industrial workers in towns during periods of trade slump and high unemployment. The Act aroused strong opposition, and a mass revolt prevented the introduction of the new poor law

B *Workhouse timetable and punishments*

Timetable

6.00 a.m.	Rise, wash, dress, rollcall
6.30 a.m.	Prayers; Breakfast (eaten in silence)
7.15 a.m.	exercise in the yards
8.00 a.m.	Work
11.00 a.m.	Prayers, Bible reading, hymns
12.00 noon	Lunch (eaten in silence)
12.30 p.m.	Exercise in yards
2.00 p.m.	Work for adults; school for children
4.00 p.m.	Prayers, religious instruction
5.00 p.m.	Hymn singing; giving thanks to God
6.00 p.m.	Supper (eaten in silence)
6.30 p.m.	Religious service
9.00 p.m.	Bed

Name	Offence	Punishment
Twenty-nine women at the mill	Neglecting and refusing to work	Dinner and supper milk stopped
Owen Trainor	Stealing onions	Flogged
James Acheson	Going to town without permission	Six hours in lock-up

in many towns. Anti-Poor Law Associations were formed to organize resistance and the Act was never fully operational in the industrial districts.

During periods of industrial depression, the Guardians in many areas administered poor relief to the able-bodied outside the workhouse in return for some kind of work. By the mid-nineteenth century, only one pauper in eight received relief in a workhouse.

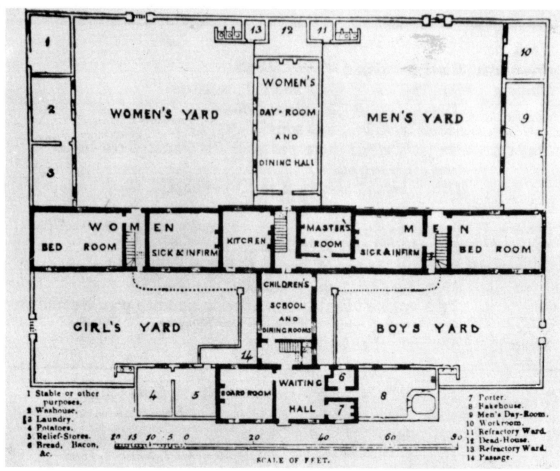

The plan shows the following labelled rooms and areas:

- WOMEN'S YARD
- WOMEN'S DAY-ROOM AND DINING HALL
- MEN'S YARD
- WOMEN BED ROOM
- SICK & INFIRM
- KITCHEN
- MASTER'S ROOM
- SICK & INFIRM
- MEN BED ROOM
- CHILDREN'S SCHOOL AND DINING ROOMS
- GIRL'S YARD
- BOYS YARD
- BOARD ROOM
- WAITING HALL

Numbered key:

1 Stable or other purposes.
2 Washhouse.
3 Laundry.
4 Potatoes.
5 Relief-Stores.
6 Bread, Bacon, &c.
7 Porter.
8 Bakehouse.
9 Men's Day-Room.
10 Workroom.
11 Refractory Ward.
12 Dead-House.
13 Refractory Ward.
14 Passage.

SCALE OF FEET.

C *Workhouse plans*

Q (a) What evidence can you find to show that families were split up on entering a workhouse (**C**)?

(b) Did the children receive any school instruction in the workhouse? How do you know?

(c) Using the numbered items on the workhouse plan can you suggest the main items of food that made up the daily diet in the workhouse?

(d) Find the washhouse (2) and laundry (3) on the plan. Who do you think did the washing and drying in the workhouse?

(e) The 'Master' was responsible for running the workhouse. Comment on the position of his room in the centre of the workhouse.

(f) The local Board of Guardians of the Poor Law Union was concerned with the general organization of the poor law. In which room did they meet?

(g) Using the sources at **B** and **C** (timetable; workhouse plan and punishments) write a short account of life in a workhouse. Why do you think some people preferred to starve to death rather than enter a workhouse?

The survival and legacy of the new poor law

The principles of the 1834 Act survived as the basis of poor relief until the early twentieth century. Yet, although conditions in the workhouses were harsh, not all were cruel. The worst effects of the new poor law were lessened by the general expansion of industry, transport and trade, especially the boom in railway construction, which all provided employment. The total cost of poor relief fell from £6 million in 1834 to £5 million in 1850. By that time the unpopular Poor Law Commission had been replaced by a Poor Law Board, the head of which sat in Parliament and was a member of the Government.

Gradually, some of the harshest features of the workhouses were changed. Yet, despite such changes, one of the greatest fears of the poor in Victorian times was that they might end their days in a workhouse.

QUESTIONS

A Multiple choice Choose the correct answer for each question and write it into your book.

1 The name given to the system of poor relief between 1795 and 1834 was:
(a) monitorial system;
(b) Speenhamland system;
(c) *laissez-faire*.

2 The village which gave its name to the system was situated in:
(a) Yorkshire;   (b) Kent;
(c) Berkshire;   (d) Cornwall.

3 Under the system, poor relief was granted according to the size of a man's family and the price of:
(a) milk;
(b) bread;
(c) meat.

4 The author of *Essay on Population* (1798) which greatly influenced poor law authorities was:
(a) Adam Smith;
(b) Edwin Chadwick;
(c) Thomas Malthus.

5 The Poor Law Amendment Act of 1834 was much influenced by the ideas of:
(a) Francis Place;   (b) William Wilberforce;
(c) Richard Oastler;   (d) Edwin Chadwick.

6 God never meant that the idle should live upon the labour of the industrious. . . . He hath therefore permitted a state of poverty to be everywhere introduced; that the industrious might enjoy the rewards of their diligence; and that those who would not work, might feel the punishment of their laziness.
(from a sermon by Richard Watson, Bishop of Llandaff)

The writer blamed unemployment on
(a) the level of trade;
(b) a rising population;
(c) individual laziness;
(d) lack of education.

7 The idle man who will not work at all and whom no one will employ, receives the whole amount from the Parish. Where then is the _____ for the good labourer to work? He would fare just as well being idle.
(evidence of a witness before Royal Commission on Poor Law 1833)

Which word fills the blank:
(a) opportunity;   (b) chance;
(c) challenge;   (d) incentive?

8 It is to a labourer's advantage to marry as young as possible and have many children. The more mouths he has to feed the greater the supplement he receives from the parish. Thus, the population increases more rapidly than ever.
(David Ricardo: Principles of Political Economy 1817)

To which system of poor relief does this refer?

9 We recommend . . . that . . . all relief to able-bodied persons or families, otherwise than in well-regulated workhouses, shall be declared unlawful and shall cease.

This is an extract from
(a) Poor Law Amendment Act 1834;
(b) Decision of Berkshire magistrates 1795;
(c) Report of Royal Commission on Poor Law 1833.

10 At Bourne a poor man applied to the Guardians for relief. They offered him a place in a workhouse but he refused. A week later he was found dead in a field having chosen death by starvation rather than enter a workhouse under the present system. *(Baxter: Book of the Bastilles)*

Is this extract an example of *fact* or *opinion*? Give reasons for your answer.

11 *I'm Stephen Witcher, labouring man — of Andover I be,*
A pauper of the workhouse, and a cripple in the knee,
The Guardians there have sent me out, in the cold and rain,
To sit all day, a breakin' stones in agony and pain.
(Punch 1848)

Why was Witcher forced to go into the workhouse? (a) he was lazy; (b) he was old; (c) he was lame.

B Essay topic: Why was the Poor Law Amendment Act of 1834 passed? State the terms of the Act and show its importance.

14 Education and schooling

In the eighteenth century the State played no part in the provision of schooling. The Church of England, other religious groups, private individuals and voluntary societies were all involved, in various ways, in attempts to provide schools and schoolteachers. By the mid-nineteenth century the State was beginning to take an increasing interest in education and in the provision of schools.

■ Education in the eighteenth century

Forms of schooling available included public schools, private schools, grammar schools, dissenting academies, parish schools, charity schools and dame schools (**A** and **B**).

A *A parson's school*

B *An eighteenth-century childhood*

My mother . . . took me under her own pedagogy untill I could read in my Bible . . . I soon began to take some notice of several historical passages in the Old Testament . . . .

And now, my . . . mother went with me to Kirk-Sandal school, where . . . master . . . placed me amongst some little ones . . . he finding me better than he expected, removed me higher, asking my mother if she had brought me an Accidence [a little book with Latin and English grammar] . . . I suppose it might be in June 1704 . . . I was not quite five years of age.

. . . February 1709 . . . my brother . . . and I were sent to Stoney Stainton, where we were under the care of . . . a very good schoolmaster, and I think grounded his scholars in their grammar rules the best that I ever knew . . . Here we continued till . . . February 1713 . . . and I had made an entrance into Greek . . . .

The next school we were sent to was Doncaster free school . . . until January . . . 1714 . . . We were boarded at Doncaster . . .

And now, my father thinking that I had got as much of the learned languages as would be of any service to a tradesman . . . sent me to Pontefract, to learn to write and accompt which I did with one Joshua Marsden, a quaker . . . I had learn'd some little to write before, but nothing of accounts . . . I went through most of the rules of vulgar arithmetick, and decimal fractions, with some little of practical geometry . . .

. . . my parents next care was to put me to some trade . . . by which I might get an honest living in the world . . . at last concluded to take me to my father's business . . . and . . . I was put to rive [split] laths and hew wood, for a little time, with my father's workmen, who had always the benefit of what little work I could do, for instructing me.

From Country Diary of James Fretwell

Q (a) List all the items which the children are using in the schoolroom. Which lesson do you think is being studied (source **A**)?
(b) How are the children being taught?
(c) Using source **B** copy and complete this chart to show the stages in the schooling of James Fretwell.

An eighteenth-century education		
Age	School/Teacher	What was taught
under 5	*his mother*	*reading Bible*
5–9	(to be	completed)

(d) In what ways have the stages in your own education differed from those which James Fretwell passed through? Are there any similarities?

The public schools

Many of the public schools had been founded in the later Middle Ages. Often the teachers were Church of England clergymen and they concentrated on teaching Latin and Greek (known as the 'Classics'). Among the best known of the public schools – at which the scholars boarded – were Eton, Winchester, Rugby, Charterhouse, Westminster, Shrewsbury and Harrow. Conditions for the boys were often harsh and cruel. In 1808 the boys at Harrow rebelled against the headmaster; and at Winchester in 1818 the army was called in to put down a riot. Bullying was common in public schools, and older boys were often used to discipline younger boys. Two headmasters, Dr Thomas Arnold of Rugby and Samuel Butler of Shrewsbury carried out reforms in their schools and introduced the teaching of more modern subjects such as mathematics and modern languages. A novel written in the nineteenth century, *Tom Brown's Schooldays* (1857), describes the situation at Rugby school.

The public schools were attended by the sons of the upper class and nobility, and by the sons of some merchants and industrialists.

Private schools

Private schools and academies were mostly attended by children from the middle classes. Private boarding schools for girls of wealthy families were established in London and the larger county towns. Such schools concentrated on moral training, etiquette (good manners and behaviour) and feminine accomplishments. They were often kept by a maiden or widowed gentlewoman. Lessons in singing, dancing, music, writing and French might be taught by visiting masters.

Some of the private schools were badly run and the teachers themselves were often poorly-educated. Many had a notorious reputation for neglecting their pupils. Charles Dickens wrote about some of the worst examples in *Nicholas Nickleby* (1839).

Grammar schools

Like the public schools these concentrated on the teaching of the Classics. In the eighteenth century there was a growing demand for more varied subjects to be taught. Parents in the industrial towns wanted their sons to learn subjects which would be useful in trade and business, such as mathematics, accounting and modern languages. However, the charters by which the grammar schools had been founded often limited teaching to the Classics.

Dissenting academies

These were founded and run by nonconformists (religious sects other than the Church of England) who were themselves forbidden to teach in grammar schools and universities because of their religious beliefs. The dissenting academies usually gave a general education more suited to the world of business and some of their pupils were later to become important industrialists. The dissenting academies were popular with many of the middle class.

Charity schools

Charity schools were established in towns and in larger villages by religious or 'caring' groups. Children were taught reading, writing, arithmetic, sewing and simple crafts such as shoe-making, as well as studying the Bible.

It was hoped that poor children would learn to be obedient and to accept their place, however lowly it was, in society. The movement for charity schools was co-ordinated by the Society for the Promotion of Christian Knowledge which had been founded in 1699.

The dame schools

For many children the only education they received was at small dame schools, usually run by elderly women in their own homes. They charged very small fees and were often little more than child-minding places with some teaching of reading, sewing and knitting.

Sunday schools

Many of the children of the poor received no schooling at all. Robert Raikes, a newspaper editor, was convinced that the only way to make sure that child workers became law-abiding adults was to teach them Christian principles on their only free day, namely Sunday. He founded the first Sunday school in Gloucester in 1783.

The Sunday schools provided simple reading, religious instruction and, in a few instances, writing. For many children it was the only schooling they received. In Wales many adults also attended the Sunday schools. The movement, which spread rapidly, was encouraged by the Anglicans, the Methodists and some factory owners. The Sunday schools were funded largely by voluntary contributions.

■ Experiments in education

How did the Industrial Revolution affect schooling?

The rapid growth of population and the movement of people from the countryside to the towns meant that there was a serious shortage of schools in some of the industrial areas. In many industrial towns the overall standards of schooling declined.

A new system of day schooling – monitorial schools

Two men can lay claim to pioneering the monitorial system. In 1798 Joseph Lancaster, a Quaker, and Andrew Bell, an Anglican vicar set up schools in London. Under the monitorial system the teacher taught the older pupils, or monitors, who would then in turn instruct and

C *Borough Road School*

Q (a) Identify the main features of this school by linking the numbers in the picture with the correct descriptions below.

Feature	Number (1–4)
The master supervising the school The older pupils or monitors standing The rows of seated pupils A kite and other toys given as rewards	

(b) By what name was this kind of school known?
(c) What part was played by the master in such a school?
(d) What part was played by the monitors in such a school?
(e) Why were the younger pupils not likely to receive a good education?
(f) Why would discipline in this type of school need to be very strict?
(g) Which subjects were most likely to be taught in this way?

---

test the younger children. The system was largely one of simple rote learning (learning by repetition) and sometimes neither the monitors nor the younger children understood what they repeated. However the new system provided a cheap form of education, since one teacher, with the minimum of books and materials, could instruct and supervise, through the use of the monitors, hundreds of pupils. Discipline in the monitorial schools was strict although there was a system of rewards as well as of punishments (**C**).

Voluntary elementary schools

From the second decade of the nineteenth century, elementary day schooling was increas-

ingly provided by the 'voluntary schools'. These were associated with the National Society and the British and Foreign Schools Society. Rivalry between these two voluntary societies led to keen competition to set up new monitorial schools, in which reading, writing, arithmetic and religious instruction were the principal subjects taught.

At first the monitorial schools were funded by voluntary subscriptions from individuals, by collections at churches and by small fees paid weekly by the pupils. The new system was supported by many people, including Robert Owen, the industrialist, who was particularly concerned with the provision of infant schools (**D** and **E**).

D *Robert Owen's schoolroom at New Lanark*

E *Evidence of Robert Owen to Select Committee on the state of Children in Manufactories (1816)*

Owen: I am principal proprietor . . . of the establishment of New Lanark in Scotland . . . .

Questioner: Do you give instruction to any part of your population?

Owen: Yes . . . to the children from 3 years old upwards . . . . There is a preparatory school, into which all the children, from the age of 3 to 6 are admitted at the option of their parents. There is a second school in which all children of the population from 6 to 10 are admitted. The schools are supported immediately at the expense of the establishment.

Questioner: What employment could be found for the children of the poor, in these situations, till ten years of age?

Owen: It does not appear to me necessary for children to be employed under ten years of age, in any regular work.

Questioner: If you do not employ them in any regular work, what would you do with them?

Owen: Instruct them and give them exercise.

Questioner: Would there not be a danger of their acquiring, by that time, vicious habits, for want of regular occupation?

Owen: My own experience leads me to say that I have found quite the reverse, that their habits have been good in proportion to the extent of their instruction.

■ The State and education

How and why did the State begin to take an interest in education?

A number of politicians were against any measures to support schooling for the children of the poor (**F** and **G**). However, there was a number of government inquiries into educational provision.

One clause in the 1833 Factory Act stated that children working in cotton mills were to receive two hours instruction a day in school (extended to three hours in 1844) and during the 1830s and 1840s a number of factory schools were set up for 'part-timers'.

There was a Government decision, also in 1833, to give £20,000 a year to be shared between the National Society and the British and Foreign Schools Society. This annual grant was increased to £30,000 in 1839 and by 1860 had reached £500,000. In order to have some influence over the way the grant was used, the Committee of the Privy Council on Education was set up in 1839. Its first secretary was James Kay-Shuttleworth, one of the most important educational reformers in the nineteenth century. To check that the schools in receipt of Government grants were organized efficiently the new Committee of the Privy Council appointed a number of inspectors.

Schoolteachers

One factor which prevented the raising of educational standards was the shortage of well-qualified teachers. Partly to overcome this the pupil-teacher system was started by Kay-Shuttleworth in 1846. Under this system pupils at the age of 13 or 14 could become apprentice teachers for a period of five years. Each day they were to teach pupils under supervision and receive instruction from the teachers. At the end of five years' apprenticeship the pupil-teachers might win a Queen's scholarship to be trained at one of the teacher training colleges. Pupil-teachers soon replaced the monitors and, by the 1850s, there were more than 10,000 pupil-teachers.

F *From* History of Hull *(1788) by G. Hadley*

The working poor are by far the most numerous class of people, and when kept in due subordination, they compose the riches of the nation. But there is a degree of ignorance necessary to keep them so . . . What ploughman who could read . . . would be content to whistle up one furrow and down another, from the dawn in the morning, to the setting of the sun? . . .

G *From* A General view of the Agriculture of the East Riding of Yorkshire *(1812) by H. E. Strickland*

The deficiency of education among the lower classes is greatly to be regretted, many being unable to read, and still more of course to write or keep accounts. This is productive of much inconvenience to the individuals, unfitting them for many situations, for which their natural abilities might otherwise qualify them, and leaving them an easy target to numerous temptations.

Q In the late eighteenth and early nineteenth centuries opinions were deeply divided on the extent to which the labouring or working classes should be educated.
  (a) For what reasons did the writer of source **F** oppose the education of the working poor and claim that the extension of schooling was harmful?
  (b) For what reasons did the writer of source **G** support the spread of education among the lower classes?

QUESTIONS

A   Multiple choice   Choose the correct answer for each question and write it into your book.

1 What was the name given to schools like Eton, Winchester and Rugby:
  (a) ragged schools;
  (b) mechanics' institutes;
  (c) dissenting academies;
  (d) charity schools;
  (e) public schools?

2 With what type of school is the name Robert Raikes usually associated:
  (a) national schools;
  (b) ragged schools;
  (c) Sunday schools;
  (d) public schools?

3 At New Lanark, Robert Owen:
  (a) set up schools for his workers' children;
  (b) taught only reading, writing and arithmetic;
  (c) made schooling compulsory to the age of sixteen years?

4 Joseph Lancaster and Andrew Bell were founders of:
  (a) charity schools;
  (b) the pupil-teacher system;
  (c) the monitorial system?

5 In which year did an Act of Parliament make £20,000 available to the voluntary societies for education:
  (a) 1802;   (b) 1819;   (c) 1833;   (d) 1844?

6 Which system provided better education for the poor in the early nineteenth century:
  (a) the monitorial system;
  (b) payment by results;
  (c) Government inspection?

7 With what type of school in the nineteenth century is the name of Dr Arnold associated:
  (a) national schools;   (b) ragged schools;
  (c) Sunday schools;   (d) public schools?

8 Copy the chart below. Fill in details of all the educational improvements which are mentioned in the chapter and arrange in chronological order.

Educational improvements		
Date	Improvement	Importance
1699	*Formation of Society for Promotion of Christian Knowledge* (to be completed)	

B   Paragraph answers   Write a paragraph in answer to each of the following questions.

1 In 1833 there were 12,117 children in a working-class area of Manchester but only 252 attended day schools. What sort of schools might these children have attended? What kind of education would they have received?

2 In 1833 the government made its first ever grant towards the cost of education. How much money was to be paid, and who was to receive it? How did the Factory Act of 1833 affect education?

3 It has been estimated that in 1850 nearly 50 per cent of the population was completely illiterate. In which sections of the population would most illiterates be found? Explain why.

4 If children attended school before 1850, what types of school were available to them? Name *four* different types, describe their origins and the sort of children who would attend each of the schools you have named.

The following questions refer to sources **D** and **E** on page 88.

Q (a) How much schooling did the children receive at New Lanark (source **E**)?
  (b) What kinds of pictures are shown on the walls of the schoolroom (source **D**)? Can you suggest how they might have been used?
  (c) What does the map of Europe on the wall indicate about the range of subjects taught at Owen's school (source **D**)?
  (d) What evidence can you find that Owen's school was concerned in the teaching of 'music and movement' as well as reading, writing and arithmetic (source **D**)?
  (e) Owen called his school an 'Institution for the Formation of Character'. Using the evidence in source **E** can you say why Owen attached such importance to education?
  (f) What do you think of Owen's methods?
  (g) From your knowledge of other factory owners, do you think that Owen's factory was typical or not?

15 Law and order

The eighteenth and early nineteenth centuries were a disorderly period of history. There were many criminals, and crime was often organized on a large scale. There was no proper police force to maintain law and order, and the prisons were squalid and overcrowded. By the mid-nineteenth century a better system of policing was in use. This, and a number of other factors, led to some reduction in crime.

■ Crime and punishment

Threats to law and order in the eighteenth century

The period was one of lawlessness, particularly in London and the larger towns. Most of the people who turned to crime did so in order to survive rather than to make their fortunes. Children were often involved in crimes such as pickpocketing and prostitution. The commonest crimes were theft, often with violence, highway robbery (**A**), poaching and smuggling. A rogue, Jonathan Wild, organized criminal gangs in London until he was executed at Tyburn in 1725. Dick Turpin, a highwayman, was an apprentice butcher before he turned to crime. He became a poacher, thief, robber, highwayman and, finally, a murderer. He was caught and then hanged at York in 1739.

How was law and order maintained?

The magistrates (or Justices of the Peace) appointed a constable in each parish. The constable was an unpaid officer who had to serve for one year. In the larger towns, watchmen or 'charlies' were also employed. Although the watchmen were paid, the amounts were so small that the work was usually left to the elderly. They often carried a rattle to raise the alarm. The watchmen were often made fun of, and they were unable to keep order in the growing towns.

By offering rewards the authorities hoped that ordinary people would help the constables. An informer could receive from about £5 to about £40 (depending upon the crime) for the conviction of a criminal. Citizens could also arrest a criminal.

How did the Fielding brothers improve law and order in London?

Henry Fielding, a novelist, became a London magistrate in 1748. He did not receive a salary, and previous magistrates had made money by accepting bribes from criminals who were brought before them. Fielding referred to it as the 'dirtiest money upon earth' and set out to

A *A highway robbery*

establish a more honest form of justice. He also trained a small force of detectives or constables who operated from his office in Bow Street. They became known as the 'Bow Street Runners' and made many arrests for crime.

Henry Fielding blamed the high level of crime on cheap gin, gambling, the inadequate system of poor relief and the defects in the way the criminal law worked. In 1751 an Act was passed by Parliament which forbade distillers to sell gin directly to the public. The licensing of public houses was regulated, and a heavy tax was put on gin.

Henry Fielding died in 1754 and his blind half-brother John Fielding took over as chief magistrate. He continued his brother's work and also formed two other groups of police – the Bow Street Foot Patrol and the Bow Street Horse Patrol – to protect the roads in and out of London from highwaymen.

Growing criminality and lawlessness

As towns grew in size it became more difficult to catch criminals. An increasing number of people found that they could make a living from crime. Many young criminals learned their 'trade' from 'old hands' in thieves' dens. However, there were even more serious problems of law and order, and at certain times, riots occurred. During the Gordon Riots in London (1780), which lasted six days, hundreds of people were killed and much damage was done before order was restored.

How was crime punished?

Parliament made punishments severe in order to deter people from becoming criminals. Whipping and the pillory (a wooden frame into which a prisoner was secured and displayed for public scorn), and sending a criminal to prison were used, but most offences were punishable by transportation or death. Parliament kept increasing the number of crimes punishable by death. Many of these were trivial: for example, stealing something worth six shillings, impersonating a Chelsea pensioner (ex-soldiers connected with the Chelsea Royal Hospital) or writing on Westminster Bridge. Executions were held in public in the mistaken belief that this would deter other people from committing a crime (**B**). However, they were attended by large crowds and many crimes which merited the death penalty were committed in the crowd while a prisoner was being hanged.

The law courts were often reluctant to pass the death sentence for a trivial offence, so they sometimes found the prisoner not guilty, or ordered him to be transported to one of the penal colonies, such as Botany Bay in Australia (**C**).

What were prison conditions like in the eighteenth century?

Newgate was the largest prison in London and it had been specially built. In many towns, old castles or toll booths were used to house prisoners. Prisons were often damp and without proper water supplies or sanitation. Often, prisoners were crowded together and disease was common. Sometimes prisoners were brutally treated and occasionally starvation occurred. Those who had money could pay for better accommodation, conditions and food. The gaolers were usually unpaid and made money by charging the prisoners fees or selling them alcohol.

Not all those sentenced to transportation left the country. Some prisoners were kept in floating prison ships or 'hulks' moored on the rivers Thames and Medway. Conditions on board these ships were appalling.

■ A better system of law and order

Who tried to reform the prisons?

John Howard, sheriff of Bedfordshire, made a tour of prisons in various parts of the country. His investigations showed that children were often kept with hardened criminals and, in some prisons, inmates were chained to the floor and unable to move. He published his report, *The State of Prisons in England and Wales* in 1777, and the public were shocked by it.

Howard died of gaol fever in 1790, but his work was continued by another reformer, Elizabeth Fry, a devout Quaker. She visited the female prisoners in Newgate and tried to help them to lead better lives. She set up a prison school, and also improved the conditions for transportees.

B *Execution at London (Tyburn)*

Q (a) Identify the main features of the public execution by linking the numbers in picture **B** with the correct descriptions in the chart.

Feature	Number (1–6)
The gallows at Tyburn surrounded by constables with staves The prisoner in the cart The coffin brought to the place of execution The preacher comforting the prisoner The spectator sending off a carrier pigeon with the news A woman selling newsheets with details of the crime and the prisoner	

(b) Why was the presence of the constables and horsemen necessary?

(c) How does the engraving show that public executions were attended for entertainment?

(d) Using all the information in the illustration, write a report of the execution for an eighteenth-century newspaper.

C *Prisoners in a prison ship*

How were prisons reformed?

The prison reformers persuaded Parliament to pass a number of Acts dealing with the inspection and cleaning of gaols. Efforts were also made to standardize prison rules. None of the early Acts was very effective, although in 1835, Inspectors of Prisons were appointed to see that the rules were obeyed. Gaolers were expected to make an annual report to the Home Office. However, the work which the prisoners were given to do remained harsh and monotonous. Some, for example, picked oakum (untwisted the tarred rope used on ships) and their hands became cut and blistered. Others were made to 'work the treadmill' by treading continuously on wooden steps inside a large hollow cylinder to make it revolve. It could be used to pump water or to grind corn.

How was the system of law and order improved?

Despite the strict penalties and harsh prison conditions, crime continued to rise. A number of reformers worked to improve both the penal (punishment) system and the policing of the country. However, many people were afraid that if a new police system was created it might be used by the Government to restrict freedom.

Some reformers argued for a reduction in the number of crimes which merited severe punishments. An opponent of the extensive use of capital punishment was Sir Samuel Romilly who succeeded in getting the death sentence lifted for the crimes of picking pockets or stealing cloth. Even more important were the reforms of Sir Robert Peel. During the years that he was Home Secretary (1822–7 and 1828–30) the death penalty was abolished for more than 100 offences.

The development of an effective police force

The development of an effective police force began in London, where it was recognized that the Bow Street Runners had made some difference to the level of crime. In 1829 the Home Secretary, Sir Robert Peel, persuaded Parliament to pass an Act setting up a new police force in London (**D** and **E**). Members of this Metropolitan Police Force were popularly called 'peelers' or 'bobbies' after the Home Secretary.

In 1835, the Municipal Corporation Act was passed. It required all boroughs to appoint a watch committee which, in its turn, appointed constables. A further Act in 1856 made the setting up of a police force compulsory in all parts of the country.

What other factors led to a reduction in crime by the 1850s?

By the mid-nineteenth century some social changes had occurred which led to a reduction in crime. The installation of street lighting in many towns, and the development of a better and safer means of travel reduced the opportunity for criminal activity. By the 1850s employment prospects were improving and the standard of living was rising. The introduction of reformatory and industrial schools in the 1850s led to a fall in juvenile crime.

D *Speech of Sir Robert Peel, House of Commons, Hansard, 15 April 1829*

If they took any series of years . . . on which the police committee had reported, they would find crime had not only increased in the metropolis more than in the other parts of the country, but had far outstretched the rate of increase of its inhabitants.

It was not easy to determine what the causes were which had led to this frightful difference between the increase of crime and of population but he [Sir Robert Peel] feared that . . . the mechanical improvements which had so distinguished the country and were a great source of its prosperity, aided criminals by enabling them to travel a great distance in a few hours.

The wealthy and populous district of Kensington not less than fifteen miles in extent was dependent on the protection of three constables some of whom, after they were in office for a time, became not very remarkable for their abstinence from intoxicating liquor. It was not surprising that three drunken beadles should be no preventive of housebreaking and thievery. The situation was the same all over London as it was in Kensington.

Q (a) Upon what evidence did Peel base his speech (**D**)?
  (b) Why was he so concerned?
  (c) What difference had he found in the level of crime in London and in other parts of the country?
  (d) What *causes* did he give to explain the different levels of crime?

E *The figures below show the detected crimes committed in London Metropolitan District expressed in percentages*

	1825	1835
Felonies	45.14	48.83
Common Assault	18.13	13.82
Larceny	8.08	10.19
Unlawful Possession	2.04	4.00
Issuing or Possessing Base Coins	2.69	3.69
Soldiers tried by Court Martial	2.51	2.62
Fraud	3.41	2.39
Assaults on Police Constables	—	1.94
Assaults on Women and Children	2.00	1.16
Misdemeanour in Workhouse	0.50	0.93
Begging or Sleeping in the Open Air	0.50	0.77
Unlawful Collection of Dust	—	0.61
Wilful Damage	0.51	0.61
Drunk and Disorderly	0.56	0.55
Conspiracy to Defraud	0.41	0.55
Cutting or Maiming	0.36	0.47
Illegally Pawning	0.24	0.38
Excise Offences	0.46	0.30
Indecent Exposure of the Person	0.46	0.30
Dog Stealing	0.12	0.24
Furious Driving and Insolence to Passengers	0.15	0.15
Leaving Families Chargeable to Parish	0.15	0.15
Abduction	0.08	0.08
Unnatural Assaults	0.08	0.08
Bastardy	0.08	0.08
Cruelty to Animals	1.46	0.08
Keeping Brothels	0.02	0.08
Stealing Fruit, Plants or Trees, etc.	1.00	0.07
Trespassing, Fishing, Poaching Game, etc.	1.00	0.06
Obtaining Money by False Pretences	0.05	0.05
Total Number of Crimes Committed	317 214	210 416
Total Population of London	1 416 407	1 803 214

Q (a) What happened to the total population of London between 1825 and 1835 (**E**)?
  (b) What happened to the total number of crimes committed in 1825 and in 1835?
  (c) Felonies are more serious crimes. Although the percentage *increased* between the two years, what happened to the *number* of serious crimes?
  (d) What happened in 1829 which might account for the decrease in the number of crimes committed (the text may help you)?
  (e) Which crime was nil in 1825 but is shown as 1.94 per cent in 1835? Can you suggest any reasons which might account for this?
  (f) Write down any questions you would like to ask about the figures. Now suggest (or find out) answers to your questions.

QUESTIONS

A Multiple choice Choose the correct answer for each question and write it into your book.

1 Criminals were often transported to which of the following:
(a) the West Indies;   (b) New Zealand;
(c) Nova Scotia;   (d) Cape of Good Hope;
(e) Botany Bay?

2 John Howard is remembered for his work in:
(a) improving the police system;
(b) improving factory conditions;
(c) reforming the penal code;
(d) improving prison conditions?

3 Who was the famous woman who began visiting Newgate prison regularly in the early nineteenth century:
(a) Jane Austen;   (b) Florence Nightingale;
(c) Charlotte Bronte;   (d) Elizabeth Fry?

4 In the early nineteenth century a large number of crimes carried the death penalty because:
(a) the public enjoyed seeing public executions;
(b) it was cheaper to execute people than to keep them in prison;
(c) the Australian colonies refused to accept any more transported convicts;
(d) the authorities relied on a system of heavy punishment to deter criminals because offenders were seldom caught;
(e) the standard of behaviour expected of people was much higher than in the twentieth century?

5 The founder of the Metropolitan Police and a leader of penal reform was:
(a) the Duke of Wellington; (b) Francis Place;
(c) Robert Peel;   (d) Edwin Chadwick?

6 Which *one* of the following statements was true of the Metropolitan Police Force when it was founded:
(a) they were unpaid volunteers under the control of the magistrates;
(b) fears of the Chartists led to the first recruitments;
(c) they were not allowed to carry firearms;
(d) they were popularly known as the Bow Street Runners;
(e) they were under the control of the army?

7 In 1830 criminals could be punished in each of the following ways *except*:
(a) death;   (b) hard labour;
(c) imprisonment;   (d) probation;
(e) transportation?

B Essay topics

1 Explain how and why Britain became a more orderly country in the nineteenth century.

2 Write an account of the reforms carried out by Sir Robert Peel during his period as Home Secretary from 1822 to 1830 in connection with
(a) Prisons;
(b) Criminal Law;
(c) Police.
In each case your answer should show the reasons for the reforms, and how effective they were, as well as giving details of the reforms.

3 Select one of the illustrations in this chapter: A highway robbery, Execution at London (Tyburn) or Prisoners in a prison ship, and write a short imaginary essay setting out the events which led up to one of the scenes shown.

4 Write a petition explaining that you have been wrongly convicted of a crime and sentenced to transportation, and complaining of conditions on board the convict ship (**C**).

16 Parliamentary reform and Chartism

In the eighteenth and early nineteenth centuries the right to vote was limited, and only about one male adult in 40 had that right. The system of voting varied from one part of the country to another. Constituencies (districts) varied in size, and in the numbers of people who were represented. By the early nineteenth century a growing number of people felt that Parliament should be reformed. After a bitter political struggle, a Reform Act was passed in 1832 which gave the wealthier members of the middle class the right to vote. However, the working class, in particular, were still excluded from the election system and many of them turned to a new political movement which came to be known as Chartism.

■ The unreformed Parliament

In what ways was the unreformed voting system unfair and open to abuse?

The voting system was complicated. Each *county* sent two MPs to the House of Commons, whatever the size of the county or the numbers of people living there. The MPs for the counties were elected by male 'freeholders', who owned property worth at least 40 shillings (£2) per year.

Other MPs were elected by 'boroughs' (towns). Voting rights varied enormously from one borough to the next. In about a dozen, almost every man was allowed to vote; in others, the right to vote was limited to a small number of men. All voting was open, so it was easy for candidates to bribe or bully their electors – the poll books could be checked afterwards, to see how the votes had been cast!

The so-called 'rotten boroughs' were particularly subject to corruption. No one actually lived in Dunwich in East Anglia, or Old Sarum in Wiltshire; yet the local landowners continued to return two MPs. In the 'pocket boroughs' a rich landowner owned enough property to be able to control the election – no one would dare oppose him or the candidate of his choice.

Many growing industrial towns, such as Manchester, Birmingham, Leeds and Sheffield had large populations but no MPs because they were not Parliamentary 'boroughs'.

■ The struggle for Parliamentary reform

Who were the early Parliamentary reformers?

The voting system was first seriously challenged towards the end of the eighteenth century. In the 1780s, numerous pamphlets were published in favour of reform.

One of the most outspoken of the early reformers was John Wilkes, a Radical MP who used his paper *North Briton* to attack the Government. Wilkes was outlawed, and fled to France. On his return he was imprisoned for a short time. He was four times elected MP for Middlesex, but the House of Commons refused to admit him and finally declared his opponent elected. However, Wilkes was strongly supported by the working and middle classes and he was eventually allowed to take his seat in Parliament.

Other early reformers included Edmund Burke and William Pitt. Burke was a moderate Whig reformer who opposed the attempts of King George III to dominate English politics and Parliament. William Pitt was a Tory statesman who became Prime Minister in 1783, but whose proposals for Parliamentary reform were defeated.

The Government feared that disturbances might lead to revolution, as had happened in France, and they acted harshly. But industrial and farming changes at the time added to the feeling of discontent and riots and disruption occurred in some parts of Britain.

In the textile-producing areas, for example, a group of workers whose jobs were threatened by the introduction of machinery, smashed the new machines and destroyed factories. These machine-breakers were known as Luddites, after their leader Ned Ludd (though it is doubtful if such a person existed). The Government made machine-breaking a capital crime, and several Luddites were hanged (**A** and **B**).

A *Official Proclamation 12 February 1811*

Any person . . . who shall wilfully and maliciously . . . break or destroy any machinery in any mill used or employed in the preparing or spinning of wool or cotton or other material for the use of the stocking or lace manufactory, on being lawfully convicted . . . shall suffer death.

B *This paper was pasted up in Nottingham on Saturday Morning 9 May 1812*

Welcome Ned Ludd, your case is good,
Make Perceval your aim;
For by this Bill, 'tis understood
It's death to break a Frame –

With dexterous skill, the Hosiers kill
For they are quite as bad;
And die you must, by the late Bill –
Go on my bonny lad!

You might as well be hung for death
As breaking a machine
So now my Lad, your sword unsheath
And make it sharp and keen –

We are ready now your cause to join
Whenever you may call;
So make foul blood run clear and fine
Of Tyrants great and Small!

p.s.   *Deface this who dare*
      They shall have Tyrants fare
      For Ned is every where
      And can see and hear –

Q (a) What name was given to the people who destroyed machinery?
(b) In which industries were the Luddites most active?
(c) How did the Government attempt to deal with machine-breaking?
(d) Set out the case *for* and *against* the Luddites.
(e) Against whom, and in which county were the Luddites particularly active in 1812 (source **B**)?
(f) Why were the Luddites prepared to use violence?
(g) Which kinds of machinery did the Luddites want to destroy, and why?

The demand for Parliamentary reform

Parliament was largely controlled by the land-owning classes. Only a few of the middle classes, and none of the working classes, were allowed to vote. The Combination Acts (see page 61) prevented unified working-class actions, so the only way the working classes could voice their discontent was through disturbances.

In 1816 a meeting of reformers at Spa Fields, in London, turned into a riot when gunsmiths' shops were raided. The disturbance was put down by troops.

In 1817 the Government, faced with much unrest, suspended Habeas Corpus, which meant that people could be kept in prison without being charged with an offence. A march to London was organized by Lancashire cotton workers to present a petition against the suspension. However, the march was halted at Stockport and the leaders were arrested. Later in the same year there were serious riots in Derbyshire against low wages and local unemployment.

In 1819, a large public meeting was held in St Peter's Field in Manchester to demand the reform of Parliament (**C** and **D**). The gathering was peaceful but the magistrates who had declared it illegal, decided to arrest the speakers, including Henry 'Orator' Hunt. When the yeomanry (a volunteer cavalry force) tried to force their way through the crowd, eleven people were killed and many hundreds were injured. Following this 'Peterloo Massacre' the Government passed stricter laws which made it more difficult to hold demonstrations.

In 1820 a plot was hatched in Cato Street, in London, to murder a number of Government ministers, capture the Bank of England and set up a provisional government. The conspirators were betrayed, and the leaders were either hanged or sentenced to life transportation.

After 1820 life in England slowly improved. Trade increased, unemployment fell, and many workers were less willing to attend meetings or join processions for Parliamentary reform.

C *A cartoon of the 'Peterloo Massacre', 1819*

D *Lieutenant Joliffe's description of how the hussars were sent in to rescue the Yeomanry*

. . . the Manchester troop of Yeomanry . . . were scattered singly or in small groups over the greater part of the Field, literally hemmed up and hedged into the mob so that they were powerless either to make an impression or to escape; in fact, they were in the power of those whom they were designed to overawe, and it required only a glance to discover their helpless position, and the necessity of our being brought to their rescue.

Q (a) Copy out all the captions in cartoon **C**.
(b) Does the cartoon give the impression that there were many more marchers (60,000) than yeomanry and hussars? YES/NO
(c) Does source **D** support or contradict the cartoon? Explain your answer.
(d) On what grounds was the intervention of the hussars justified?
(e) In what ways might the evidence pose problems for the historian?
(f) What was the purpose of the Manchester meeting at St Peter's Field?
(g) Using the text and sources what do you think really happened?
Who do you think was really to blame?
Could the massacre have been prevented?

Note: When the Manchester Yeomanry and Special Constables arrested 'Orator' Hunt and tried to seize the standards and caps of liberty the crowd panicked. The badly trained Yeomanry were unable to control the crowd or their own horses. Therefore the magistrates ordered the well-trained regular cavalry, the Hussars, to assist the Manchester Yeomanry and disperse the crowd.

Q (a) Which people and interests were well represented in the unreformed House of Commons (source **F**)?
  (b) Which classes of people and interests were *not* well represented in the unreformed House of Commons (source **F**)?
  (c) Identify the main features of the cartoon (source **E**) by linking the number with the descriptions and, where appropriate, writing out the captions.

Feature	Number (1–5)	Caption
The Sovereign, King William IV, who had to accept the Whig Government and the Whig reforms		No caption
The Whig Prime Minister whose party passed the Reform Act		
A Whig politician alarmed at the widespread unrest in many parts of the country		
The Sovereign's former Tory coachman whose party opposed the Reform Bill		
A follower of the ideas of reform and its philosophy		

  (d) How do the captions show different attitudes towards reform in the Whig Party?
  (e) What evidence was there that the country was 'unruly' in the early 1830s?
  (f) Why did many opponents of parliamentary reform argue that 'the present system had proved itself to be the best which ever had stood the test of experience'?

F *Declaration of the Birmingham Political Union, 1830*

The House in its present state is too far removed in habits, wealth and station from the lower and middle classes of the people. The aristocratic interests of all kinds are well-represented there. The landed interest, the church, the law, the monied interest are all there. But the interests of industry and trade have scarcely any representatives at all. It is essential to the national welfare that this be changed.

Why was there a clamour for electoral reform in the 1830s?

The middle classes who had prospered from the industrial development of Britain – industrialists, financiers, merchants – now felt that power should not be concentrated in the hands of the landowners. In many of the growing industrial towns political unions were formed.

In 1830 a Whig government came into power, and in March 1831 introduced a Bill for the reform of Parliament (**E** and **F**). The Bill was strongly opposed in the House of Commons by MPs in the opposition Tory Party and was eventually defeated.

In April, the King dissolved (ended) Parliament and there was another general election, which the Whigs won easily. They put forward a new Reform Bill which was passed by the House of Commons but thrown out of the House of Lords. This provoked widespread unrest. In Nottingham the mob burned down the castle and there was also burning and looting in Bristol. Many feared that if Parliament was not reformed there might even be a revolution.

When a third Bill was introduced, the House of Lords again threatened to reject it and the Whig Prime Minister resigned. The Tories, under their leader the Duke of Wellington, were unable to form a government, for public opinion was firmly against any government except a Whig one. The king had to ask the Whigs to take office once more. He promised that, if the House of Lords continued to oppose reform, he would create enough new lords to make sure that the Bill passed. Finally, the House of Lords gave in and the Reform Act became law in June 1832.

How were voting rights extended by the 1832 Reform Act?

A large number of the smaller boroughs lost either one, or both of their MPs, while the growing industrial towns were given more.

The 1832 Act extended the vote to those males who owned property, mainly the middle classes. In the counties, the vote was given to many copyholders (farmers who were tenants and whose farms were passed down from father to son) and to the wealthier leaseholders. In the boroughs, the old system was abolished and replaced by a simpler voting qualification, namely for all male householders whose property had a value for rating purposes of at least £10 a year. The property qualification meant that the vote was still confined to the wealthy. However, the number of voters increased from about 440,000 to about 660,000.

How did the 1832 Reform Act affect Parliament?

The Act was the first stage in the reform of Parliament. Elections were still conducted openly, and corruption and bribery remained features of the voting system. The Act left most of the working classes, and all women, without the vote. Thus the working class achieved no real benefit from the Act for which they had campaigned.

■ The Chartists

Why did many people become Chartists in the 1830s and 1840s?

Many of the working-class supporters of Parliamentary reform were disappointed with the 1832 Act.

The attempts to establish Poor Law Unions and workhouses, in which conditions were harsh, were bitterly resented. It seemed that the unemployed might have to choose between starvation and the workhouse. There was also dissatisfaction concerning working and living conditions. Some people had hoped for improvements through the activities of trade unions. However, the trade union movement suffered a setback with the collapse of the Grand National Consolidated Trade Union and the Tolpuddle Martyrs (see page 63).

Many working- and middle-class people therefore turned to a new political movement which came to be known as Chartism.

What were the aims of the Chartists?

In 1836, the London Working Men's Association was formed by a group of skilled craftsmen and small tradesmen. The secretary was William Lovett, a cabinet maker. In 1838 a meeting in Birmingham was attended by representatives from all over the country. Lovett, Feargus O'Connor (the editor of the newspaper *Northern Star*), Thomas Attwood (a banker and founder of the Birmingham Political Union), and some others drew up a list of rights and a programme of reform (**G, H** and **I**). The People's Charter (hence Chartists) had six points:
1 voting rights for all adult males over 21 years of age; 2 the use of a secret ballot to prevent bribery at elections; 3 no property qualifications for Parliamentary candidates so that working men might stand; 4 constituencies of equal size in terms of numbers of people represented by each MP; 5 a salary for MPs; 6 annual elections so that MPs would have to take more account of the wishes of the voters.

G *From* Hansard

Mr T. Attwood said, in rising to present this very extraordinary and important petition . . . to the House with 1,280,000 signatures . . . the men who signed the petition were honest and industrious – of sober and unblemished character – men who had always obeyed the laws. Gentlemen whose wants were provided for by the estates to which they succeeded from their fathers, could have no idea of the privations suffered by the working men of this country . . . whether they were handloom weavers, artisans (*skilled craftsmen*) or agricultural labourers . . . . Although he most cordially supported the petition . . . he washed his hands of any idea of any appeal to physical force, he repudiated all talk of arms – he wished for no arms but the will of the people, legally, fairly and constitutionally expressed . . . .

H *The People's Charter, 1837*

The Six Points
OF THE
PEOPLE'S
CHARTER.

1. A VOTE for every man twenty-one years of age, of sound mind, and not undergoing punishment for crime.

2. THE BALLOT.—To protect the elector in the exercise of his vote.

3. NO PROPERTY QUALIFICATION for Members of Parliament—thus enabling the constituencies to return the man of their choice, be he rich or poor.

4. PAYMENT OF MEMBERS, thus enabling an honest tradesman, working man, or other person, to serve a constituency, when taken from his business to attend to the interests of the country.

5. EQUAL CONSTITUENCIES, securing the same amount of representation for the same number of electors, instead of allowing small constituencies to swamp the votes of large ones.

6. ANNUAL PARLIAMENTS, thus presenting the most effectual check to bribery and intimidation, since though a constituency might be bought once in seven years (even with the ballot), no purse could buy a constituency (under a system of universal suffrage) in each ensuing twelve-month; and since members, when elected for a year only, would not be able to defy and betray their constituents as now.

I *A cartoon from* Punch, *1848 (Note: The house is the House of Commons; John, the 'butler', is the Prime Minister)*

NOT SO *VERY* UNREASONABLE!!! EH?"

John. "My Mistress says she hopes you won't call a meeting of her creditors; but if you will leave your Bill in the usual way, it shall be properly attended to."

Q (a) Draw a diagram to show the main factors which contributed to the rise of Chartism.

(b) Explain what each of the Six Points meant to the Chartists, and why they included them in their Charter (source **H**).

(c) Why is the Charter (source **I**) so large?

(d) What kinds of people joined the Chartist movement?

(e) By what peaceful means did the Chartists try to win their demands?

(f) How does the cartoonist suggest that the Chartists were 'not so *very* unreasonable'?

(g) Why was Parliament unwilling to agree to the Chartists' demands?

(h) At which times, and why, did the Chartists seem to present a serious threat to law and order?

(i) Draw a diagram to show why the Chartist movement failed.

By what methods did the Chartists attempt to win their demands?

The Chartists' six points were presented to Parliament as huge petitions in 1839, 1842 and 1848. On each occasion the petitions had between one and two million signatures but they were rejected by the House of Commons.

The Chartists were divided between those who favoured 'moral force' (peaceful methods) and those who were prepared to use 'physical force'. William Lovett preferred peaceful means. He used persuasion, through pamphlets and demonstrations, to promote the Chartist cause. The 'physical force' Chartists called for more violent action.

After the rejection of the Petitions there were riots. In 1839, there were riots in Birmingham and a serious uprising of miners and iron-workers at Newport in Wales. Here an attempt was made to free a number of Chartists held in prison. The marchers, led by John Frost, were met by soldiers and special constables in Newport and more than a dozen of the demonstrators were killed. Frost and a number of his supporters were sentenced to imprisonment or transportation.

The rejection of the second Chartist petition in 1842 was also followed by riots, the most famous of which were the Plug riots in Lancashire. These were so named because the rioters went round the mills removing the plugs from the boilers which supplied the power.

Chartists worked to change society in other ways. They set up the Co-operative Land Society (1845) which bought land and set up villages where it was hoped everyone would have an equal plot of land for cultivation. Families who moved into the communities bought their plots on an instalment plan over a long period of years. However, within a few years the Co-operative Land Society collapsed.

Why did the Chartist Movement fail?

1   Parliament ignored its demands and the Government acted firmly against it.
2   Many workers were apathetic (disinterested) and took no part in Chartist activities.
3   Other movements, the trade union movement, the Ten-Hour Movement for factory reform, and the Anti-Corn Law movement (see page 109), were important counter-attractions.
4   When workers were unemployed they would attend meetings, sign petitions, join demonstrations or even, in the last resort, riot. As economic conditions improved, support for the Charter dwindled.
5   The churches often taught that people should accept the position into which they had been born.
6   The signatures on the three petitions were sometimes fictitious or forgeries (Queen Victoria's name appeared on the 1848 Petition; so too did the name 'Pug Nose').
7   The Chartists were often scorned in the newspapers, and the movement was ridiculed.

When were Chartist aims (the Six Points) achieved?

The Acts of 1867, 1884 and 1918 gradually gave the vote to all adult males. The Acts of 1918 and 1928 extended the vote to women. There was some redistribution of constituencies, so that they were more equal in terms of the number of voters returning each MP. In 1872, open voting was replaced by the secret ballot and, shortly afterwards, the property qualifications necessary for a candidate to stand for Parliament were abolished. Under an Act of 1911 MPs were to be paid.

The idea of annual Parliaments was impractical but in 1911 the life of Parliament was shortened to a maximum of five years.

■ Cooperative Movement

In the nineteenth century, a number of groups of consumers and producers were formed to organize the sale and production of goods. The most famous group was the 'Rochdale Pioneers', who opened a shop in 1844. The money to run the store was provided by working-class members. Profits from the store were divided among members in proportion to the amount they spent. The movement spread rapidly mainly because of the popularity of the 'dividend' system and by 1851 there were 15,000 members.

QUESTIONS

Parliamentary representation before 1832
Total number of MPs = 658 in House of Commons

consisting of

English counties	84	(2 MPs each county)
English boroughs	405	
Wales	24	
Scotland	45	(1707 Act of Union)
Ireland	100	(1800 Act of Union)
		(2 MPs each county)

1 (a) How did county representation in England and Ireland differ from that of Wales and Scotland (see table above)?

(b) County A (see map) was the smallest county in England and County B was the largest county. What did they have in common?

(c) The area marked ▨ was greatly under-represented. Can you name the area?

(d) How did representation in the area marked ▨ contrast with the representation of the six counties of South-West England?

(e) 'Boroughs' such as Old Sarum, Dunwich, and Grampound were criticized by those who wanted Parliamentary reform. What term was used to describe such boroughs? How were these boroughs affected by the 1832 Reform Act?

(f) What did the towns marked ▣ have in common before 1832? Where were they mainly located, and why? How were these towns affected by the 1832 Reform Act?

(g) What happened in 1831–2 in the towns marked ▲ ? Can you explain why?

2 Using the information above, write an account of the way in which the House of Commons was represented before 1832. Why did many people think the system was unfair? How did the Reform Act attempt to improve the situation? How much of the unreformed system remained after 1832?

3 Write short paragraphs on each of the following topics:

(a) Secret ballot (1872);

(b) Elections to be held at least every five years (1911);

(c) Payment of MPs (1911).

4 Copy and complete this chart to show the extension of the franchise in the nineteenth and twentieth centuries (the bar graph will help).

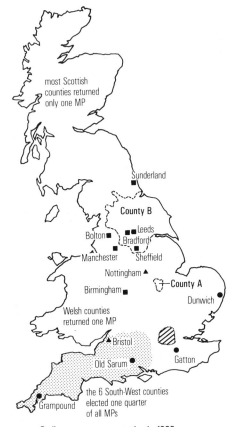

Parliamentary representation in 1830

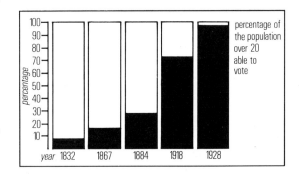

Date	Terms	Importance/ Groups given the vote	Percentage of the population able to vote
1832	(to be	completed)	

17 Commerce, trade and the Industrial Revolution

In the eighteenth and nineteenth centuries trade was organized and controlled by a complicated system of laws and tariffs (taxes). This system is often described as one of protection, or *mercantilism*. However, many people believed that restrictions and tariffs hindered the expansion of trade and, by the 1850s, Britain had become a Free Trade country.

■ Trade and commerce

British overseas trade in the eighteenth century
A feature of the eighteenth century was the growth of the British Empire in North America, the West Indies and India. The colonies provided markets for British goods and supplied Britain with a wide variety of raw materials.

The value of Britain's imports and exports increased sevenfold. British industry required more imported raw materials and more markets for the sale of finished goods. The main imports included shipbuilding materials, iron, naval stores, cotton, sugar, tobacco and dyestuffs. By the 1790s Britain had ceased to be a corn exporting country and had begun to import corn.

Woollen cloth was the most important export item during the eighteenth century, but cotton textiles overtook woollens as an export soon after 1800. In the later eighteenth century there was a marked rise in the export of iron and coal. A growing proportion of British shipping was devoted to the slave trade.

Commerce and banking
Banking developed in Britain from the seventeenth century onwards. The foundation of the Bank of England in 1694, and its gradual development, helped to establish a degree of financial stability previously unknown. Some people did invest in unreliable schemes, however, such as the short-lived South Sea Company which collapsed in a financial crisis known as the 'South Sea Bubble'. But despite such setbacks, banking and commerce continued to expand.

The growing industries of Britain were also supported by private provincial banks.

The protective system
Parliament tried to protect old-established industries (especially woollen cloth manufacture) and agriculture by imposing tariffs on imports, and encouraging exports. The growth of new industries was encouraged and British shipping was protected by the Navigation Acts, which forbade the import of any goods not carried in British ships or in the ships of the country where the goods were produced.

Mercantilists, that is, those who believed in the protective system, accepted that the tariffs on imports should be used to support agriculture, manufactures and trade. Export bounties or rewards were given to encourage the export of agricultural produce, and import duties protected British farmers from foreign competition. Trade regulations stated that certain commodities from Britain's colonies – especially sugar, tobacco and dyestuffs – had to be sent to Britain first before being exported elsewhere.

The eighteenth century was a golden age for merchants, who benefited from the protective system. High import tariffs also provided a golden age for smugglers. Import duties on items such as silks, tea, tobacco, wine and brandy made smuggling very profitable.

■ Free trade

The Wealth of Nations, 1776
Adam Smith, a Professor at Glasgow University, wrote a book in 1776 entitled *The Wealth of Nations* in which he argued that trade and industry should be freed from restrictions and protection (**A** and **B**). He believed that people should be left to follow their own interests in their own way (a policy known as *laissez-faire*).

The ideas of Adam Smith influenced a number of politicians, especially William Pitt the younger who became Prime Minister in 1783. Pitt reduced the duties on a number of

A *Children making pins in the eighteenth century*

B *From* The Wealth of Nations *by Adam Smith*

. . . To take an example from a very trifling manufacture . . . the pin-maker; a workman not . . . acquainted with the use of the machinery employed in it . . . could scarce make one pin in a day, and certainly could not make twenty . . . This business is now . . . divided into a number of branches . . . One man draws out the wire, another straights it, a third cuts it, a fourth points it, a fifth grinds it at the top for receiving the head; to make the head requires two or three distinct operations; to put it on is a peculiar business, to whiten the pins is another; it is even a trade by itself to put them into the paper; and the important business of making a pin is, in this manner, divided into about eighteen distinct operations . . . I have seen a small manufactory . . . where ten men only were employed, and where some of them consequently performed two or three distinct operations. But though they were very poor, and therefore but indifferently accommodated with the necessary machinery, they could, when they exerted themselves, make among them about twelve pounds of pins in a day . . . those ten persons, therefore, could make among them upwards of forty-eight thousand pins in a day . . .

In every other art and manufacture, the effects of the division of labour are similar . . . though, in many of them, the labour can neither be so much subdivided, nor reduced to so great a simplicity of operation . . . How many different trades are employed in each branch of the linen and woollen manufactures from the growers of the flax and the wool . . . to the dyers and dressers of the cloth. . . .

Q (a) Can you name any of the working processes shown in illustration **A**?

(b) Using source **B** calculate how long it would take an inexperienced worker – producing 20 pins a day – to make as many pins as one worker could produce in a day in a pin-making manufactory employing ten men.

(c) What is the division of labour? What are its advantages? What are its disadvantages?

goods. In 1786 Britain made a trade treaty with France, whereby each country agreed to reduce duties on certain goods. As a result of Pitt's measures, smuggling became less profitable.

The campaign to end the slave trade

By the end of the eighteenth century there was growing concern about this human trade, which had brought great profits to the merchants of ports such as Bristol and Liverpool. Slaves were bought or exchanged (bartered) on the West African coast for British manufactured goods (**C**). The slaves were then shipped to the West Indies or the American states. Many slaves died in appalling conditions on the long sea journey.

In 1807, largely through the efforts of the MP William Wilberforce, an Act was passed which abolished the trade in slaves. Slavery itself was finally abolished throughout the British Empire in 1833.

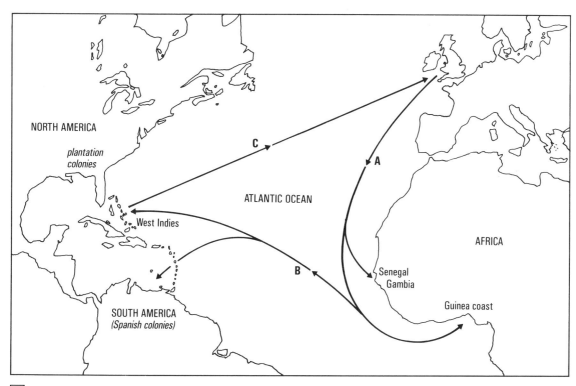

C *The triangular trade*

Q (a) Rearrange the information in the table below correctly and copy it into your book.

Route	Letter (A–C)	Cargo carried
C	Middle Passage: West Africa to West Indies	sugar, cotton, coffee, mahogany timber
B	Inward Passage: West Indies to Britain	brandy, cloth, muskets, gunpowder, bar iron handcuffs, leg irons, beans
A	Outward Passage: Britain to West Africa	negro slaves

(b) What was the triangular trade?

(c) Name two of the main British ports concerned in the slave trade.

(d) Which articles were carried from Britain to be exchanged for slaves in West Africa?

(e) Can you explain why handcuffs, leg irons and beans formed part of the cargo on the outward passage from Britain?

(f) What were conditions like for slaves on the Middle Passage?

(g) Why were slaves needed to work on the plantations of the West Indies and the American Colonies?

(h) Which goods were brought back to Britain on the Inward Passage?

(i) What arguments were there for and against the abolition of the slave trade?

The wars against France 1793-1815

Pitt's commercial policy of removing trade restrictions was interrupted by the outbreak of war against France in 1793. The revenue from import tariffs was needed to pay for the long years of war.

The Corn Laws

After 1815, European countries were again free to export corn to Britain. This foreign corn was cheaper than that grown at home, so the price of bread should have come down. But landowners and farmers used their great influence in Parliament to protect themselves against foreign competition. In 1815, the Tory Government passed the Corn Laws (**D**) which prohibited the import of foreign corn until the price of British corn had risen to the high price of 80 shillings (£4) per quarter (a measure equal to 291 litres). Farmers were careful to keep the price of corn below £4,

but this still had the effect of making bread expensive for the poor.

The revival of the movement for free trade

The movement towards free trade grew stronger after 1820. Manufacturers and merchants in the rapidly expanding industries such as cotton, iron and pottery became increasingly confident of their ability to sell goods in world markets.

Q (a) Copy out all the captions in cartoon **D**.
   (b) Can you suggest what is being carried in the ship?
   (c) What is the price at which the product is being offered?
   (d) Are the English politicians willing to accept the imports? Can you say why or why not?
   (e) What is the viewpoint of the cartoonist towards the English politicians? Give reasons for your answer.

D

The Blessings of Peace or the Curse of the Corn Bill.

Opposition to free trade came from the older industries such as silk and paper, which were not in a strong competitive position. The strongest opponents of free trade were the landowners who were determined that British agriculture should be protected against the importation of cheap foreign corn.

The work of William Huskisson

William Huskisson was MP for the port of Liverpool and, when he became President of the Board of Trade, he removed many of the duties on imports. However, Huskisson was not in favour of complete free trade.

The Corn Laws continued to cause controversy. The price of corn varied greatly from year to year and even from month to month. Huskisson wanted more stable prices and proposed a sliding scale. The landowners strongly opposed Huskisson's proposals and he was forced to resign. In 1828, a sliding scale was introduced, but it differed from the one that had been proposed by Huskisson. As the price of corn rose, the rate of duty decreased. This sliding scale was not a success, although it continued in operation until 1842.

The Anti-Corn Law League and the struggle for repeal

In 1839 a pressure group was established in Manchester. This was the Anti-Corn Law League which worked for the repeal of the Corn Laws. The main leaders were Richard Cobden, a Manchester cotton manufacturer who became known as 'the Apostle of Free Trade'; and John Bright, the son of a Rochdale carpet manufacturer, who was a great orator (public speaker). The Anti-Corn Law League was well funded, particularly by the manufacturers, and it conducted a propaganda campaign.

Manufacturers and workers hoped that if the Corn Laws were repealed the price of bread would fall. Manufacturers wanted cheap bread so that workers could live on lower wages. Industrialists also argued that if foreign countries sold their corn to Britain they would have money to buy British goods, and this would lead to an expansion of trade and industry.

The work of Robert Peel and William Gladstone

Robert Peel, Conservative Prime Minister, and William Gladstone, President of the Board of Trade, wanted to abolish import tariffs which caused higher prices. The budgets of 1842–5 removed duties from all exports and from most imports. As a result, foreign trade increased. To make up for the loss of revenue that followed the removal of tariffs, income tax was introduced (**E**).

E *From* Punch *1846*

PEEL'S CHEAP BREAD SHOP,

Q (a) Write out all the captions in source **E**. Can you explain what happened when the cheap bread shop opened in 1846?
(b) Who was the baker?
(c) Where was the shop situated?
(d) When was the shop opened?
(e) What was the shop for?
(f) Why was there a great fall in bread?
(g) What were the results of the repeal of the Corn Laws?

The repeal of the Corn Laws in 1846 was due to (a) the efforts of the Anti-Corn Law League; (b) a poor harvest in the summer of 1845; and (c) a potato famine in Ireland, which finally forced Peel to act. The repeal of the Corn Laws split the Conservative party and both Peel and Gladstone were among those who resigned.

William Gladstone, as Chancellor of the Exchequer in the Whig Governments, used his budgets to encourage trade and industry, and by 1860 Britain was virtually a free trade country. In 1860, under the terms of the Anglo-French Cobden Treaty, France agreed to reduce duties on a wide range of British goods; and Britain agreed to admit all French manufactured goods duty free. This treaty was a great success.

■ The workshop of the world

1 In the mid-nineteenth century Britain produced one-third of the world's output of manufactured goods, owned one-third of the world's shipping, and controlled a quarter of the world's trade. Britain was the first nation to industrialize and became the world's first urbanized society.

2 The Great Exhibition of 1851 (**F–H**) showed that Britain was the world leader in many branches of technology and industry.

3 The expansion of trade, and the industrial and agricultural changes of the eighteenth and nineteenth centuries enabled Britain to support a much larger population.

4 In the short term, living and working conditions for the majority of the population were often bad, with hardship and unemployment in some trades.

F   *The opening of the Exhibition 1 May 1851*

A fine day for the opening . . . I was struck by the number of foreigners in the streets . . . I went to the Park and along the Serpentine. There were immense crowds on both sides of the water . . . there must have been near three hundred thousand people in Hyde Park . . . The boats . . . darting across the lake; the flags; the music; the guns; – everything was exhilarating . . .

    I made my way into the building; a most gorgeous sight; vast; graceful; beyond the dreams of the Arabian romances. I cannot think that the Caesars ever exhibited a more splendid spectacle.

Q (a) What was the purpose of the Great Exhibition of 1851?

   (b) Were visitors impressed by the Exhibition (source **F**)?

   (c) Did Queen Victoria enjoy the Great Exhibition (source **H**)?

   (d) Design the front page of a programme or catalogue for the Great Exhibition, showing the date, place, price of admission, and other details.

G   *The Great Exhibition 1851*

H *Queen Victoria's Exhibition Journal*

. . . The tremendous cheering, the joy . . . on every face, the vastness of the building . . . its decorations and exhibits . . . and my beloved husband, the creator of this peace festival . . . a day to live for ever . . .

QUESTIONS

1 Trace the map below into your book. In the four boxes write down the name of the industry and the name of the industrialist associated with each place.

2 In the early eighteenth century areas A and B were noted for which manufacture?

3 Name the area shaded ▨ which had become the main centre for woollen cloth manufacture by the early nineteenth century.

4 Name the old centres of the iron industry marked C and D on the map.

5 Name the ports marked E and F which were important in the slave trade.

6 (a) Name river G which was important in the iron industry.

(b) Which trade is indicated by arrow H on the map?

(c) Which metals were mined at J and K on the map?

(d) Name the type of mixed cotton/linen textiles manufactured in area L.

(e) Town M was the centre of knitted stockings manufacture — what is its name?

(f) Who built bridge N and the road to London marked – – – – – ?

(g) Which towns were connected by the railway line O marked ———— on the map?

(h) With which towns, marked on the map, were each of the following connected: John Kay (flying shuttle); John Wilkinson (iron and cannon foundries); James Hargreaves (Spinning Jenny); Richard Crawshay (iron foundries)?

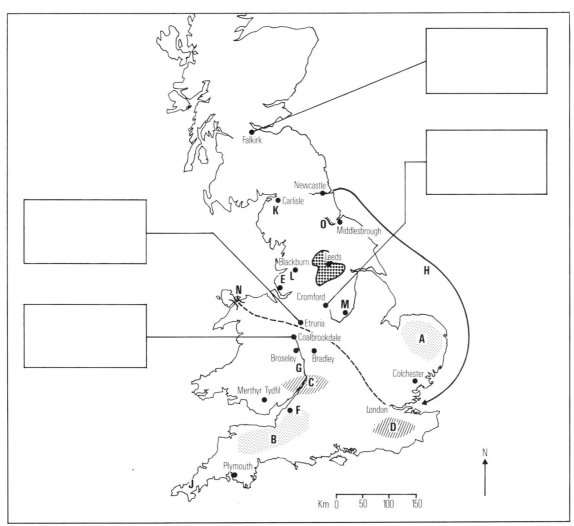

PART TWO

18 The changing fortunes of agriculture

The changing fortunes of agriculture from the mid-nineteenth century to the present day have depended on a number of factors. These include the demand for, and the price of, food; variations in weather conditions; the volume of food imports; and the particular circumstances of two World Wars. Mechanization and the use of scientific farming methods have increased the amount of food produced on the land.

■ A period of prosperity

High farming and the 'Golden Age' of agriculture

Farmers had warned that the repeal of the Corn Laws in 1846 would lead to the ruin of British agriculture (**A**). In the first years after repeal their forecasts appeared to be right. Between 1846 and 1849 the import of foreign corn doubled and prices fell.

However, by the mid-nineteenth century a new period of prosperity was beginning for British farmers. The continued growth of population and the rising standard of living of many industrial workers led to a growing demand for more foodstuffs. The rapid growth of the railway system in the 1840s opened up new markets, and enabled farmers to sell larger quantities of farm produce. The railways also made it easier for farmers to obtain fertilizers, cattle food and agricultural machinery.

In the 1850s and 1860s a number of the countries that might have exported corn to Britain were engaged in wars and had little surplus (extra) grain to export. At the same time, the cost of importing foodstuffs was still high. Thus British farmers had the advantage over foreign competitors and produced about half of the wheat and most of the meat and dairy produce required for the home market. This was a 'Golden Age' for British agriculture.

What were the main features of the 'Golden Age'?

In 1849 James Caird, a Wigtownshire farmer, published a pamphlet called *High Farming*. In it he recommended that any challenge from foreign competition could best be met by improved systems of mixed farming, that is by both the raising of livestock and the growing of crops. During the 'Golden Age' mixed farming, which could respond to changes in prices, became fashionable (**B** and **C**).

Aided partly by relatively cheap government loans, landlords spent more than £20 million on underground drainage and pipes and on other

A banquet showynge Ye Farmers Friend impressynge on ye agricultural interest that it is ruined.

A *A sketch by Richard Doyle*

Q (a) Write out the captions of the sketch.
   (b) What evidence can you find that a banquet is taking place?
   (c) Who are the people attending the banquet?
   (d) Where are the women sitting?
   (e) What is the speaker, 'Ye Farmers' Friend', telling the audience?
   (f) Do the guests appear to be rich or poor? What evidence can you find to support your answer?
   (g) Did the cartoonist believe that English farmers were 'ruined'? If not, what was he really trying to say about agriculture?

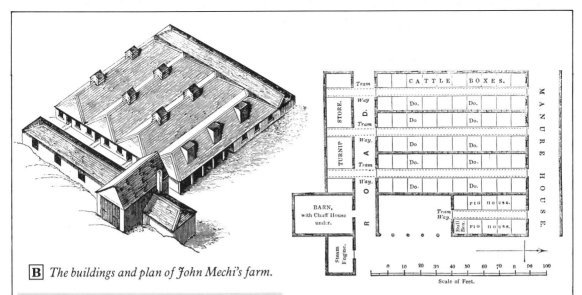

B *The buildings and plan of John Mechi's farm.*

C *John Mechi's farm*

John Mechi owned a farm at Tiptree. He drained the farm with inch pipes (2.5 cm) at five feet (1.5 m) deep and fifty feet (15 m) apart, removed all hedges and trees, laid out square fields with hard roads, and engaged as many men as applied to work to dig his land. Ten years later when there were fewer unemployed he subsoiled his fields by steam power. Periodically his steam engine pumped manure on to his fields, and it also powered his thresher, grinding mills and feed cutters.

Mechi decided that animals out in the rain and sun wasted food and manure.

By the application of liquid manure and other substances he steadily raised the fertility of his land. In the eighteen sixties he obtained average yields of six quarters of wheat, seven quarters of barley and up to forty tons of mangolds [a variety of beet used as cattle food] per acre. He normally kept thirty to forty bullocks, about two hundred sheep and a large number of pigs and poultry.

Q (a) How did the farmer make sure that his land was fully used (**C**)?

(b) How did Mechi fertilize the land (**C**)?

(c) Copy and complete the chart below to show the products raised on Mechi's farm.

Farm product	Quantity
Wheat	6 quarters per acre
(to be completed)	

(d) What evidence can you find that Mechi had a mixed farm?

(e) For what purposes was steam power used on the farm (**C**)?

(f) Where do you think Mechi kept his animals and why?

(g) What do you think the tramways were used for (**B**)?

(h) How many cattle and pigs could be housed (**B**)?

(i) What was the main food of the animals?

improvements to the land. Landowners granted long leases to their tenants and encouraged them to improve their farms.

New ideas and technical improvements led to increased output to meet the demands of the growing towns. Progress in mechanization included the introduction of varieties of plough and more widespread use of steam-driven machines, particularly the threshing machine.

Another important feature of the Golden Age was the increasing use of artificial fertilizers to improve the soil. Such ideas were introduced into Britain by Sir John Lawes, who set up a factory in London to manufacture these fertilizers.

In 1838 the Royal Agricultural Society was set up to encourage farming on scientific principles. The Society arranged agricultural shows, and offered rewards for new discoveries. In 1842 Sir John Lawes founded the Rothamsted Agricultural Research Station. The station conducted experiments on manuring, strains of seeds, crop rotation and stock-breeding, and did much to enhance the use of artificial fertilizers.

D *Inside a farm labourer's cottage in the middle of the 19th century*

Mr. Punch (to landlord). *"Your stable arrangements are excellent! Suppose you try something of the sort here! eh?"*

Q (a) Write out the caption underneath picture **D**.
  (b) Three visitors are shown (standing up). Who do you think they are?
  (c) How many people do they find living in the cottage?
  (d) What season of the year do you think it is?
  (e) Why do you think the farm labourer's family are in bed?
  (f) Describe the living conditions in the cottage.
  (g) Do you think the cartoonist approves of the way the landlord houses his farm labourers?
  (h) How does the cartoonist suggest that the landlord took more care over his animals than over his farm labourers?

Although many farmers prospered during the Golden Age, the farm labourers did not benefit greatly (**D**). Many labourers were forced to send their wives and children out to work to supplement their income.

The end of the Golden Age

By the later 1860s new factors were emerging which presented a serious threat to landowners and farmers. Prices fell and the import of foodstuffs increased. British farmers began to suffer seriously from overseas competition.

■ A period of depression

What were the causes of the depression in British farming in the later nineteenth century?

Agricultural prosperity ended in the 1870s, coinciding with much wet weather, poor grain harvests, and the outbreak of animal diseases.

After free trade had been established, imports had been allowed to come into Britain unrestricted by tariffs. Successive goverments refused to re-introduce protection for British agriculture in the form of tariffs on imports.

From the 1870s onwards, foreign food was imported in increasing quantities, in particular from North America, Australia and New Zealand. Railways in the newly developing countries, and the improvements in steamships, enabled foreign farmers to undercut British farm prices, and to sell more food in Britain. Falling prices for foodstuffs benefited the growing numbers of town dwellers and industrial workers (**E–G**).

What were the effects of the depression?

Although foreign competition affected all farming, its effects varied between regions, and from one farming activity to another (**H**).

The most severe effects were felt in the corn-producing regions, in the south and east of England. Some farmers, who had borrowed money to improve their farms during the good years of the Golden Age, went bankrupt, leaving farming for good. Others invested less money in drainage or fertilizers so that the quality of their land declined.

Some farmers turned from arable (growing crops) to pastoral (rearing animals) farming, where the effects of foreign competition were less severe. However, as imports of wool from Australia and New Zealand increased, the prices of English wool fell. Competition in meat was less severe and, until the 1880s, the pastoral farms of the north and west highland zones were relatively prosperous. However, the development of refrigeration ships, and meat canning on a large scale led to increasing imports of meat from North America, Argentina, New Zealand and Australia (**I**). Nevertheless, some British farmers continued to do well from the raising of beef cattle, for many people preferred to eat fresh rather than frozen or canned meat.

E *Changing prices of bread and wheat 1870, 1895*

Year	Price of loaf (4 lbs)	Price of wheat (quarter)	Total of wheat used Imported	Home grown
1870	8d (4p)	58s (£2.90p)	40%	60%
1895	5d (2½p)	22s (£1.10p)	80%	20%

Q (a) How did the price of bread and wheat change between 1870 and 1895?

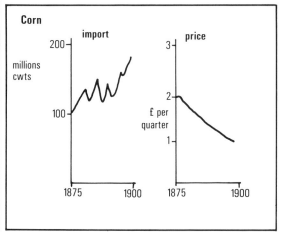

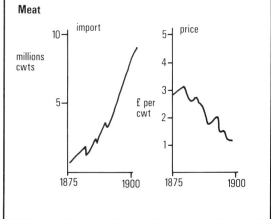

F *Corn imports and prices 1875–1900*   G *Meat imports and prices 1875–1900*

Q As imports of corn and meat increased, what happened to prices?

H *Numbers of people working on the land (England and Wales) – figures from census returns*

	Farmers and Graziers	Farm Labourers
1871	249 735	988 824
1891	223 610	798 912
1911	208 761	665 258

Q (a) How many farmers, graziers (who rear cattle for market) and labourers left the land in the period 1871 to 1891?
(b) Explain the connection between increasing imports, falling prices and the decline in the numbers of people working in British agriculture.

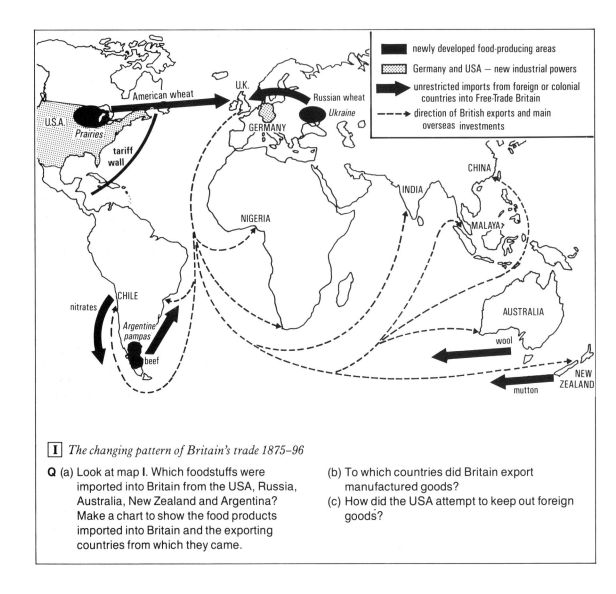

I *The changing pattern of Britain's trade 1875–96*

Q (a) Look at map **I**. Which foodstuffs were imported into Britain from the USA, Russia, Australia, New Zealand and Argentina? Make a chart to show the food products imported into Britain and the exporting countries from which they came.

(b) To which countries did Britain export manufactured goods?

(c) How did the USA attempt to keep out foreign goods?

Although some dairy products were imported from Holland and Denmark, competition in milk and milk products was much less severe. British dairy farmers benefited from the increased demand for milk from the growing population, and by the development of the railway network. Urban growth and higher living standards also encouraged the development of market gardening, vegetable farming and fruit growing near large towns.

What was the attitude of the Government?

In 1879, and again in 1894, Royal Commissions were set up to investigate the causes of the agricultural depression but they did little except set up a Board of Agriculture to help British farmers with research and advice.

The agricultural depression, particularly in the corn-growing districts, meant that many farmers employed fewer agricultural labourers. Many labourers left the land to work in the towns, while others emigrated abroad. In an attempt to persuade small tenant farmers and agricultural labourers to remain on the land, Parliament passed a number of Acts. In 1892, for example, a Small-holdings Act was passed which helped some labourers to become small farmers.

■ A brief recovery

Agricultural recovery during the First World War 1914–18

During the First World War there was an urgent need to increase the production of home-produced food. This became especially important after 1916 when the German submarine campaign became more deadly and British shipping losses increased. For a short period, in 1917, Britain had only six weeks' food supply left. Under such circumstances, imports fell, prices rose, and farmers' profits increased.

Government intervention

During the war years, the Government encouraged a 'plough policy' – the ploughing-up of grassland in order to grow crops. In 1917 the Corn Production Act guaranteed farmers certain minimum prices for their crops.

One problem for agriculture was the shortage of labour, for many farm workers enlisted into the armed forces. During the War, the Agricultural Wages Board was set up to fix legal minimum wages for farm workers. By the end of the War, the labour force on the land included many women, and volunteers of all ages, including children (**J**). Some prisoners of war had also volunteered to work on the land.

What were the main achievements during the war years, 1914–18?

The 'plough policy' was successful. By 1918 about 2.5 million additional acres of land had been brought under cultivation. The number of allotments was also increased. Despite the shortages of labour, horses, machines and materials, there was a great increase in farm output.

■ Problems for British agriculture 1918–39

Changing farming patterns

During the inter-war years many farms were neglected. Much of the land which had been ploughed up and cultivated during the war years returned again to grass or fallow. However, the output of sugar beet increased and the production of dairy produce, poultry and eggs, vegetables and market garden crops greatly expanded.

Farm workers

During the inter-war years many more farm workers moved to the towns. The numbers of agricultural workers in Britain fell from 1.5 million in 1911 to 1.3 million in 1921 and to 1.2 million in 1931.

Mechanization

After 1918 the mechanization of farming was accelerated with the increasing use of machines such as tractors and combine harvesters. So, despite the decline in the numbers of agricultural labourers, farming productivity increased.

[J] *Helping with a harvest during the First World War.*

Q (a) At what time of the year was this photograph taken?
  (b) What work is being carried out?
  (c) Is the work being done by
    (i) agricultural labourers,
    (ii) women workers or
    (iii) Boy Scouts?
  (d) Give reasons for your choice and, from the evidence, suggest the period in which the photograph was taken.

How did agricultural policies change in the 1930s?

In the 1930s, the attitude of the Government towards British agriculture changed, the new policies being marked by the ending of total free trade, and the provision of more aid and protection for farmers. It was hoped that Britain's dependence on imported food could be reduced and that, at the same time, the ties with the Commonwealth and Empire could be strengthened. The methods used to effect the changing policies included tariffs, import quotas (restrictions), subsidies (money grants) and the regulation of home production and price-fixing.

Government assistance and subsidies

Under the Derating Act (1929) farm buildings and farm land were exempted from the payment of local rates. The Government also supported the production of sugar beet, which had been subsidised since 1924. In 1935 the sugar factories were amalgamated into a single, semi-public company, the British Sugar Corporation.

The Agricultural Marketing Acts (1931, 1933) authorized the Government to regulate imports and the home supplies of agricultural produce. Marketing Boards, with compulsory powers over output and prices, were set up for hops, potatoes, pigs and bacon. The most famous of the Boards was the Milk Marketing Board (**K**). Such measures helped to bring about the recovery of British livestock farming. The output of meat and milk products also increased.

In 1932 a Wheat Act was passed to assist British cereal producers and farming prices slowly recovered. However, by the end of the 1930s almost 90 per cent of the wheat consumed in Britain was still being imported.

What was the importance of the new agricultural policies?

The Government measures of the 1930s marked the beginning of a new phase in the development of British agriculture. Positive state policy had replaced many of the *laissez-faire* views which had prevailed since the mid-nineteenth century. From here on British farming was to be subsidized by the taxpayer.

K *Advertisements from around 1925*

Q (a) Which Marketing Board published these advertisements?
(b) What was the purpose of their advertisements, and how might they benefit British farmers?

■ Increased support for agriculture

How did the Government encourage food production during the Second World War 1939–45?

Even before the outbreak of war in 1939, the Government had urged farmers to increase food production and to plough more land. During the war, shipping was needed for carrying war materials rather than for importing food. Again, there was a shortage of labour because many workers left the land to join the armed forces but the Women's Land Army and volunteer prisoners of war helped to overcome this (**L** and **M**). More farming machinery came into use.

Increased production

Farmers were offered subsidies to plough up their grassland and the Government guaranteed prices for crops. During the years 1939–45 the amount of land ploughed by British farmers increased by more than 50 per cent. Food output went up by 70 per cent and agriculture flourished. Although much of the increase was in mainly wheat, barley and potatoes, milk production was maintained. Thus Britain was able to survive the threat posed by the German submarine U-boat campaign which had been designed, partly, to starve Britain into submission.

British agriculture since 1945

Since the Second World War, successive British governments have continued the policy of assisting agriculture. The more food that British farmers could produce, the better. Governments considered that, after the dangers of the two World Wars, it was important not to be too dependent on imports.

Q (a) Look at **L**. During which years did the Government want people to 'Dig for Victory'?
  (b) Can you explain the meaning of the poster?
  (c) Why was much of the 'digging' carried out by women (**M**)?

L *Government poster*

M *Working on the land during the Second World War.*

N

Q (a) In **N**, what product is being pumped into the container lorry? Can you suggest where the lorry might be going and for what purposes the product is used?

(b) In **O**, what is being kept in the cages? What is battery farming?

(c) Using the illustrations and statistics, describe some of the ways in which farming has become mechanized.

O

Numbers employed on British farms	1914	1946
Horses	1¼ million	½ million
Tractors	500	203,000
Combine Harvesters	Nil	3,500
Labour Force	1½ million	1 million

What were the main Government policies?

One of the most important measures since the Second World War was the Agriculture Act (1947), which guaranteed British farmers fair and fixed prices for most farm produce. The Government policy of fixed price support provided a long period of stability for agriculture. The Government also made grants available to encourage farmers to use more advanced machinery on the land.

Features of modern British agriculture

Since the Second World War there has been a revolution in British farming methods. Although much land has been used for the expanding towns and new motorways the production of food has continued to rise.

Mechanization has continued rapidly with tractors, combine harvesters, grain dryers and mechanical milking (**N** and **O**). At agricultural colleges and British universities there has been much scientific research into farming. The stan-dards of British farming have been highly regarded abroad. Farm machinery and pedigree animals – especially cattle – have been exported to many countries.

What criticisms were made of British farming?

By the early 1970s the system of Marketing Boards, together with the use of subsidies to keep up farmers' incomes cost more than £300 million per annum and led some critics to claim that British governments had 'feather-bedded' farmers at the expense of the taxpayers. Others complained that farmers had failed to properly conserve the countryside, for example, by destroying hedges in order to gain more land and to use larger machines.

Finally, not all those involved in agriculture have shared in the growing wealth derived from the land. Although the Agricultural Wages Act (1947) guaranteed farm workers' wages, the levels of pay are still lower for those employed in agriculture than for town workers.

QUESTIONS

1 (a) Why was it believed that farmers would be ruined after 1846?
  (b) Why were many farmers prosperous in the years after 1850?

2 How did farmers benefit from the work of the Royal Agricultural Society?

3 (a) What developments made it possible for overseas countries to export foodstuffs to Britain?
  (b) What effects did the increasing imports of foodstuff have on farmers and on British agriculture?
  (c) Which sections of the British population gained from the fall in food prices?

4 What measures were taken to protect British farmers in the 1930s?

5 (a) Why did the Government encourage the ploughing-up of grassland and pasture land during the war years?
  (b) Why was farming prosperous during the war years?

6 (a) At which dates do you think photographs **A** and **B** were taken? Give reasons for your answer.

Photograph A	Photograph B
1850	1850
1890	1890
1940	1940
1970	1970

  (b) List as many differences in the photographs as you can.
  (c) List as many similarities in the photographs as you can.
  (d) There were many reasons why the changes shown in the photographs took place. Can you suggest some of the reasons?

7 (a) In the period between the photographs, farming in Britain underwent great changes. Describe the changes that took place in Government policies, farming methods, and in the labour force.
  (b) Do you think that all the changes have been beneficial? Give reasons for your answer.

8 **Essay:** Compare the life and work of an agricultural worker in 1850 with that of a modern farm worker. Include some or all of the following points: the organization of work; the products of farming; hours of work; conditions of work; machinery and equipment; skills and training.

Photograph A
Photograph B

19 The iron and steel industry

In the later nineteenth century there were few changes in the processes of iron making. In contrast, there were a number of technical advances in the production of steel and output had greatly increased by the early twentieth century. During the two World Wars both industries prospered but in the inter-war period, and after 1945, they found it difficult to compete in world markets.

■ An age of steel

The superiority of steel

Steel is a blend of iron and carbon, which provides a tougher and more pliable metal than iron. Until the mid-nineteenth century, the cost of manufacture prevented the large-scale use of steel and it was only used for fine products. However, iron could not withstand stress as well as steel could so there was a need to find ways of producing steel more cheaply and in large amounts. This was achieved through the technical developments of a number of inventors.

The work of Sir Henry Bessemer

Bessemer was an inventor. He manufactured cannons during the Crimean War and soon came to recognize the strength of steel.

In 1856 Bessemer developed the converter, a technique which is still associated with his name (**A** and **B**). A cylindrical vessel was used, into which molten pig iron was poured. A hot blast was driven through the molten metal (via holes in the base) to burn out the impurities.

At first, his converter could not produce a commercially usable metal. However, a metallurgist (someone who knows about metals), Robert Mushet, pointed out the need to add a small quantity of manganese containing carbon to the molten metal in the converter and what was known as mild steel was produced.

The work of William Siemens

Siemens was a member of a famous German engineering firm, who had settled in England.

In 1866 he invented the open hearth method of steel-making. During this process, the hot blast – on its way to the furnace – passed through chambers which brought the metal to a very high temperature. Gas was used as a source of heat and it was possible to control the temperature easily and accurately. This meant that the open hearth process produced better quality steel than the Bessemer technique and, after improvements carried out by two Frenchmen, Pierre and Emile Martin, it was preferred in Britain after the 1870s. Siemens founded a company to produce steel in large amounts at Landore, Swansea.

What resulted from the early inventions?

The Bessemer and Siemens-Martin processes made it possible to produce mild steel cheaply and in bulk. The two new processes marked a new phase in the development of steel and brought to an end the age of universal iron. However, the changeover from iron to steel was not immediate. Many of the resources required for steel production, for example machinery and labour, were tied up in iron making, and the setting up of new steel works was expensive. Some steel was used by the railway companies for rails; and upwards of twenty steel ships had been launched by 1865.

The two rival processes (Bessemer and open hearth process) had one disadvantage – they could not use iron ores containing phosphous. This was a serious drawback, for most British iron ore contained phosphorus. It was therefore necessary to import large quantities of phosphorus-free iron from Sweden and Spain, and the new steel works were established close to the ports in the Clyde valley, South Wales and at Middlesbrough on the Tees.

The work of Sidney Gilchrist-Thomas

In 1878 a London magistrates' clerk and amateur scientist, Sidney Gilchrist-Thomas, and his cousin P. C. Gilchrist, a works chemist, discovered a device that would permit the use of phosphoric iron ore in steel making. To extract

A *A Bessemer converter*

Q Identify the main features of the Bessemer process by linking the numbers in the picture with the correct description in the chart below.

Feature	Number
Converter in position for charging (filling)	6
Liquid iron in container	
Converter in blowing position	
Large white flame	
Man filling a mould	
Mould broken open	

B *The four main stages of the Bessemer process*

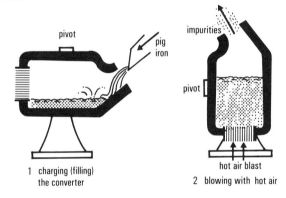

1 charging (filling) the converter

2 blowing with hot air

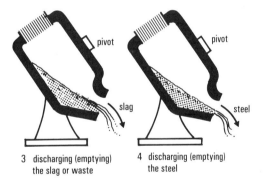

3 discharging (emptying) the slag or waste

4 discharging (emptying) the steel

the phosphorus from the iron ore a basic lining of limestone was put inside the converter. This 'basic method' of steel making could be used in both the Bessemer and the Siemens processes and meant that Britain could now use its own phosphoric iron ore in the manufacture of steel.

With the adoption of the Gilchrist-Thomas process, the cost of producing steel was further reduced and this encouraged the use of steel rather than wrought iron for railways, ships, boilers, bridges, machinery and armaments. It also led to important changes in building construction when steel and reinforced concrete were combined. Even the slag waste of the new process proved valuable for manure in agriculture.

■ Changing patterns of trade in iron and steel

The growth of foreign competition

Although the significant technical developments took place in Britain, other countries adopted the new processes more quickly and on a much larger scale. In 1870, British pig iron accounted for more than half of the world's supply but by 1900 this had fallen to only 20 per cent (**C** and **D**). The Gilchrist-Thomas process was valuable to Britain, but many British manufacturers had invested in the Bessemer and Siemens-Martin processes and were reluctant to invest the additional capital required for a new method. By 1914, both USA and Germany were larger steel producers than Britain. In those countries, important commercial developments took place in the production of steel alloys.

War and peace

Due to the demand for arms, equipment and ships to fight the First World War the iron and steel industry prospered, as did engineering and nearly all the metal industries. However, during this period, many foreign markets had been lost. A general fall in trade and a slump in ship-building badly affected the industry. Much British plant (factories) and machinery were old-fashioned and production costs were high.

Thus, within two years of the ending of the war, the iron and steel industries had entered a period of depression.

However, in the 1930s, tariffs were imposed on many imported iron and steel goods which protected the British industry and enabled it to make a modest recovery. In 1932, in response to Government pressure, the employers formed the British Iron and Steel Federation, which controlled planning and output in the iron and steel industry, and limited price competition between firms in Britain. As the iron fields of the Midlands became more important, changes also occurred in the location of the industry and

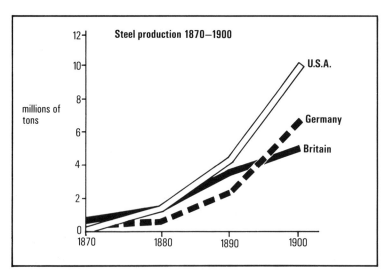

C *Steel production 1870–1900*

Q Look at **C**.

(a) By how much did British steel output grow between 1870 and 1900?

(b) Which country was the world's leading steel producer in 1870?

(c) Which country had become the world's leading steel producer by 1900?

(d) In which year did steel production in Germany overtake the level of British output?

(e) What was Britain's percentage of world steel production in 1851 (**D**)?

(f) What was Britain's percentage of world steel production in 1901 (**D**)?

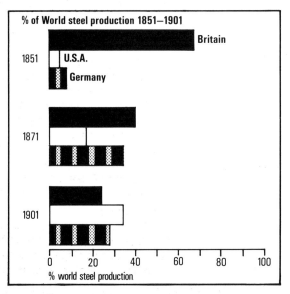

D *Percentage of world steel production 1851–1901*

important new steel works were established at the new town of Corby in Northamptonshire.

With the beginning of rearmament (building up defences and weapons) in the 1930s, the industries grew stronger. Steel output rose from 5 million tonnes in 1931 to 13 million tonnes by 1939. During the Second World War, as in the First World War, the iron and steel industries flourished.

■ Iron and steel since 1945

The traditional manufacture of iron and steel has found it increasingly difficult to compete in world markets in the post-war years. By the 1980s the industries had greatly reduced their capacity and workforce. However, some branches of engineering have prospered, particularly by providing materials for some of the newer industries.

QUESTIONS

A Multiple choice   Choose the correct answer for each question and write it into your book.

1 Which of the following was an advantage of the open-hearth process over the Bessemer converter:
(a) the waste or slag could be sold as fertilizer;
(b) gas was used as a source of heat;
(c) it allowed for the use of scrap steel?

2 Which of the following were directly changed by the Gilchrist-Thomas process:
(a) the puddling furnace;   (b) Bessemer converter;
(c) Open Hearth furnace; (d) the electric furnace?

3 Which of the following help to explain the slow development of the British steel industry:
(a) large amounts of money had been invested in iron manufacture;
(b) there was insufficient capital to develop a new industry;
(c) British steel inventions lagged behind those of other countries;
(d) ships could not be built of steel until the 1880s?

4 Which *two* of the following were largely to blame for the decline of the British iron and steel industries by 1914:
(a) insufficient modernization of plant;
(b) inferior British workmanship;
(c) over-reliance on exports;
(d) free trade?

5 Which of the following remedies would have been most appropriate for the British iron and steel industries:
(a) a smaller workforce;
(b) higher wages to workers;
(c) import duties;
(d) cheaper furnaces?
Give reasons for your choice.

B

1 Match each of the items in List A with the appropriate item from List B.

List A

Sidney Gilchrist-Thomas
Henry Bessemer
William Siemens

List B

1856 developed the Converter
1866 invented Open Hearth method
1878 basic lining process

2 (a) What effect did Bessemer's converter have on steel production?
(b) What was the main disadvantage in using British iron ore in the manufacture of steel?
(c) How did the Gilchrist-Thomas process help Britain's steel industry?

3 'Thirty years ago [1851] England had almost a monopoly of the manufacturing industries of the world. She produced more of everything than she needed; other countries produced very little. The rest of the world had to buy from Britain because it could not buy anywhere else. Well, that was thirty years ago. Now, France and America have got machinery – our machinery. Each year they sell an increasing volume of their goods here in Britain. On the other hand, year by year, these countries are closing their markets to our exports.'
(a) How had Britain's trading position changed between 1850 and 1880?
(b) How did the writer account for the changes?

4 Essay topics
(a) Describe the changing fortunes of the British steel industry in the period 1850–1980.
(b) What effects did the changed methods of producing steel have on British industry?

20 Shipping and shipbuilding

During the nineteenth century two important changes occurred in the shipbuilding industry. Iron and steel instead of wood were increasingly used in the construction of ships and, gradually, the use of sail was replaced by steam power. Britain became the world's leading shipbuilder and remained so until the First World War. Today, the British shipbuilding industry can only survive with Government support.

■ From wood and sail to iron and steam

The early development of steamships

The early steamships, which had paddles on one or both sides of the ship, were built of wood and were propelled by Boulton and Watt steam engines (**A**). The first successful passenger steamer in Britain was Henry Bell's vessel, *Comet* (1812), which was used on the river Clyde. The early steamers also carried sails as the engines were sometimes unreliable.

After 1818, wooden steamers carrying sails

A *An early British paddle-steamer, the* 'Charlotte Dundas'. *It was designed by William Symington and, from 1802, worked regularly on the river Clyde in Scotland.*

operated between Dover and Calais. In 1819 the 'Savannah', an American ship, crossed the Atlantic in 25 days but used its engines for less than 15 per cent of the total crossing time. It was not until the late 1830s that the Atlantic was crossed using steam alone. In 1839 a propeller under the stern (back of the ship) was first introduced and this, known as the 'screw propeller', soon replaced the paddles. It soon became clear that iron ships were better able to withstand the vibrations of the screw propellers.

Iron ships

The first iron barge had been constructed as early as 1787 by John 'Iron-mad' Wilkinson. In 1817 the first iron ship was built on the river Clyde. The development of iron steamships is particularly associated with one of the great engineering figures of the nineteenth century.

Isambard Kingdom Brunel

Brunel was the engineer responsible for many important bridges, such as the Clifton Suspension Bridge, Bristol; and the Royal Albert Bridge over the river Tamar. He was also the engineer for the Great Western Railway, which ran between London and the port of Bristol. In

Q (a) What is the boat in **A** built of?
  (b) How can you tell that the boat was powered by steam?
  (c) How is the boat being steered?
  (d) Is the paddle wheel at the fore (front) or aft (back) of the boat?
  (e) In what ways might this evidence be of use to an historian?

1835, Brunel suggested that the railway line should be extended beyond Bristol by means of 'a steamboat to go from Bristol to New York, and call it the 'Great Western'' (**B**). By 1838 Brunel's steamboat, 'Great Western', was ready, and crossed the Atlantic Ocean in 15 days. However, it proved a financial failure. It carried fewer than one hundred passengers and failed to gain the government's contract for carrying mail, which went to the American, Samuel Cunard.

Nevertheless, Brunel designed and built a number of transatlantic steamships, including the 'Great Britain' and the 'Great Eastern'. Brunel's 'Great Britain' (1845) was the first large iron ship to use a screw propeller instead of a paddle-wheel. The 'Great Eastern' (1858) at 20,000 tons was one of the biggest iron ships ever made and Brunel designed it to carry 4,000 passengers in comfort. In 1860 the 'Great Eastern' crossed the Atlantic in a record-breaking time of 11 days.

How was the efficiency of steamships improved?

In 1854 the compound engine was patented by John Elder. It required less coal, which enabled steamships to go much faster and to travel longer distances. (The main problem with early steamships was that the length of their journey was dependent on how much coal they could carry.) (**C**)

At the end of the nineteenth century marine (sea) engines were revolutionized as a result of the work of Sir Charles Parsons who developed the steam turbine engine (patented 1884). This led to a great increase in speed.

The change from sails to steam and from wood to iron and steel was slow. It was not until the 1860s, for example, that the British navy was prepared to construct iron battleships. Developments in the steel industry led to great reductions in the cost of the raw material. By the end of the nineteenth century, vessels were increasingly built of steel rather than iron. As a result, ships were lighter, used less fuel and could carry more cargo.

B *Advertisement for Brunel's steamship, the* 'Great Western', *1838*

Q (a) Between which two countries, and which two cities, did the *Great Western* operate?
(b) How long did the sea journey take?
(c) What fares were charged to passengers?
(d) Which people travelled at half fare?
(e) How much did it cost to transport goods?
(f) What evidence can you find that the ship did not rely only on steam power?
(g) The captain had formerly served in the Royal Navy. How do you know?
(h) Why did a surgeon travel with the ship?

C *D. A. Wells,* Recent Economic Changes, *1892*

Prior to about the year 1875 ocean steamships had not been very satisfactory as freight-carriers. The marine engine was too heavy, occupied too much space, consumed too much coal. For transportation of passengers, and of freight having large value in small space, they were satisfactory; but for performing a general carrying trade of heavy and bulky articles they were not satisfactory.

Q Why were the early ocean steamships unsatisfactory for carrying heavy or bulky goods?

D *A clipper, the* 'Cutty Sark'

Q (a) How was this ship (**D**) powered?
  (b) Two of the crew (at **A**) are carrying out difficult and dangerous work. What are they doing?
  (c) What were the advantages of wind and sail power?
  (d) What evidence can you find that the ship was probably travelling at maximum speed?
  (e) On which trade routes were clippers most commonly used and what cargoes did they carry?
  (f) What was the main disadvantage of the sailing ship?
  (g) Why and when did the clippers decline?

The survival of sail

Sailing ships managed to compete with steamships until nearly the end of the nineteenth century. One reason was that their source of power (the wind), was free.

The fastest sailing ships were not British, but American 'clippers', which were able to cut down, or 'clip' from, the time taken by their competitors. British clippers were also built, particularly from the 1830s onwards (**D**).

Some clippers could reach 16 knots (29 kph) in full sail. Although clipper ships specialized in the carriage of tea from China they also brought wool and grain from Australia.

The main disadvantage of the sailing ship was the need to 'tack', that is, to change direction or sail to gain the benefit of the wind. The opening of the Suez Canal in 1869 favoured the steamships. There was little room for tacking operations in the Suez Canal, and so sailing vessels had to be towed through.

Although sailing vessels and clippers survived until the 1870s, the opening of the Suez Canal, improvements in steamships, and the building of coaling stations (where ships could take on fuel) along the main trade routes all favoured the steamship. Nevertheless, small sailing ships survived much longer in the coasting and river estuary trades (**E**).

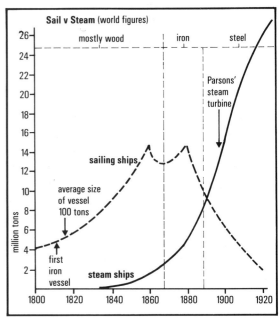

E *Sail v steam*

Q (a) In which year was the tonnage of sailing ships at its peak?
  (b) By which year was the tonnage of sailing ships and steam ships approximately equal?
  (c) From which year did sailing ships begin to decline rapidly?
  (d) From which decade were all new ships built of steel?

■ The triumph and decline of British shipbuilding

The world's shipbuilder

Throughout the nineteenth century, shipbuilding was one of Britain's main industries. Merchant ships carried British manufacturing exports on sea routes around the world, and returned with raw materials and food produce. Luxury liners could carry passengers to almost anywhere in the world.

By 1860 Britain was the world's leading shipbuilder. Ships built in Britain were purchased by many other countries. By the time the First World War broke out, Britain was the world's largest trading country and British companies owned about 60 per cent of the world's shipping.

Shipping and shipbuilding after 1914

During the First World War the British shipbuilding industry worked to replace merchant shipping destroyed by German submarines and to supply ships to the Royal Navy, despite shortages of materials and workers. Immediately after the war, British shipyards were very busy but by 1920 the industry was entering a prolonged period of depression. The sharp fall in international trade meant that many merchant ships were laid up and the demand for new ships slumped. There was also less demand for shipbuilding for the Royal Navy during peacetime. The decline in Britain's coal exports reduced the demand for shipping capacity. Britain's shipyards were not equipped to produce the new oil-burning ships, oil tankers and motor ships which were coming into more general use. Britain found it difficult to compete with other shipbuilding countries, particularly the USA and Japan (**F**).

Britain's shipyards during the great depression

By 1933 nearly two-thirds of Britain's shipbuilding workers were unemployed and many shipyards on Tyneside and Clydeside had closed. The effect on the workers was appalling. The closure of Palmer's shipyard at Jarrow (**G** and **H**) in 1934 meant that over 70 per cent of the workers were unemployed and Jarrow became known as 'the town that was murdered'.

F *Output of the British shipbuilding industry*

Year	Output in tons weight
1913	1 000 000
1938	500 000

G *Speech in Parliament, 2 November 1936*

During the last fifteen years Jarrow has passed through a period of unparalleled industrial depression . . . where 8,000 persons were once employed, only a hundred are now employed.

H *Jarrow marchers on their way to London, 1936*

Q (a) Can you explain the connection between the figures in source **F**, the speech in Parliament in source **G** and the marchers in the picture **H**?

(b) Which regions of Britain were most affected by the changes in output of the British shipbuilding industry?

(c) In what work had the 8,000 persons been employed (source **G**)?

(d) What did the unemployed workers of Jarrow do to draw attention to their problems?

(e) Put the information given in the photograph into a written paragraph bringing out the most important features.

Despite some Government assistance, Britain's shipbuilding industry never fully recovered and the labour force in shipbuilding declined by one-third in the inter-war years.

One exception to the depression in shipbuilding was the construction of a number of superior luxury liners which were launched in the 1930s, including the 'Queen Mary' and the 'Queen Elizabeth'.

The Second World War brought about a revival in the shipbuilding industry, which was also maintained for a short period afterwards.

Shipbuilding since 1945

Immediately after the end of the Second World War, British shipyards were launching about half of the world's new tonnage. However, Britain failed to take the necessary initiatives to maintain its position. British shipbuilders did not modernize either their shipyards or their methods of management. The workforce continued to be dominated by demarcation disputes (disputes about who does what job).

By the mid-1950s Britain's production of world shipping tonnage had fallen while the position of Japan and Germany had strengthened. Today a much reduced British shipbuilding industry can only survive with Government financial support.

The hovercraft

The hovercraft (**I**) rides on a cushion of air. The air is drawn in above the craft and is blown out along the lower edge to create a high pressure air pad. Running round the lower edge of the craft is a 'skirt' which helps to contain the air. The hovercraft can travel over land and water. It was invented in the 1950s by Christopher Cockerell and made its first Channel crossing in 1959. Cross-channel services began in 1966.

I *A hovercraft*

QUESTIONS

1 Match each of the items given in List A with the appropriate item from List B.

List A	List B
Charles Parsons	'Cutty Sark'
Henry Bell	'Charlotte Dundas'
I. K. Brunel	'The Queen Mary'
William Symington	'Great Britain'
Christopher Cockerell	'Comet'
Sailing clipper	The hovercraft
Luxury liner	The steam turbine engine

2 In any account of the development of shipping in the nineteenth and twentieth centuries a number of individual ships may be considered of particular importance. Select *five* of those ships, place them in chronological order, and write *three* sentences about each one to show why they were important. Your work should be presented in the form of a chart as set out (right).

3 (a) Who invented the hovercraft?
(b) When was the hovercraft first used to make a Channel crossing?

4 **Essay topic:** Describe and explain the changing fortunes of British shipping and shipbuilding in the twentieth century by linking the following: the impact of two World Wars; the change from coal to oil fuel; the increase in the size and speed of ships; the development of the great liners; the decline of British merchant shipping; competition from air travel.

Date	Name of ship	Importance

21 New forms of power

Britain has been fortunate in its energy reserves. The industries of the industrial revolution used water and steam power and were often located on the coalfields. In the later nineteenth and twentieth centuries new forms of power such as gas, electricity, oil and nuclear power were developed, making it possible for industry to be located away from the coalfields.

■ Gas

Coal gas

Gas made from coal was first used for street and some house lighting (**A** and **B**). The Gas Light and Coke Company was set up in London in 1812. The manufacture of gas, which soon spread to other towns, created new jobs both at the gasworks and in the industries which made

A *A peep at the Gas Lights in Pall Mall*

Q (a) Copy out the captions in the cartoon (source **A**).
(b) Design a poster or advertisement setting out all the benefits of gas lighting, which might persuade people to invest money in the Gas Company (**B**).

B *Lady Bessborough to the British Ambassador*

What can occasion such a ferment in every house, in every street, in every shop, in every garret about London? It is the Light and Heat Company. It is Mr Winsor and his lecture, and his gas, and his patent, and his shares . . . That strong light that has lit up Pall Mall for this year past has all at once blaz'd up like a comet . . . .

C *Michael Faraday giving a Christmas lecture for young people, 1855*

Q (a) Identify the main features of the Royal Institution's Children's Christmas Lecture by linking the numbers in the picture **C** with the correct descriptions in the chart.

Feature	Number
Michael Faraday Experiment bench Lecturer's assistant Prince Albert (Prince Consort) Prince of Wales (later Edward VII)	

(b) Why was the lecture theatre suitable for showing experiments to audiences?

(c) Which kind of people attended the lectures? How can you tell that they regarded the lectures as a social occasion?

(d) What evidence can you find that Faraday was a popular lecturer?

(e) How can you see that Faraday believed in giving practical demonstrations of science?

(f) Which items of chemical apparatus do you recognize? Are any of the items still used today?

(g) How was the lecture theatre lit?

---

use of the 'waste' products, for example coal tar for the chemical industry. By 1914 gas was being used for cooking and heating, as well as for lighting.

Natural gas

Until the 1950s nearly all gas was produced from coal and it was expensive compared to some other fuels. However, from the 1960s the industry developed the use of 'natural gas'. At first, natural gas was imported in liquified form from North Africa and Algeria, but in 1965 natural gas was discovered beneath the North Sea. Special floating rigs were set up and the gas was brought ashore and distributed to many parts of Britain by pipeline. The changeover from coal gas to natural gas made it necessary to 'convert' existing gas appliances, so that they could safely burn natural gas. Once this was done, gas consumption greatly increased.

■ **Electricity**

The development of electricity

An Englishman, Michael Faraday, was a pioneer in the development of electricity (**C**). His research led to an electric battery (1812) and the first dynamo (1831).

Sir Charles Parsons developed a 'turbo-alternator', which made it possible to drive a dynamo much faster. The system of transmitting power by alternating current was developed by Sebastian de Ferranti. The work of Parsons, Ferranti and Siemens (see page 122) helped to make electricity more generally available for public use and in 1881 the first central electricity generating plant was built.

The early uses of electricity

In 1878 30,000 spectators were able to watch a football match in Sheffield played under the light of four electric arc lamps. However, arc lamps were not suitable for indoor use. Joseph Swan and the American inventor Thomas Edison helped to overcome this problem by the invention of the incandescent electric lamp, which permitted electric lighting in the home.

Partly because of its high cost in its early years, Britain was slow in developing the use of electricity. It was not until the later nineteenth century that methods were found to use electrical power for industrial and domestic purposes.

What advances were made in the production and use of electricity?

In the early 1920s there were more than 400 different organizations which provided electricity and there was little uniformity in voltage. Some organizations supplied alternating current (a.c.) while others supplied direct current (d.c.).

In 1926 the Electricity Supply Act was passed by Parliament. This established the Central Electricity Board. The Board was to standardize the different voltages that were in use in different parts of Britain and to close some of the smaller and inefficient power stations.

The National Grid

In 1926, in order to provide electricity more cheaply in all parts of the country, the Board set up a network of power lines known as the National Grid. The Board bought electricity from the private companies generating electricity at the power stations. This was fed into the 'grid', and then sold to users. Through the grid, the Board could transmit electricity to all places at all times. The National Grid was completed in 1934.

The improvement of the electricity supply and the building of the National Grid provided work for 100,000 people, at a time of high unemployment. Gradually, more and more houses changed to electric lighting and a number of new industries produced electrical goods for use in the home (**D**). Equally important was the growth of industries manufacturing

D *Advertisement for electrical goods*

Q (a) At what time of the year did this advertisement (**D**) appear?
    (b) How might the gifts advertised have made life in the home easier?
    (c) How would the following tasks have been carried out before the use of electricity: carpet cleaning, heating, cooking, ironing?
    (d) What do the letters G.E.C. stand for?

equipment needed in the production of electricity and in electrical engineering. Factories in electrical engineering often employed a large workforce.

Developments since 1945

The electricity supply industry was nationalized in 1947, under the control of the Central Electricity Generating Board. (To nationalize an industry means to transfer it from private ownership to boards of managers appointed by the Government.) The country was divided into areas, and each area had its own electricity generating board. Nationalization meant that money could be spent on research to keep the industry up to date.

After the 1960s, a number of different fuels were being used to produce electricity. Most power stations used coal (**E**), but a growing number used oil (**F**) and nuclear power. Some coal-fired power stations used oil or gas to boost the electricity supply when demand was particularly high. A small proportion of electricity (less than five per cent) was produced by means of hydro-electric power (where falling water rather than steam engines was used to drive the dynamos).

E *Coal-fired power station*
F *Oil-fired power station*

Q Identify the main features of a modern power station by linking the numbers in the pictures **E** and **F** with the correct descriptions in the chart below.

Feature	Numbers	
	Coal-fired	Oil-fired
Coal store/oil storage tanks		
Boiler house where steam is produced from water to turn turbines coupled to generators to provide electricity		
Chimney/s for discharging exhaust gases		
Cooling towers		

How has electricity affected people's lives in the twentieth century?

Electricity has provided a clean and convenient source of power which has contributed to a greatly improved standard of living, particularly since the Second World War. Electrical goods include televisions, stereos, hair driers and a range of cooking and cleaning equipment. One of the most important electrical devices of the past generation has been the computer. Many electrical devices are also used in motor vehicles.

The development of electricity has transformed industry over the past fifty years. Electricity and the National Grid have freed industry from location on the coalfields. Many industries became located in new areas, such as the Midlands, the South-East and the South of England.

■ Oil

Increasing use of oil

By the early twentieth century the demand for oil was growing. Petrol was needed for motor vehicles, and some ships changed from coal to oil which was cleaner and easier to use.

After the Second World War, oil imports increased rapidly. As well as petrol, oil was used for domestic and industrial heating and in power stations. In addition, a wide range of by-products such as detergents, plastics and man-made fibres were manufactured from oil. Much of the crude (raw) oil was imported from the Middle East (**G**) and then refined (purified) in Britain. This process became an important industry and large refineries were built at some of the main ports. These were operated by the great international oil companies such as British Petroleum (BP), Esso and Shell.

The increasing use of oil led to a fall in the demand for coal; and oil has replaced coal as the most valuable of the fossil fuels (fuels which are formed from the remains of dead plants and animals).

North Sea oil

The Middle East oil crisis of 1973 led to a sharp increase in the price of imported oil. But Britain's own oil reserves had been discovered under the North Sea. Although the reserves are very great, extracting oil from the North Sea is difficult and expensive, and involves the construction of oil rigs which operate at sea. Britain is now able to export oil. However, unless new reserves are discovered and worked, oil production, which has reached its peak, will begin to decline.

G *World production of crude oil*

Q By how much did world production of crude oil increase between (i) 1915–25 and (ii) 1960–70?

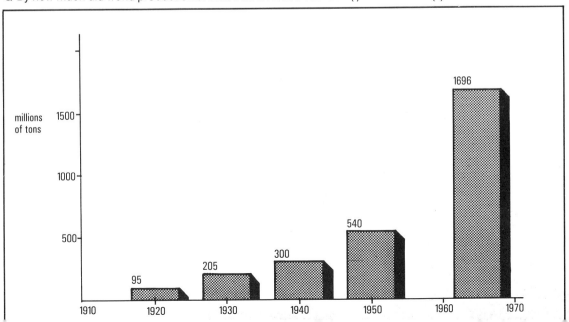

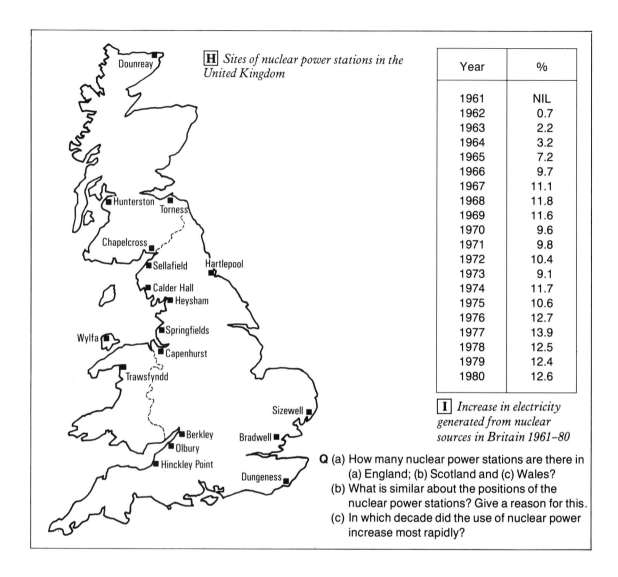

H Sites of nuclear power stations in the United Kingdom

Year	%
1961	NIL
1962	0.7
1963	2.2
1964	3.2
1965	7.2
1966	9.7
1967	11.1
1968	11.8
1969	11.6
1970	9.6
1971	9.8
1972	10.4
1973	9.1
1974	11.7
1975	10.6
1976	12.7
1977	13.9
1978	12.5
1979	12.4
1980	12.6

I Increase in electricity generated from nuclear sources in Britain 1961–80

Q (a) How many nuclear power stations are there in (a) England; (b) Scotland and (c) Wales?
(b) What is similar about the positions of the nuclear power stations? Give a reason for this.
(c) In which decade did the use of nuclear power increase most rapidly?

■ Alternatives to fossil fuels

Nuclear power

When atoms of uranium are split, immense heat is released. This can be used to produce steam for driving the turbines of electricity generators and is known as atomic energy or nuclear power. In Britain, atomic energy, and its uses, are controlled by the United Kingdom Atomic Energy Authority. The first large-scale nuclear power station was opened at Calder Hall in Cumbria in 1956. By the early 1980s, Britain was generating about 15 per cent of its electricity in eighteen nuclear power stations (H and I). Many people argue that nuclear power is relatively cheap, clean and safe. Others maintain that there may be dangers from radioactivity as a result of accidents or leaks at the power stations, or from the disposal of nuclear waste.

Alternative sources of energy

In the 1980s there is considerable interest in the development of alternative sources of energy – tidal power, wave energy, wind energy, geo-thermal energy (using the Earth's internal heat) and solar energy (using the sun's rays). However, such sources are likely to make only a small contribution to Britain's future energy needs. As oil and gas reserves fall, the country will need to rely on coal and, probably, on nuclear energy.

QUESTIONS

Total Energy Consumption in the United Kingdom
(These figures are calculated in millions of tonnes-coal equivalent)

	1959	1971	1978	1979
Coal	190	139	120	130
Petroleum	58	151	139	139
Natural Gas	0.1	29	65	71
Nuclear Energy	0.5	10	13	14
Hydro-Electricity	1.5	1.8	2.1	2.2
Total	250.1	330.8	339.1	356.2

Total Fuel Production in the United Kingdom
(These figures are calculated in millions of tonnes-coal equivalent)

	1959	1971	1978	1979
Crude Oil	0.1	0.4	91.8	132
Natural Gas	0	28	58	58
Coal	210	149	124	122

Source: Government Statistical Service.

1 (a) Look at the tables above. Which form of energy
has decreased in both consumption and
production between 1959 and 1979? Can you
suggest reasons for this decline?

(b) What happened to the consumption of
petroleum in the 1970s? Can you explain why?

(c) By how much did total energy consumption
increase in the period 1959–79? Can you give
reasons for this increase?

(d) Which forms of fuel were not produced on any
great scale in 1959 but are very important
today? Can you explain the reasons for the
change?

2 (a) Look at map **J**. Write down the numbers and
names of *three* of the coalfields.

(b) Name a coalfield in Britain where production
has declined in recent years and explain why
this has happened.

(c) Why is the Yorkshire-Notts-and Derbyshire
coalfield the leading producer of coal? Why
has the coalfield been extended eastwards?

(d) Name *two* of the nuclear power stations shown
on the map.

(e) What source of power is located beneath the
North Sea at the area marked A?

(f) What source of fuel is located at the areas
marked B?

(g) Name *one* oil refinery and describe the
advantages of its site.

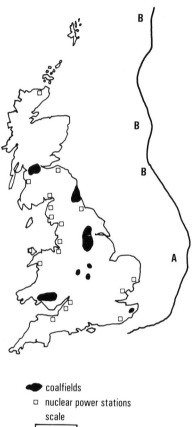

coalfields
nuclear power stations
scale
0   50 km

J *Britain's fuel resources in the 1980s*

3 **Essay topics**

(a) What are the arguments for and against the
increasing use of nuclear power?

(b) The total amount of energy consumed has
risen more rapidly than the total amount of
energy produced in Britain. If this trend
continues, what other forms of power might be
developed?

22 Trade unions

After the mid-nineteenth century, permanent trade unions of the skilled workers or craftsmen developed. After 1880 the semi-skilled and unskilled workers also established more permanent unions. There was a rapid rise in trade union membership, from 750,000 in 1888 to 8 million by 1918. In the period between the Wars, large-scale unemployment became a serious problem. There were many strikes, the most significant being the General Strike of 1926, but with massive unemployment the trade unions could do little for their members. During the Second World War trade unionists co-operated with employers and the Government. Since 1945, the power and influence of trade unions has fluctuated (risen and fallen).

■ 'New model' unionism

The revival of trade unionism
In general, from the 1850s to the early 1870s employment conditions were good and the demand for labour increased. Trade union organization among skilled craftsmen grew, particularly where the units of employment or production were large.

Amalgamated Society of Engineers (ASE), 1851
This union, which consisted largely of steam-engine and machine makers, grew out of the earlier local trade societies (**A**). It set a new standard of stability with high contributions paid by members, a system of benefits, centralization of control, and the business-like approach of its General Secretary, William Allen. The ASE was one of the first unions of a new type, which came to be known as the 'new model' craft unions. The ASE was soon copied, for example by the Amalgamated Society of Carpenters and Joiners (1861) under its General Secretary, Robert Applegarth.

AMALGAMATED SOCIETY OF ENGINEERS, MACHINISTS, MILLWRIGHTS, SMITHS, AND PATTERN MAKERS.

A *Trade union emblem*

Q (a) Which kinds of workers did this Society represent?
(b) What was the motto of the Society?
(c) What kinds of work are being carried out in the emblem of the Society?
(d) What were the benefits of belonging to such a Society?
(e) Describe the two figures representing war and peace. Which is being welcomed and which is being rejected?

What were the main features of the 'new model' unions?

The craft unions, or 'new model' unions, were organized on a national basis, with strong central executive committees. The union officials were paid and administration was efficient. The new model unions consisted mainly of skilled workers, who could afford to pay high subscriptions. Sick pay and other benefits were provided for members in need. The unions wanted to secure better wages and hours for their members through an understanding with employers and without strikes.

Some working-class leaders considered that the new model unions of skilled craftsmen were out of touch with the great mass of the semi-skilled and unskilled workers.

What was the Junta?

In 1860 the London Trades Council was reorganized as an unofficial cabinet of the skilled craft unions. This was known as the 'Junta'.

The Junta, which included the national secretaries of the leading 'new model' unions, campaigned to improve the legal position of trade unions. The Junta supported the Second Reform Act (1867), which gave the vote to working-class men in towns, and increased trade union influence on Parliament.

Crisis for the trade union movement

In Sheffield, the masters employed non-union workmen in the cutlery trades. Some union members reacted violently and in 1866 the house of a non-unionist was blown up. The public was shocked and started to regard trade unions as dangerous organizations.

The Hornby v. Close judgement of 1867 refused the Bradford branch of the Boiler-makers' Society permission to prosecute their treasurer for stealing the funds. This judgement meant that if a union's funds were stolen by an official, the officers or members could not take legal action against the thief for recovery of the money.

The Royal Commission

In 1867 the Government set up a Royal Commission to examine the position of trade unions. The members of the Junta, particularly William

Allen and Robert Applegarth, gave evidence to the Commission that trade unions could provide benefits for their members; that most trade unions were peaceful bodies; and that industrial relations between employers and workers were often better if trade unions existed. In its report (1869) the Royal Commission came out in favour of the 'new model' unions.

The Trades Union Congress (TUC)

Not all trade unionists were content to follow the methods of the Junta. In 1868, 34 delegates representing 118,000 trade unionists met at a 'Congress' in Manchester to discuss trade union matters (**B**). Members of the London-based Junta did not attend but, in the following Congresses the craft unions and Junta were more strongly represented. Efforts were concentrated on exerting pressure on Parliament, and the TUC gradually became accepted as the central organization for trade unions.

How did trade unions gain full legal recognition?

Under the Trade Union Act of 1871, unions became full legal organizations and union funds were protected from dishonest officials. However, another Act was passed in the same year, the Criminal Law Amendment Act (1871), which prohibited picketing. This weakened the strike weapon and angered trade unionists. In the 1874 general election, many trade unionists voted for the Conservatives – who had promised to improve the position of trade unions – in protest against the Liberals, who had passed the Criminal Law Amendment Act.

In 1875 the Conservative Government passed the Conspiracy and Protection of Property Act, which permitted trade unions to use peaceful picketing during strikes.

The legislation of the 1870s was a great triumph for the working classes. It established the power of the trade unions, which could organize effective strikes if peaceful bargaining failed.

■ The new unions

New unionism of unskilled workers.

Unskilled workers were often opposed to the type of trade union organized by skilled workers

PROPOSED CONGRESS OF TRADES COUNCILS

AND OTHER

Federations of Trades Societies.

MANCHESTER, FEBRUARY 21st, 1868.

FELLOW-UNIONISTS,

The Manchester and Salford Trades Council having recently taken into their serious consideration the present aspect of Trades Unions, and the profound ignorance which prevails in the public mind with reference to their operations and principles, together with the probability of an attempt being made by the Legislature, during the present session of Parliament, to introduce a measure detrimental to the interests of such Societies, beg most respectfully to suggest the propriety of holding in Manchester, as the main centre of industry in the provinces, a Congress of the Representatives of Trades Councils and other similar Federations of Trades Societies. By confining the Congress to such bodies it is conceived that a deal of expense will be saved, as Trades will thus be represented collectively; whilst there will be a better opportunity afforded of selecting the most intelligent and efficient exponents of our principles.

It is proposed that the Congress shall assume the character of the annual meetings of the British Association for the Advancement of Science and the Social Science Association, in the transactions of which Societies the artizan class are almost entirely excluded; and that papers, previously carefully prepared, shall be laid before the Congress on the various subjects which at the present time affect Trades Societies, each paper to be followed by discussion upon the points advanced, with a view of the merits and demerits of each question being thoroughly ventilated through the medium of the public press. It is further suggested that the subjects treated upon shall include the following:—

1.—Trades Unions an absolute necessity.
2.—Trades Unions and Political Economy.
3.—The Effect of Trades Unions on Foreign Competition.
4.—Regulation of the Hours of Labour.
5.—Limitation of Apprentices.
6.—Technical Education.
7.—Arbitration and Courts of Conciliation.
8.—Co-operation.
9.—The present Inequality of the Law in regard to Conspiracy, Intimidation, Picketing, Coercion, &c.
10.—Factory Acts Extension Bill, 1867: the necessity of Compulsory Inspection, and its application to all places where Women and Children are employed.
11.—The present Royal Commission on Trades Unions: how far worthy of the confidence of the Trades Union interest.
12.—The necessity of an Annual Congress of Trade Representatives from the various centres of industry.

All Trades Councils and other Federations of Trades are respectfully solicited to intimate their adhesion to this project on or before the 6th of April next, together with a notification of the subject of the paper that each body will undertake to prepare; after which date all information as to place of meeting, &c., will be supplied.

It is also proposed that the Congress be held on the 4th of May next, and that all liabilities in connection therewith shall not extend beyond its sittings.

Communications to be addressed to MR. W. H. WOOD, Typographical Institute, 29, Water Street, Manchester.

By order of the Manchester and Salford Trades Council,

S. C. NICHOLSON, PRESIDENT.
W. H. WOOD, SECRETARY.

B *Invitation sent out to bring together the first Trades Union Congress*

Q Look at **B**.
(a) Where was the Congress to be held?
(b) In which year was the Congress or meeting held?
(c) Why was Manchester an appropriate place to hold a Congress?
(d) Why did Manchester and Salford Trades Council call the Congress?
(e) The invitation to attend the Congress included a list of twelve subjects for discussion. Which *three* subjects might a trade unionist at the time have considered to be most important, and why?

and, after the 1870s, 'new unions' of unskilled workers developed.

The main features of the new unions were low subscriptions, a membership consisting of lower-paid and unskilled workers, and a socialist outlook. The unions paid no sick benefits, nor did they include the traditional friendly society activities. They concentrated on shortening working hours and increasing wages. To gain these objectives, they were prepared to use the strike weapon.

One of the earliest of these 'new unions' was the Agricultural Labourers' Union started in 1872 by Joseph Arch, a hedge-cutter and Methodist preacher in Warwickshire. However, many farmers refused to recognize the new union and by 1876 it had virtually collapsed.

Unions for the semi-skilled and unskilled workers were more successful in areas of concentrated labour. In the 1880s the coal miners of Yorkshire and Lancashire formed the Miners Federation. They demanded a minimum wage and a reduced working day and were prepared to take strike action.

Sensational and successful strikes

The London match-girls strike (1888) The girls who made matches at Bryant and May's factory in London were paid low wages and worked in bad conditions (**C**). The phosphorus fumes which were produced during the match-making caused gangrene (decay) of the jaw, and many of the girls suffered from a terrible disease called 'phossy jaw'. In 1888 Annie Besant, a journalist and member of the Fabian Society (see page 142) encouraged the match-girls to strike for better working conditions and wages. Public opinion was on the side of the match-girls, and their strike was successful.

The London Dockers Strike (1889) London dockers were paid low wages and their regular employment was always dependent upon the number of vessels in the port. Ben Tillett, leader of the General Labourers Union, organized a campaign to ensure that labourers on the docks, who were largely unskilled, would be paid a minimum of 6d (3p) per hour, and that no docker should be employed for less than four hours at a time. When the dock employers refused, a strike followed.

The strike for the 'docker's tanner' (6d) won public support, and financial aid for the strikers was received from as far away as Australia. Marches and demonstrations were organized in London, and the intervention of a leading churchman, Cardinal Henry Manning, as mediator (someone who talks to both sides in a dispute and tries to bring about a solution), made the strike more respectable. After a strike of five weeks, the dockers were successful in their demands.

The London Gas Workers Strike (1889) The un-skilled men at the London Gas Light and Coke Company were organized into a Gas Workers Union by William Thorne, a working-class member of the Social Democratic Federation. The threat of a strike was sufficient for the Company to reduce the working day from twelve hours to eight without a reduction in pay.

The success of the London strikes encouraged the growth of new unions of unskilled workers.

C *Girl matchmakers (1888)*

Q (a) What is being sold by the person holding the tray in **C**?
(b) Where do you think the girls worked and what did they make?
(c) Do they look well- or badly-paid?
(d) How were the women and girls dressed?
(e) Why were the match-girls in the news in 1888?
(f) What was the outcome of their strike?

■ Trade unions and the rise of the Labour Party

The political activities of the trade unions

In the last quarter of the nineteenth century a number of working men were elected as members of Parliament. They were known as the Lib-Labs, because of the support they received from their local Liberal Associations. The Lib-Labs were usually prominent trade unionists of the craft unions. However, they often had little contact with the mass of the working classes and they opposed radical social reform.

At the same time, a number of new socialist societies were established. In 1881 the Social

Democratic Federation (SDF) was founded, by a wealthy Marxist (someone who believes in the teachings of Karl Marx), H. M. Hyndman. It was prepared to work towards the overthrow of society by violent revolution. A number of the leaders of the new unions were members of the SDF.

The Fabian Society, founded by a small group of socialists in 1884 was more moderate. They believed in the gradual spread of socialism and the formation of a socialist state. Early Fabians included George Bernard Shaw, Annie Besant, H. G. Wells, and Sidney and Beatrice Webb.

Keir Hardie and the Independent Labour Party

Keir Hardie was a self-educated Scottish miner. In 1892, Hardie was elected MP for a London seat, as an Independent Labour candidate. He arrived at the House of Commons in a cloth cap, carrying a red flag, and with a brass band. In 1893 Hardie called a meeting of the local Labour parties and the various socialist parties. From this meeting there emerged the Independent Labour Party (ILP) (**D**). The ILP sought to work with the trade unions and to tap trade union funds to help gain Parliamentary power. At first, the ILP worked with the Liberals.

D *Membership certificate of the Independent Labour Party*

Q (a) Where and when was the Independent Labour Party founded?

(b) Why was the Conference of 1914 a time for celebration?

(c) Who was the Chairman of the ILP?

(d) To which countries do the flags marked 1 and 2 belong?

(e) Why are many different flags shown?

(f) Complete the following: 'Socialism – The Hope . . . .'

(g) The word *weal* means *happiness* or *welfare*. Can you explain the motto: *'There is no weal save commonweal'*?

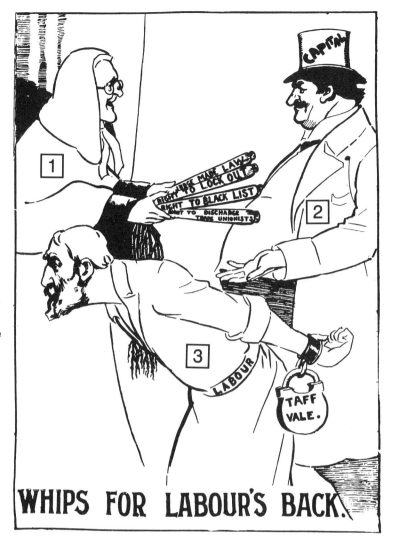

WHIPS FOR LABOUR'S BACK.

Q Look at **E**.

(a) In what ways was the Taff Vale Judgement a threat to the trade unions?

(b) What type of source is source **E**?

(c) Who are the people shown as 1, 2, 3?

(d) What 'rights' are being handed to *capital*?

(e) How might these rights be used against employees (*labour*)?

(f) Does the illustration show *labour* in a strong or weak position? How can you tell?

(g) Why were trade unions handcuffed by the Taff Vale Judgement?

(h) Is the source biased? Give reasons for your answer.

The Labour Representation Committee (1900)

In 1899 the Trades Union Congress agreed to a proposal from Keir Hardie that a Conference should be held, with a view to getting more working-class MPs elected. The Conference was held in London in 1900, with delegates from trade unions, socialist societies (SDF, Fabians), the ILP, local Labour parties, and the Co-operative Society. This Conference agreed to form the Labour Representation Committee, which changed its name, in 1906, to the Labour Party.

The Taff Vale Judgement (1901)

In 1901 the Amalgamated Society of Railway Servants was ordered to pay damages of £23,000 to the Taff Vale Railway Company for destruction caused during a strike. The union appealed against the judgement, but the decision was confirmed by the House of Lords (**E**). This judgement meant that trade unions could not strike without fear of being sued by employers, and this weakened their legal position.

Trade unions campaigned for Parliament to restore their position and looked, particularly, to the Labour Representation Committee. In the 1906 General Election, the trade unions raised funds to promote the return of Labour MPs to Parliament. In all, 23 Lib-Labs, and 30 LRC members were elected.

The new Liberal Government passed the Trade Disputes Act of 1906, which protected the unions against claims for damages by their employers, as had happened with Taff Vale.

The Osborne Judgement (1909)

W. V. Osborne, a local secretary of the Amalgamated Society of Railway Servants, was a Liberal. He objected to his union's paying a political levy (sum of money) to the funds of the Labour Party and took them to court. He won his case and the House of Lords confirmed the decision, forbidding the handing over of any trade union funds to a political party. This was a great setback for the Labour Party because the political levy was its main source of income. Labour MPs were determined to fight against the House of Lords' judgement.

In 1911, an Act was passed which provided an annual salary of £400 for MPs. This greatly benefited the Labour Party, as it made it possible for working-class men to support themselves as MPs. In 1913 the Trade Union Act made the political levy of trade unions legal.

Individual trade unionists could 'contract out' of the political levy by signing a form saying they did not wish to pay. The Act meant that financial support from the trade unions for the Labour Party was secure.

Syndicalism

In the years 1910–14 prices rose more rapidly than wages, and unemployment increased. It was a period of unrest, particularly among the larger and more militant unions. Extreme socialists argued that only a policy of syndicalism (worker control of industry) would bring improvements for the working class. They believed that the strike weapon could be used to overthrow society and take over the factories and workshops. The majority of trade unionists did not support such extremist ideas. The syndicalists aroused the hostility and fear of employers and also of politicians.

Although syndicalism failed, the larger unions worked more closely together against the employers. By 1914, the miners, transport workers and railwaymen were working together as a Triple Alliance. It was agreed that if one of the three unions was involved in a dispute, the others would come out on strike in sympathy.

A period of industrial truce 1914–18

During the First World War, leading trade unions co-operated with the employers and the Government. At factory level, the influence and power of union officials grew. At local and national level, union leaders became involved in the war effort, and some union leaders even served in the Government. Trade unions became more acceptable in society.

However, even during the period of industrial truce there had been some unofficial strikes, such as those by shipbuilders on Clydeside, miners in South Wales and the police in London. At the end of the war, workers had many grievances; and the trade unions were stronger than ever before.

■ Trade unions 1918–39

Position of trade unions after 1918

By 1918, membership of trade unions had risen to 8 million. The so-called Triple Alliance of miners, railwaymen and transport workers was renewed, and a number of smaller unions amalgamated (joined together) to form bigger unions.

Despite an appearance of strength, the trade unions had a number of serious weaknesses. Widespread unemployment gave the employers the advantage in bargaining over wages and conditions. In practice, the Triple Alliance was a sham, because the big unions did not stand together in times of crises as they had agreed to do. By 1926, trade union membership had fallen to just over 5 million.

What factors led to the national coal strike?

During the 1914–18 war the Government had taken control of the coal mines. After 1918, the unions did not want the industry handed back to private owners. During the war many export markets had been lost for coal, and other countries produced increasing quantities of coal for themselves. In 1919 the Government appointed a Royal Commission under Sir John Sankey to investigate the situation in the coal industry. The Sankey Commission recommended that the mines should be nationalized, but the Government refused to act and the coal industry faced increasing competition from foreign markets. Between 1914 and 1939, British coal exports fell by 50 per cent. At the same time, new forms of fuel and power were being developed. The introduction of mechanization, and the investment in new techniques, was much slower in Britain than in the USA and some other countries.

Faced with falling demand from home markets and declining exports, the mine owners sought to cut costs in order to maintain their profits. In 1921, the miners were threatened with a reduction in wages and they came out on strike. There was talk of a 'general strike', with the Triple Alliance giving support. However, the railwaymen and transport workers withdrew their support for the miners on the so-called 'Black Friday', and the miners were left to fight alone. After three months on strike they were forced to accept the owners' demands.

The General Strike: background to the crisis

In 1925 Britain returned to the Gold Standard (which linked the value of the pound to the value of gold), which increased the prices of its goods and seriously damaged its export trade, especially in coal.

The mine owners proposed immediate wage cuts and a longer working day. In an effort to avoid a strike, the Government appointed a Royal Commission under Sir Herbert Samuel to investigate the situation. It was agreed that while this Commission carried out its investigations a subsidy should be paid to make up miners' wages to their previous level.

The Samuel Commission supported the mine owners' proposals of a cut in wages and one extra hour's work each day. The miners rejected the report's recommendations. The secretary of the Miners' Union, A. J. Cook, used the slogan, 'Not a penny off the pay, not a minute on the day' (**F**).

The nine days' strike

Talks involving the Government, the TUC, the miners' union and the mine owners broke down and the TUC called a General Strike in support of the miners, which began on 3 May 1926. A number of vital industries – docks, railways, road transport, iron and steel, chemicals, printing, building, electricity and gas – went on strike (**G** and **H**). The General Strike, which was neither revolutionary nor violent, quickly collapsed and, after nine days, it was called off by the TUC. The miners were left to struggle on alone for six months until poverty and hunger forced them to accept lower wages and longer hours.

Why did the General Strike fail?

The Conservative Government had made plans to resist the workers. Long before the strike was called, the Government had created a secret 'Organization for the Maintenance of Supplies'. Many members of the Government wanted a showdown with the unions.

The Government was able to win over public opinion. It set up its own newspaper, the *British Gazette*, edited by Winston Churchill, to put forward its point of view. It also used the new wireless broadcasting service, the BBC, to reach the public. Assistance was given to the Government by volunteers, particularly from the

F *Facing the facts*

Q (a) Which industry faced 'remorseless foreign competition' in the years after 1918 (**F**)?
  (b) Who was A. J. Cook and what slogan did he use?
  (c) How does the cartoonist (**F**) suggest that the miners and the mine owners might have different views of 'hard economic facts'?

G *Bus leaving the garage under police escort during the General Strike, 1926*

Q (a) Is the bus being driven by the regular driver (**G**)? How can you tell?
  (b) Why is there a policeman riding with the driver?
  (c) Where was the regular bus driver?
  (d) Why was a soldier guarding the route?
  (e) Why were the buses travelling in a convoy?

H *Convoy of supplies during the General Strike*

Q Look at **H**.
  (a) Why was it necessary to use troops to carry supplies?
  (b) What evidence can you find that the Government was expecting trouble during the General Strike?
  (c) Why were goods being moved about in convoys?

middle classes, to keep essential services going. Some key workers, for example in electricity and water supply, did not go on strike. The Government also called in the troops to run necessary services. The churches too, condemned the strike.

In contrast, the TUC had not made adequate preparations, although it did publish a news-sheet, the *British Worker*. The Labour Party was divided over the General Strike and some of its members feared anarchy (complete disorder).

Q (a) The headlines and extracts below appeared in *either* the *British Gazette*, which was published by the Government, or the *British Worker* which was the news bulletin of the Trades Union Congress. Draw a chart and put the extracts in the correct columns (the first entry has been done for you).

British Gazette	British Worker
5 May This is not a dispute between employers and workers, it is a conflict between Trade Union leaders and Parliament and that conflict must . . . end . . . in . . . victory for Parliament.	*5 May* The workers' response has excelled all expectations. All the essential industries and all the transport services have been brought to a standstill.
(to be completed)	

5 May There are already many signs that the strike is by no means as complete as its promoters hoped.

6 May The strike is intended as a direct hold-up of the nation to ransom. It is for the nation to stand firm.

6 May The working class is holding quietly and tenaciously to the position it has taken up.

10 May . . . the talk about revolution is rubbish . . . the dispute concerns miners' wages . . . .

11 May Order and Quiet through the land . . . Increasing numbers of men returning to work.

(b) How do the extracts show the different attitudes towards the General Strike of the Government and the trade union movement?

What were the results of the General Strike?

The General Strike left many of the working classes feeling betrayed and defeated. Many workers were victimized for having gone on strike. The strike had cost the trade unions £4 million, and the number of trade union members declined. The Government and the employers considered that they had been victorious.

In 1927 the Trades Disputes and Trade Union Act was passed. This declared that general strikes, or strikes called in sympathy with other workers, were illegal. The police and other essential workers were forbidden to strike. The Act also forbade the civil service unions from joining the TUC.

In future, workers were to 'contract in' if they wanted to pay the political levy to support the Labour Party. As a result, the income of the Labour Party fell by one-third.

After the defeat of the General Strike and the miners' strike, the emphasis in industrial relations was on negotiation rather than confrontation. For the time being, the unions were prepared to work through Parliament and the Labour Party.

■ Changing fortunes of trade unions since 1939

Trade unions during the Second World War

In some ways the position of trade unions during the Second World War was similar to that of the First World War. A number of trade union leaders, for example, Ernest Bevin of the Transport and General Workers Union, served in Churchill's Coalition Government. There was a serious labour shortage in the coal industry during the war and, to overcome this difficulty, some males were conscripted into (forced to work in) the mines. They became known as 'Bevin boys'. Membership of trade unions had risen to 8 million by 1944.

Post-war reconstruction

The conditions in the years after 1945, for example fairly full employment, favoured the growth of trade union power.

The 1945 General Election resulted in a decisive victory for the Labour Party, which brought in a programme of Welfare State reforms in which the trade unions co-operated fully. Trade unions made substantial contributions to Labour Party funds and financed or sponsored a number of individual MPs. In 1946 the Labour Government repealed the Trades Disputes Act (1927) which meant a return to the principle of 'contracting out' of the political levy (see page 144). The trade unions became powerful and the TUC was requested to give advice on many aspects of national policy.

The trade unions and TUC were anxious to show that they could act responsibly and in 1961 the trade unions co-operated with the Conservative government when it formed the National Economic Development Council ('Neddy'). However, the trade unions were unwilling to co-operate with proposals to regulate wages.

Demands for trade union reform
From the 1960s onwards there were confrontations between the Government and the trade unions. By the mid-1960s the slower rate of growth of the British economy made the Government want to reduce the power of trade unions and prevent high wage increases. A number of unofficial or 'wildcat' strikes, in which some union' members called strikes against the wishes of other members, set public opinion against the trade union movement. In addition, there were a number of demarcation disputes (about who does what job) between the members of different unions. The so-called 'closed shop' system, which restricted employment in certain industries to trade union members only, was also criticized.

Between 1965 and 1968 a Royal Commission looked into the trade unions. In its Report, the Commission hoped that the trade unions would carry out improvements voluntarily. These hopes were disappointed and Governments felt it necessary to take stronger measures.

In Place of Strife
In 1969 the Labour Government proposed some measure of trade union reform in a white paper called *In Place of Strife*. These included ballots (votes) before strikes and the idea of a 'cooling off' period before workers took industrial action. However, the white paper was strongly opposed by the trade unions and the proposals were withdrawn.

Trade union confrontation with the Conservative Government 1970–4
Attempts were made by the Conservative Government to reduce the power of the trade union movement. The Industrial Relations Act (1971) attempted to end unofficial or wildcat strikes; to break the closed shop practices; to make sympathetic strikes illegal; to make sure that trade union members were balloted before strikes were called; and to provide a compulsory 'cooling-off' period. In order to obtain and retain their rights and privileges, trade unions were to be compelled to register.

Opposition to the Industrial Relations Act
The trade unions were strongly opposed to the Act of 1971 and the TUC advised unions to adopt a policy of non-co-operation. The Act provoked a number of serious strikes among the miners, railwaymen and dockers. In 1974 a second major strike by the miners led to a crisis in the supply of power, which resulted in the introduction of the three-day working week.

The 1974 General Election was fought partly on the issue of 'who should govern the country' – the Government or the trade unions. The Conservatives were defeated and the Labour Party was returned to power.

Trade unions and the Labour Government 1974–9
The Labour Government repealed the 1971 Act. However, the Employment Protection Act (1975) and the Trade Union Act (1976) increased the involvement of the Government in industrial relations. The Advisory, Conciliation and Arbitration Service (ACAS) was set up to arbitrate in industrial disputes (talk to both sides and attempt to find a solution).

Rising unemployment and high inflation in the 1970s meant that the Government were unable to stand by while high wage settlements were being agreed. Between 1974 and 1978, various attempts were made by the Labour Government to control the wage demands of the trade unionists.

The 'winter of discontent'

In 1978–9 the trade unions rejected the Labour Government's 5 per cent limit on wage increases and a series of strikes occurred. This period became known as the 'winter of discontent'. Many members of the unions and of the general public became dissatisfied with both the trade union movement and the Labour Party. The Conservatives promised to carry out major trade union reforms, and in the General Election of 1979 they were returned to power.

Trade union reforms of the 1980s

Since 1979 the Government has intervened more often in industrial relations and in the affairs of trade unions. Parliament and the law are being used to regulate trade unions.

The 1984 Trade Union Act made provision for the funding of secret ballots for the election of senior trade union positions, and before industrial action was taken. Picketing was to be limited to the establishment at which strikes were taking place. Union members were to be consulted as to whether or not they wished to contribute to Labour Party funds.

However, industrial disputes continued and, in 1984, plans for the closure of 'uneconomic pits' in the coal industry sparked off the longest and most bitter strike in British industrial history.

QUESTIONS

1 Copy and complete the following passage by choosing (from the list provided below) the correct words or initials. (NB: there are more words and initials than spaces.)

The Amalgamated Society of Engineers, one of the first of the _____ unions, consisted mainly of skilled workers who could afford to pay high _____ . The national secretaries of these unions worked together in the _____ to improve the position of trade unions. In 1868 trade union delegates meeting at Manchester decided to set up the _____ to agree policy and organize the activities of the trade union movement. In 1875 the _____ Act permitted trade unions to use peaceful picketing during strikes. In the 1880s many _____ of unskilled workers were formed. The _____ Judgement of 1901 meant that trade unions could not strike without fear of being sued for damages but the Trade Dispute Act of 1906 restored the industrial power of the trade unions. In 1909 the _____ Judgement forbade the handing over of any trade union funds to a political party but the _____ Act of 1913 made the political levy of trade unions legal.

new unions	Trades Union Congress
new model	Hornby versus Close
benefits	Criminal Law Amendment
subscriptions	Conspiracy and Protection
Taff Vale	of Property
Osborne	Trade Union
Royal Commission	ILP
Junta	

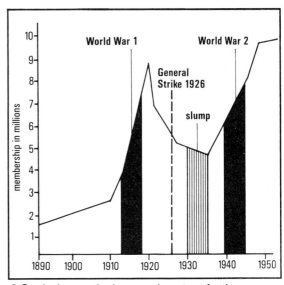

2 Study the graph above and account for the following:
  (a) the rise in trade union membership in the period around 1900;
  (b) the decline in trade union members between 1920 and 1930;
  (c) the marked rise in membership since 1940.

3 For each of the following, write a few sentences to show that you understand the meaning:

  peaceful picketing;
  sympathy strike;
  closed shop;
  wildcat strike;
  demarcation dispute.

Most towns of any size had some form of passenger transport from at least the early nineteenth century. Horse omnibuses, trams, trolleybuses, municipal bus services and the railways have all enjoyed periods of popularity before being replaced by other, newer, forms of public transport. The Government has become increasingly involved with public transport in the twentieth century.

■ Public transport on the roads

How did the public travel in large towns in the mid-nineteenth century?

The means of transport varied according to the wealth and social class of the towns' inhabitants. The wealthy owned horse-drawn carriages; the middle class hired carriages; the lower middle class used hansom cabs or hackney carriages; and the working class used the cheaper horse-drawn omnibus.

The horse-drawn omnibus service was pioneered by George Shillibeer, who operated a service in London. In the mid-nineteenth century the London General Omnibus Company was started and soon there was competition between different companies.

When did tramways come into general use?

After 1860 horse-drawn trams began to appear. These were cheaper to operate than horse omnibuses because it was easier to pull a large vehicle along a smooth rail than on a rough road.

Electrification of trams

In 1885 Blackpool electrified its tramway system. Other towns soon followed, using a system of overhead wires. The use of electric power led to a big reduction in operating costs and cheaper fares, and trams became a popular means of transport (**A** and **B**). By 1914, British towns had a total of more than 4,000 kilometres of electric tramways.

These electric trams with their cheap fares made regular urban travel possible for the working class. Their greater speed enabled more people, who worked in the centres of towns, to live in the suburbs. Towns grew outwards along routes which extended beyond the existing built up areas.

The trolleybus

Trams were limited to the tracks in the roads and often caused traffic jams. One alternative to the tram was the trolleybus which was also powered from electric cables. However, it was not restricted to a central track and could run alongside the kerb. Trolleybuses were widely used after 1918, but their routes were restricted by the system of overhead electric wires and could not be varied.

Another transport revolution – the bicycle

The early machines, which were known as 'bone shakers', were heavy, clumsy and uncomfortable to ride. The lighter penny-farthing (1879) was an improvement but it was difficult to steer and the rider was seated high off the ground.

In 1885 a bicycle was produced which had wheels of equal size and a lower saddle. Shortly afterwards pneumatic tyres (tyres with a separate, air-filled inner tube) were invented by a Belfast chemist, J. B. Dunlop, which greatly added to the comfort of cycling. Firms such as Rover, Triumph, Humber and Sunbeam began to produce bicycles on a large scale, and this led to a great reduction in the price.

For working-class people the bicycle represented an important new means of travel, both for going to work and for leisure (**C**). By the early twentieth century, cycle outings were a popular form of leisure.

When was the motor bus developed?

The first motor buses appeared at the end of the nineteenth century, and by 1910 there were over 1,000 in London. After 1918 there was a great expansion in the use of motor buses and coaches, and outings became very popular. Larger coaches were constructed and solid tyres were replaced by pneumatic ones. Some firms were able to operate long-distance coach services to rival the railways.

Q (a) When do you think each illustration was produced?

Illustration **A**						
1875	1885	1895	1905	1915	1925	1935

Illustration **B**						
1875	1885	1895	1905	1915	1925	1935

(b) Which illustration, **A** or **B**, shows the earlier scene? Give reasons for your answer.

(c) List as many differences in the pictures as you can. Are there any similarities?

(d) There were many reasons why the changes shown in the illustrations took place. Can you suggest some of these reasons?

C The invasion of England by American cyclists

How were bus services regulated?

Under the terms of the Road Traffic Acts (1930, 1933), which were concerned with passenger services (excluding London) the country was divided into regions. Within each region Traffic Commissioners had powers to issue operating licences to bus companies and to regulate safety standards and fares.

In 1933 the London Passenger Transport Board was set up to co-ordinate all of London's train, bus and tram services. As a result of the Road Traffic Acts a pattern of local bus services was established which was to be used throughout the British Isles over the following fifty years.

■ Public transport on the railways

The golden age of British railways

In the later nineteenth century, the overall length of railway line was increased with the construction of additional local and branch lines. Steel rails replaced iron ones and, in 1892, the Great Western Railway replaced its broad gauge with the standard gauge (see page 56). Technical improvements included new sidings, stations, bridges and tunnels. Signals were standardized, red for danger, green for clear line ahead.

Improvements in comfort included the introduction of steam heating, gas lighting, restaurant cars, corridor trains, lavatories, and sleeping carriages (**D**). In the third-class carriages, windows were introduced.

From 1863 onwards a system of underground (tube) trains was established in London. The main problem was that all the locomotives were steam driven and so gave out huge amounts of steam and smoke. However, this was solved when an electric underground railway was opened in 1890 and ran successfully. By 1905 all the underground lines were electrified.

Suburban railway lines were also developed in London and some of the larger cities.

D Saloon carriage of London, Brighton and South Coast Railway, 1873

Decline and reorganization

In the early twentieth century the railways experienced difficulties as a result of rising costs and cut-throat competition with other forms of transport. During the First World War the Government controlled the railways and it was realized that savings could be made by cutting out the wasteful duplication of services.

Under the terms of the Railway Act (1921) the railway system was handed back to private ownership but only after complete reorganization. The private companies which had existed before the First World War were grouped into four new companies namely, the London, Midland and Scottish (LMS), the London and North-Eastern Railway (LNER), the Southern Railway (SR) and the Great Western Railway (GWR). Within each region, the company had almost complete control so that wasteful duplicate lines could be closed.

Speedier journeys became possible with engines such as the 'Silver Jubilee', the 'Coronation Scot' and the 'Mallard'. Some lines were electrified, mainly in the Southern Region which made sufficient profit to enable it to make improvements. However, the profits made by the companies were small and they were forced to abandon some of the branch and local lines. Rail freight fell by almost 20 per cent between 1918 and 1939; while the number of passengers carried by rail fell by 60 per cent between 1920 and 1939. This decline in rail freight and passenger traffic was mainly due to competition from road transport.

The railways after 1939

During the Second World War the railways were again controlled by the Government, but there was not enough money or workers to carry out urgently needed repair of the railway system. By 1945 large stretches of track were in disrepair and rolling stock was in decay.

In 1947, under the terms of a new Transport Act, the railways were nationalized and became 'British Railways'. Although a number of steam locomotives were built in the years immediately after nationalization, it was recognized that diesel and electric locomotives had many advantages in terms of cleanliness and efficiency. From the 1960s steam locomotives were no longer thought suitable for railways in Britain.

After nationalization, more lines were electrified but the extent of modernization was limited. By the early 1960s, freight and passenger traffic had further declined and it was clear that much of the railway network needed either scrapping or replacement.

What was the Beeching Report of 1963?

Shortly after the British Railways Board was set up, its first chairman, Dr Reginald Beeching, produced a major report on the future of the railways (**E**). Under the Beeching proposals thousands of miles of track, mainly under-used local and branch lines, were to be closed, together with a large number of stations. The railways were to concentrate on the more profitable inter-city routes and suburban lines, where the track was to be electrified (**F**). Attention was also to focus on long-distance freight and heavy bulk loads for which special rolling-stock was to be designed.

E *The Beeching Report of 1963*

Stopping train services developed as the predominant form of rural public transport in the last century, when the only alternative was the horse-drawn vehicle . . . Today . . . buses carry the greater part of the passengers moving by public transport in rural areas, and . . . are fighting a losing battle against private transport. In 1938 the number of private cars was 1,944,000 and in 1961 there were 6,000,000 . . . It is questionable whether British Railways meet as much as 10 per cent of the total and declining demand for public rural transport . . . most of the trains carry an average of less than a bus-load and lose nearly twice as much as they collect in fares . . . . It is obvious that a high proportion of stopping train services ought to be discontinued as soon as possible . . . .

Q (a) Why did the rural services and branch lines present serious financial problems for British Railways (**E**)?

   (b) What did the Beeching Report recommend?

   (c) Which people might object to the closure of rural services and why?

The railways after Beeching

Many of the Beeching proposals were put into effect and more than 8000 kilometres of track were closed. More rapid modernization has taken place, particularly electrification. A network of rapid 'Inter-City' trains (**G**) and a system of high speed 'Freightliner' container trains was established.

Despite improvements, railways have found it increasingly difficult to compete with motorway traffic and large juggernaut lorries. Nevertheless, the railways have continued to play an important part in the country's overall system of public transport.

F *Leaving the station in Newcastle*

Q Look at **F**.
(a) How is this locomotive powered?
(b) Is this an illustration of (i) a London Underground tube train; (ii) a short-distance suburban train; or (iii) an 'Inter-City' express that can reach speeds of 160 kph?

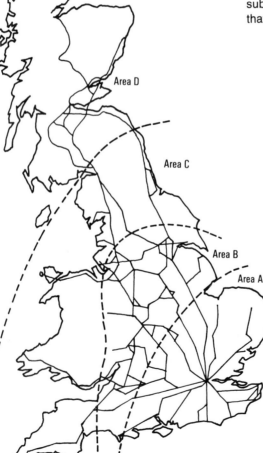

G *British Rail Inter-City services*

Q In what ways are the patterns of railways on map **G** different in areas A, B, C and D? How can these differences be explained?

■ **Why has there been a 'shrinkage' of the public transport system since the Second World War?**

1 Rising fares on public transport have tended to turn passengers away.
2 Many forms of public transport are over-used during rush hours but under-used at other times, and this can make the service uneconomic.
3 The railways have suffered from the com-petition of road transport. Juggernauts have taken away much of the freight traffic, while large comfortable coaches with video and other facilities have attracted passengers.
4 The main challenge to both rail and road public transport systems has been the development of the motor car. The increase in the personal motoring habit has badly affected the profits and the prospects of public transport.

QUESTIONS

1 (a) Why were trams so popular a form of public transport in the late nineteenth and early twentieth centuries?

(b) What were the main disadvantages of the tram?

2 What benefits did the bicycle bring to ordinary people?

H *Pie charts showing changes in the carriage of freight and other goods*

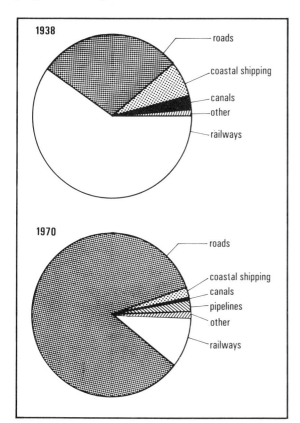

1938

- roads
- coastal shipping
- canals
- other
- railways

1970

- roads
- coastal shipping
- canals
- pipelines
- other
- railways

3 What steps have been taken since the 1960s to make the railways more profitable?

4 (a) Which form of transport increased its percentage share in goods transport (**H**)?

(b) Which method of transporting goods suffered the greatest decline?

(c) What method of transporting goods was used in 1970 but was not in use in 1938?

(d) Give examples of what might be carried by pipeline.

(e) Explain why the changes you have recorded occurred.

5 Copy out and complete the details in the time-chart below to show some of the landmarks in the development of public transport since 1850.

Date	Event	Importance
1863		Improved transport in London
1870	First London horse tramway	
	Blackpool electric tram	Big reduction in operation costs
1885		Start of bicycle revolution
1892	Great Western Railway abandons broad gauge	
	Railway Act	Amalgamation into four companies
1930		Pattern of bus services set for fifty years

24 The motor car

A *The 'Enterprise' steam omnibus, 1833*

Q (a) What is the main difference between the two methods of wheeled transport shown in illustration **A**?

(b) What other differences and similarities are there?

(c) How do you know the coach on the left is powered by steam?

(d) Which of the two vehicles attracted most attention from the bystanders? Why do you think this was so?

The first mechanically-propelled (horseless) carriages were driven by steam power. In 1769 a Frenchman, Nicholas Cugnot, drove a steam carriage through the streets of Paris. In 1860 another Frenchman, Etienne Lenoir, patented the first internal-combustion engine. The story of the modern motor car had begun.

■ Horseless carriages

When were horseless carriages first used in Britain?

The first horseless road carriages were used in Cornwall by William Murdock in 1784 and by Richard Trevithick in 1800. By about 1830, steam carriages were becoming more common and during the 1830s Walter Hancock developed a steam coach service in parts of London (**A**).

Why was there opposition to horseless carriages?

Supporters of steam railways opposed the use of steam carriages on the roads. The people dependent on horse-drawn road vehicles (such as stage-coach owners and drivers, innkeepers, landowners and farmers) feared competition. The turnpike trusts, believing that the heavy steam carriages would damage their roads, charged them very high tolls.

What were the main drawbacks of steam road carriages?

1 Steam engines were cumbersome and noisy.
2 Steam trains on the railways were much faster than anything on the roads.
3 Fares on the railways were lower than those on steam road carriages.
4 Laws were passed to restrict the speed of steam road vehicles.

What was the Red Flag Act?

In 1865 the Highways and Locomotive Act of Parliament was passed, which soon became known as the *Red Flag Act*. This limited the speed of self-propelled steam vehicles to four miles per hour (6½ kph). Every horseless carriage on the roads was required by the Act to have a man walking ahead, carrying a red flag by day and a red lamp at night.

■ The internal combustion engine

Who patented the first internal combustion engine?

In 1860 a Frenchman, Etienne Lenoir, patented the first internal-combustion engine and made a short journey using the engine fixed to a road vehicle. Like the steam engine, the internal combustion engine turns heat into energy by means of a piston moving up and down inside a cylinder. But, while the steam engine needed a boiler working *outside* the cylinder to produce the necessary heat, the internal combustion engine produced its heat *inside* the cylinder. This meant that it had the potential to be smaller, lighter and portable. However, Lenoir did not develop his invention for transport but kept his engines for his workshops.

The Austrian, Siegfried Markus also worked on the internal combustion engine. He built a car which was shown to the public at the Vienna Exhibition (1873). The cars made by Markus were only used at night when there was no other traffic. The wheels were made of iron and complaints were made about the noise. Eventually the police told him to stop using the cars.

Who became known as the 'fathers of the motor car'?

The first men to make and improve cars for public sale were two Germans, Gottlieb Daimler and Karl Benz. Daimler worked on the four-stroke engine, a system used in almost all car engines today. He wanted to make an engine which was smaller, lighter, faster and quieter than those already in use. In 1884 Daimler's engine was used to drive a motor-cycle and two years later was used on a four-wheeled vehicle. Also in 1886 Karl Benz fitted a petrol engine to a three-wheel carriage and reached a speed of eight miles per hour (13 kph). The early engines used much fuel, and were neither powerful nor smooth running. By the 1880s several inventors were experimenting with the internal-combustion engine in different parts of the world, but it was Daimler and Benz who became known as the 'fathers of the motor car'.

Why was the development of the motor car slower in Britain than in France and Germany?

In England the early motorists were restricted by the Red Flag Act. Inventors in France and Germany had more freedom and there was less opposition to the horseless carriage than in Britain.

What was Emancipation Day and how was it celebrated?

In 1896 the Red Flag Act was finally ended and motorists were allowed to travel at speeds of up to twelve miles per hour (19 kph). To celebrate their freedom, or emancipation, about forty motorists drove their cars from London to Brighton (**B**). Gottlieb Daimler came to England especially to take part in the run. However, travel conditions and the state of the roads were bad and only fourteen vehicles finished. The London to Brighton Veteran Car Run is still celebrated annually.

B *Brighton – end of Emancipation Run 1896*

Q (a) When did the first London to Brighton Run take place?
  (b) What did it celebrate?
  (c) The London to Brighton Run is still an annual event. Can you find out on which day of the year it takes place?
  (d) What is special about the cars which take part in the present-day London to Brighton Run?

What was the One-Thousand-Mile Car Trial?

In 1900, more than sixty cars travelled all over Britain to advertise the advantages of motoring and of manufacturing motor cars. This was known as the One-Thousand-Mile Trial (**C**).

What were the problems of the early motorists?

The early cars were expensive to buy and to use. Motorists had to be able to deal with the mechanical faults of their machines because there were few garages. Damaged and punctured tyres caused many breakdowns and were difficult to repair. New tyres were expensive. Brakes were only slowly improved and, at first, there were no proper radiators to keep the engine cool (**D, E** and **F**). For a long time the only way of starting the engine was to turn the handle at the front, sometimes a long and laborious task. At first, too, there were no reverse gears and if two cars met in a narrow road, one of them would have to be pushed backwards. Few of the early cars had sides or a roof and, to protect themselves from the dust thrown up by the thick rubber tyres, the early motorists wore special clothing. This added to the expense of travel.

Who were the earliest British car manufacturers?

In 1905 Herbert Austin began car manufacture in Birmingham. Two years later, C. S. Rolls and F. H. Royce built the 'Silver Ghost'. In 1912 William Morris built the first Morris Oxford car. The earliest motor cars were fine pieces of hand-built and hand-finished craftsmanship.

Why were the motoring organizations formed?

There was much opposition to motoring and in 1897 the Royal Automobile Club (RAC) was founded to help and 'defend' motorists. In the early twentieth century new motoring laws were passed. Under the terms of the Motor Car Act (1903) cars were only to be driven by licensed drivers. Cars were to be registered and were to carry number plates, lights and horns. The speed limit was raised to twenty miles an hour (32 kph) but by that time many motor cars were capable of much faster speeds. Police traps were set to catch speeding motorists.

However, in 1905, the Automobile Association was formed to organize patrols to warn motorists of the police traps. Today, the AA and the RAC, Britain's motoring organizations, provide many facilities, which include breakdown services, travel information and legal advice.

By 1914, the number of cars registered in Britain had risen from 23,000 (in 1906) to more than 130,000.

How did the First World War affect the development of motor vehicles?

Motor vehicles played an important part in moving troops and supplies behind the battlefields in Europe. Few private cars were made and many British car firms went over to the making of ammunitions (weapons and shells).

C *One-Thousand-Mile Car Trial (1900)*

Pneumatic tyres were in their infancy, and bursts and punctures were the rule rather than the exception . . . the quaint costumes . . . including goggles, veils, gauntlets, and fur collars . . . which were practically imperative on all vehicles which travelled at upwards of 20 mph [32 kph] for we had no screens in those days. Some cars were not even fitted with radiators, but filled up with water, which boiled away as the vehicle proceeded, from water tanks, generally carried at the rear of the vehicle. The brakes of my 12 h.p. Daimler car, built in 1899, were made of two pieces of wire rope to which were attached wood blocks. On going down any lengthy descent the blocks often caught fire and smouldered till they were put out with water. Wooden wheels . . . were used by everyone, for cast steel and wire wheels did not come into use till many years later.

Q (a) Why did early motorists attract so much attention?
    (b) Why do you think that motorists had to dress as they did?
    (c) What did the braking system consist of? Do you think the brakes were reliable?
    (d) How did motor car trials and road races increase the numbers of vehicles sold?

D *Repairing a motor car, 1904*

E *Extracts from the Diary of an early motorist*

9 Dec. 1895 – . . . motor sparked at once and went well. After lunch started home in motor car . . . police spotted us; awful crowd followed us . . . had to beat them off with umbrella.

10 Dec. – Policeman called at 1.30, took our names, re driving . . . without red flag ahead.

13 Dec. – Went drive round common; tyre came off.

16 Dec. – Took train . . . and proceeded to Court House . . . [solicitor] spoke up well for motors. Silly old magistrate fined us one shilling and costs, 15 *s.* 7 *d.* [78p].

27 Dec. – Frightened an unattended horse attached to a milk cart, which bolted and sent milk-cans flying in all directions.

4 Jan. 1896 – Lost nut off air valves; pushed home.

6 Jan. – Stuck again, small tube supplying petrol to carburettor choked.

14 Jan. – . . . Jack got out to hold unattended horses, and I drove the car into curb and smashed frame. Shoved into stable close by.

F *Popular music hall song*

He had to get under
Get out and get under
Then he'd get back at the wheel
A dozen times they'd start to hug and kiss,
and then the darn'd old engine it would miss
and then he had to get under
get out and get under
and fix up his automobile.

Q (a) The two sources **D** and **F** have a common theme. What is it?
(b) Using sources **D**, **E** and **F** list the main problems of motoring.
(c) How were motorists protected from dust and bad weather?
(d) What did the motorist mean in writing 'the motor sparked at once' (source **E**)?
(e) What was the purpose of the 'red flag ahead' (source **E**)?
(f) Why was the motorist fined in 1895 (source **E**)?
(g) Can you list the differences between the car in the picture (source **D**) and a modern car?

Why was there a growing demand for small cars in the period 1918–1939?

During the First World War, thousands of people had been employed in driving and servicing motor vehicles. When they returned home after the war, they were keen to have a car of their own. The tax on petrol, which had doubled during the war, was repealed in 1921. During the war, Goodyear and Dunlop had each patented a pneumatic tyre which greatly cut the cost of tyre replacement. The new Ministry of Transport, which was set up by the Government in 1919, made road building grants to local authorities out of motor taxation. The amount of tax which a car owner paid depended on engine size (£1 per horse power) so manufacturers and designers produced smaller engines.

The result was the popular 'baby cars' of the 1920s and 1930s, the Austin 7 and the Morris Minor. These small family cars could be bought for a little over £100.

William Morris, who worked at Oxford, was the first Englishman to take up the mass production and assembly line methods developed by Henry Ford in America (**G**). These methods also helped to bring cars within the reach of a larger section of the population.

In what ways were motor vehicles improved in the period 1918–39?

The most important improvements included more reliable engines and brakes; brake 'stop' lights; safety glass for windscreens and improved windscreen wipers; dipping headlights; and electric direction indicators. Greater comfort was provided for drivers and passengers.

Cars were often tested in races and competitions. International and national road and track racing became very popular at such centres as Le Mans, Monte Carlo and at Brooklands in England.

The use of motor vehicles in the Second World War

In Britain itself the number of private cars registered dropped by about sixty per cent between 1939 and 1943. Petrol rationing, shortages of parts, the difficulty of obtaining new

---

G *Henry Ford and mass-produced motor cars*

In the USA Henry Ford produced cars at a low price and in very large numbers.

1893: 'It will be large enough for the family but small enough for the individual to run and care for . . . it will be so low in price that no man making a good salary will be unable to own one.'

1908: Ford Model T ('Tin Lizzie') 'I will build a car for the great multitudes . . . The real way is to make one like another, as much alike as pins or matches . . . Any customer can have a car painted any colour that he wants so long as it is black.'

1913: Ford's first assembly line – 'In the chassis assembly line are 45 separate operations . . . Some men do only one or two small operations, others do more. The man who places a part does not fasten it. The man who puts in a bolt does not put on the nut; the man who puts on the nut does not tighten it . . .'

Q (a) Why was Henry Ford able to produce cars at a low price (**G**)?
(b) Why were the Ford cars so popular (**G**)?
(c) Which British manufacturer followed the example of mass production (**G**)?

---

vehicles and the restrictions on their use made life difficult for the motorist. However, transport was important in the war, and great use was made of motor vehicles of all kinds – tanks, armoured cars, lorries, jeeps, motor cycles.

Why and how were roads improved?

The increasing volume of road transport meant that it was necessary to have better roads with more solid foundations. In 1909 the Road Board was set up. This raised funds by taxing motor vehicles (Road Fund Licence). At first the Road Board concentrated on improving road surfaces, but later new roads were constructed.

The great expansion of road traffic after the Second World War finally prompted the Government to begin a major new road building programme of motorways. As early as 1946 the Ministry of Transport drew up a plan for motorways but it was not until the 1950s that the Preston Bypass and the motorway between London and Birmingham (the M1) were opened. Since that time a large number of other motorways have been constructed and opened, serving London, other principal cities and ports, and the industrial regions. The main features of motorways include dual carriageways of two or three lanes to permit high speed travel; 'hard shoulders' (the hard shoulder is the lane to the left of the main carriageways, where vehicles are allowed to stop in an emergency), central reservations, crash barriers and special lanes for vehicles to join and leave the flow of traffic smoothly. Certain types of traffic – learner drivers, mopeds, pedestrians, animals – are forbidden on motorways. Service areas are spaced out along the motorways and provide petrol, information and refreshments.

The post-war period has seen the construction of a number of magnificent road bridges, many of which charge tolls. These include the bridges over the Forth, the Severn, the Tamar and, most recently, the Humber.

Why and how was road safety improved?

The increase in road accidents in the late 1920s and early 1930s led to steps being taken to improve road safety and several Acts were passed.

1 'Third party' insurance (insurance against damage done to another person) was made compulsory.
2 Driving tests were introduced in 1934.
3 Pedestrian crossings, traffic lights and roundabouts were constructed.
4 'Cat's eyes' (reflective studs invented by Percy Shaw) were set along roads.
5 Speed limits were imposed.
6 The Highway Code was introduced.
7 The Road and Rail Traffic Act of 1933 established a system of licences for vehicles to carry freight.

Since the Second World War the volume of traffic has grown enormously and stricter road safety measures have been introduced:

1 Drivers of heavy goods vehicles need a special driving licence, and the number of hours they can work without a rest is limited.
2 Cars over three years of age are now subject to an annual Ministry of Transport test (the MOT) which licenses cars as roadworthy.
3 Car drivers and front-seat passengers are compelled by law to wear safety seat belts.
4 A driver suspected of having had too much to drink may be subject to a 'breathalyser' test and, if found guilty, may be disqualified from driving.

Traffic in towns

The rapid growth of motor traffic in the 1950s brought serious problems of congestion on the roads and in towns. Parking became increasingly difficult. 'No Waiting' signs multiplied, coin meters were introduced, elaborate one-way systems were started, more traffic lights appeared and special pedestrian crossings were put into use. Despite these changes, increasing amounts of traffic continued to cause problems in towns. A special committee was set up under Professor Buchanan to study the problems and produce a report.

What did the Buchanan Report recommend?

Buchanan produced a special report on *Traffic in Towns* (1963). This made important suggestions with regard to traffic problems: urban through ways, one-way systems, stricter parking regulations, more car parks, 'bus only' lanes, restrictions of right turns, ring-roads and bypasses.

What changes have occurred in vehicle design and manufacture?

After the Second World War the number of car owners rose rapidly. Manufacturers began to provide more room and comfort for drivers and passengers. Among the many new ideas and features were car heaters, window de-icers, car radios, and automatic gear-boxes. The setting up of assembly lines for new models was very costly, so fewer types of cars were produced. Automation in the car industry limited the manufacture of cars to a small number of firms (**H** and **I**). Austin and Morris combined to form the British Motor Corporation, and then later merged with Leyland Motors to become British Leyland. Of the new British cars, the 'Mini' became very popular.

H *Assembly line at Ford's Halewood factory*

I *Production at Austin Rover – cars being built by robots*

Q (a) Both factories shown in the photographs (sources **H** and **I**) show the production of a similar product. What is the product?

(b) What similarities are there between the two scenes?

(c) Make a list of all the differences you can find.

(d) How can you explain the differences you have recorded?

(e) Make a chart to show the advantages and drawbacks for *either* of the production methods.

(f) Can you name any of the car models produced by (i) the Ford Motor Company and (ii) the Austin Rover Company?

QUESTIONS

Chart showing traffic statistics 1919–1938

Year	Private Cars	Commercial Vehicles	Road Deaths
1919	132,000	82,000	*not known*
1921	242,000	128,000	*not known*
1928	885,000	300,000	6,138
1930	1,056,000	348,000	7,300
1938	1,944,000	498,000	6,648

1 (a) Look at the table above. What happened to the number of cars in use in the 1930s? How do you account for this?

(b) During the 1930s the number of deaths on the road decreased. Can you explain why?

2 (a) Using the map on the right and the text, can you explain why the British Leyland factory is based near Oxford?

(b) Select five motorways and say which towns and cities they link.

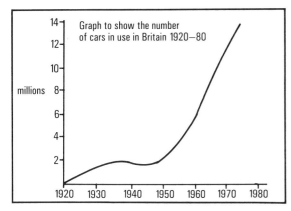

Graph to show the number of cars in use in Britain 1920–80

3 (a) Look at the graph above. At which period was there a decrease in the number of cars in use, and why?

(b) During which years did the number of cars in use increase most rapidly?

(c) What factors account for this increase?

(d) What problems have resulted from the increase in the number of vehicles on the roads?

(e) What attempts have been made to solve these problems and how might such problems be overcome in the future?

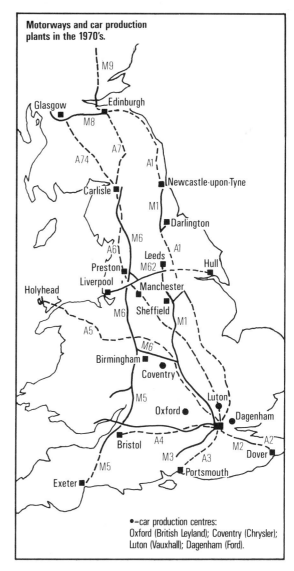

Motorways and car production plants in the 1970's.

●=car production centres: Oxford (British Leyland); Coventry (Chrysler); Luton (Vauxhall); Dagenham (Ford).

4 Using the information in the chapter design a time chart like the one below to show the main stages in the development of the internal combustion engine/motor car.

Date	Event	Importance
1769	*Cugnot's steam carriage*	
	(to be	completed)

25 The development of flight

From early times birds were studied, wings were constructed and attempts were made to fly by jumping off high places, often with fatal results. People flapped their wings but failed to realize that birds, in proportion to their size, have muscles much stronger than man. The secret of flight lay in discovering the right kind of power and how to use it. Today, air transport provides rapid communication around the world. It supports a range of activities and industries and provides opportunities for mass travel.

■ Lighter-than-air machines

When did man first fly?

In France, several attempts at unmanned flight were made using hot-air balloons, the brothers Montgolfier leading the way. The first free flight of a manned hot-air balloon took place in Paris in November 1783 (**A**). Shortly afterwards, a Frenchman flew in a hydrogen-filled balloon which was more reliable than the hot-air type. The first aerial ascent from British soil, to a height of about 100 metres, was made in 1784 by 'Balloon' Tytler. In 1785, the first balloon crossing of the English Channel was made. The reaction to manned flight in the eighteenth century was similar to that which greeted the first moon landing in the twentieth century, and 'balloon fever' spread throughout Europe.

Hydrogen balloons were used by scientists and mapmakers and were big attractions at public festivals and displays. In wartime, balloons were used for reconnaissance purposes.

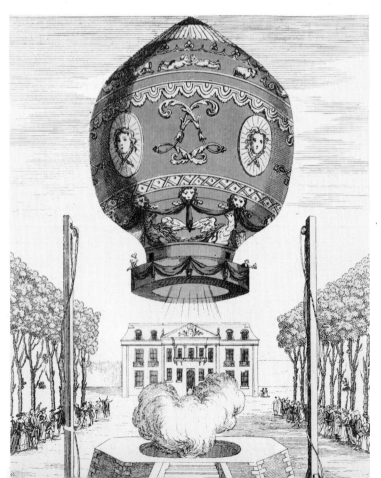

A *Up, up and away*

Information
Date: 21 November 1783
Place: Paris, France
Number of balloonists: Two
Specifications:
Height 70 feet (21 m)
Diameter 46 feet (12 m)
Fuel: Trusses of damp straw
Equipment: Forks, rope, cords, 2 pails of water, 2 sponges
Duration of flight: 25 minutes
Maximum height: 3000 feet (914 m)
Distance covered: Six miles (9·6 km)

Q Using the pictorial and written information in **A**, write a report of the first free flight of a manned balloon.

The early development of airships

Airships had an advantage over balloons in that they could be controlled by the use of propellers and engines. In 1852 Henry Giffard, a Frenchman, flew the first real airship, which was powered by a steam engine. However, steam engines proved too heavy.

The invention of the internal combustion engine (see page 157) and the use of petrol as fuel, together with more effective means of steering, provided the necessary factors for the development of airships (**B**). The most famous of the early airships were those associated with Count von Zeppelin in Germany. In 1900, the first Zeppelin was constructed and within 10 years at least five were in regular service between German cities.

During the First World War a few German Zeppelins were used to bomb London and other parts of England. Some British airships were used to protect naval convoys.

The decline of airships

After 1918 Germany once again took the lead in airship development with two intercontinental machines, the Graf Zeppelin and the Hindenburg. Unfortunately, almost all of them used hydrogen, an inflammable (easily set on fire) gas, rather than helium which was non-inflammable but more expensive. In 1930 the British airship R101 crashed on its maiden flight; and in 1937 the German Hindenburg burst into flames at its mooring tower and many lives were lost. Airships had largely been abandoned by the late 1930s. In the 1960s, Japan and the USSR experimented with nuclear-powered airships.

■ Heavier-than-air machines

The first heavier-than-air machines

By definition, an aeroplane implies an angled wing that rises as it moves through the air. Sir George Cayley, a versatile Yorkshireman, was a pioneer in aeronautics and is sometimes called the 'father of flying'. He built the first glider (an aircraft without an engine) which has been claimed by some as the first modern aeroplane. Although attempts to power aeroplanes with steam engines failed, a number of successful flying models, worked by such means as elastic or clockwork, were constructed.

The development of powered flight

Heavier-than-air machines became a practical possibility with the development of the petrol-driven internal combustion engine, which provided greater power in relation to weight and size. Two Americans, Wilbur and Orville Wright had built many gliders before they attempted to develop powered flight in a heavier-than-air machine. Their first petrol-driven controlled flight took place at Kittyhawk in North Carolina, USA, in 1903 (**C** and **D**). The flight in the Wrights' machine, 'Flyer I', lasted only 12 seconds but in 1905 their 'Flyer III' stayed aloft for half an hour.

Pioneering flights 1905–14

Other pioneers were inspired by the success of the Wright brothers. In 1909 Louis Bleriot, a Frenchman, flew across the English Channel in a monoplane (an aeroplane with one set of wings) and won a prize of £1000 offered by the *Daily Mail*.

In Britain, progress was slow. An American, Colonel Cody, made the first flight in Britain in 1908 and in the following year A. V. Roe used a motor-cycle engine to power a British-built triplane (an aeroplane with three sets of wings). In 1910 Claude Grahame-White, a British airman and engineer, made the first night flight during the London to Manchester air race, and was guided by car headlights. In 1911 the first air cargoes were flown. These were usually letters and so air mail began. In 1912, the Royal Flying Corps was founded.

C The two sources show the first petrol-driven controlled flight at Kittyhawk, USA in 1903

Q (a) The two illustrated sources are different in their *form*. What is source **C**? What is source **D**?

   (b) How and why does source **D** provide more information than source **C**?

   (c) Which source would be most useful for an historian trying to reconstruct what it was like to be present at the time of the flight? Give reasons for your answer.

The First World War

At first, aeroplanes were used for aerial recon-naissance, but later they were developed as bombers and fighters. Aeroplanes increased in power, speed and size, and by the end of the War there were many thousands in service. In 1918 the Royal Flying Corps became the Royal Air Force.

Pioneering flights after 1918

In 1919, two British former RAF pilots, John Alcock and Arthur Whitten Brown made the first crossing of the Atlantic in an aeroplane. Their flight from Newfoundland to Ireland took 16 hours. In the same year two Australians made a 28-day flight from England to Australia. One of the most sensational pioneering flights was that of the American aviator, Charles Lindbergh, who made the first solo non-stop flight across the Atlantic in the aeroplane 'The Spirit of St Louis' in 1927. In 1930 Amy Johnson, a British airwoman, flew solo from Croydon near London to Australia in 19½ days (**E** and **F**). The following year she made a record-breaking flight to South Africa.

Increasingly, metal rather than wood was used for aircraft construction, and more efficient petrol engines were developed for monoplanes. Flying boats (aeroplanes which could take off and land on water) were used for long-distance travel. The pioneering flights showed what was possible and prepared the way for the development of civil aviation.

■ Commercial development of aviation

Civil aviation in Britain

The early aviation companies found it difficult to make a commercial success of flying. The first important long-distance British airline, Imperial Airways, was formed in 1924 as an amalgamation of a number of small companies. By 1939, it operated about 80 aeroplanes to provide services all over the world.

In 1935 another company, British Airways, was formed which operated mainly in Europe. Both received a large subsidy (money grant)

E *Amy Johnson – a photograph taken in 1930*

F *Description of a flight from London to Australia in 1930*

I ran smack into a monsoon, rain such as I'd never imagined. I was soaked, sitting there in the open cockpit. I came down very low to find my way, following a railway and almost taking the tops off the signal boxes. I kept a look-out for the racecourse at Rangoon where I was to land. It was getting very dark and still pouring when I saw a big building. Down I went, blinded with rain. Too late I saw mud and goal posts, and realized I was landing on a playing field. In a flash I was in a ditch, the machine on its nose – wings, propeller, undercarriage, all broken. I burst into tears. But I couldn't have crashed in a luckier place; what I had mistaken for a racecourse was the playing field of an engineering college. Students got to work and in two days and nights we rebuilt the plane.

Q (a) Who is the woman air pilot (**E**)?
  (b) Why did she dress in this way?
  (c) What famous flight did she make in 1930, and how long did it take (**F**)?
  (d) Using source **F** make a list of the dangers and difficulties that a pioneer aviator had to face.

from the Government. In 1939–40 the Government bought out both Imperial Airways and British Airways and formed the British Overseas Airways Corporation (BOAC).

How did the Second World War affect aviation?

During the war, aircraft construction became the largest industry in Britain under the newly created Ministry of Aircraft Production. A range of aircraft were built with emphasis on speed, range of flight and power. These included the bombers such as the Lancaster and the Wellington, fighters like the Spitfire and the Hurricane, and the Mosquito fighter bomber.

Radar (radio detection and ranging), which had been used on a small scale in the late 1930s, was improved during the war, particularly through the work of Robert Watson-Watt. Radar enabled objects within a certain distance to be located by the echoes or rebounds from radio waves. One of its important early uses was the detection of enemy aircraft during the Battle of Britain in 1940. Frank Whittle, a British engineer, had worked on the jet engine in the 1930s but his ideas had been turned down at the time. However, by the end of the Second World War the importance of the jet engine had been recognized and turbo-jets had also been introduced on a small scale.

The expansion of civil aviation

After 1945 civil aviation prospered. From the 1960s, the tourist and travel market grew rapidly and, in terms of the passenger trade, the aeroplane competed successfully with shipping. The number of passenger miles flown in British aircraft rose from 300 million in 1945 to 10,000 million in 1970.

The expansion of civil aviation has influenced the growth and siting of airports. Within Britain, the main centres of population are serviced from regional airports. London is serviced by Heathrow and Gatwick but pressure has grown for a third London airport and this will be sited at Stansted in Essex.

For many years after 1945, air services were run by two public corporations, British Overseas Airways Corporation (BOAC) and British European Airways (BEA), together with a number of private companies. In 1977, Laker Airways was given permission to begin a cut-price service on the North Atlantic route, and a 'price war' developed between airlines until Laker Airways collapsed. Today, there are two main British airlines, the government-owned British Airways (formed by the merger of BOAC and BEA) and the privately-owned British Caledonian.

British aircraft manufacture

After 1945, Britain became an important manufacturer of military and civilian aircraft, with important export markets. The development of the jet engine permitted faster and higher flight.

The construction of modern aircraft requires huge sums of money and Government support is necessary. From the mid-1960s there was some attempt to co-operate internationally on projects, for example, the Anglo-French Concorde. Both the English-built Concorde and the French-built Concorde made their first flights in 1969. In terms of speed and technical achievement the Concorde is a success. However, it was more expensive to develop than had been planned, its fuel consumption is high and it operates at a loss (**G**).

Manned space flight

In 1961 the Russians sent the first man, Yuri Gagarin, into orbit round the earth, followed in 1963 by the first woman, Valentina Tereshkova. Although the British Interplanetary Society was formed in 1933, Britain has not played a major part in the development of space flight. The first steps on the moon were taken by the American Neil Armstrong in 1969.

■ Flight: its impact

1   Air transport has been one of the growth industries of the twentieth century.
2   It has stimulated a range of new air-linked activities: aircraft construction, airport services, tourism.
3   It has created a variety of employment opportunities.
4   The financial cost of aviation development, particularly in space flight, has been great.
5   The cost must also be measured in terms of noise, pollution and accidents.

G *The shape and design of this aircraft are very distinctive. It was built as a result of co-operation between Britain and France. Do you know what the aircraft is called?*

H *An Armstrong Whitworth Argosy biplane, in service with Imperial Airways between 1926 and 1935. Capable of carrying 18–20 passengers, it served mostly on the London–Paris run, and on routes through Africa.*

Q (a) At which dates do you think photographs **G** and **H** were taken?

Illustration **G**					
1920	1930	1940	1950	1960	1970

Illustration **H**					
1920	1930	1940	1950	1960	1970

(b) Which photograph (**G** or **H**) shows the earlier scene? Give reasons for your answer.

(c) List the main differences between the aircraft in the two photographs.

(d) Are there any similar features in the two photographs?

(e) There are many reasons why aircraft changed so rapidly in the twentieth century. Can you list *some* of the reasons?

(f) Which of these reasons do you consider most important in explaining why aircraft developed so rapidly?

QUESTIONS

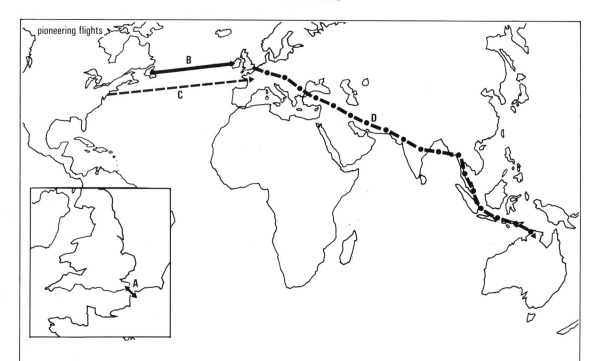

pioneering flights

1 (a) Name the following: The man who flew across the English Channel in 1909 (A); the two men who followed the route marked (B) in 1919; the man who, in 1927, made the solo flight along the route marked (C); the woman who, in 1930, made the flight along the route marked (D).

(b) In which year did she make a record breaking flight to South Africa?

(c) What was the importance of these pioneering flights in the development of air travel?

(d) Why were flying boats extensively used in the inter-war years?

2 Copy and complete the following passage using the list of words opposite (NB: there are more words than spaces).

Commercial _____ really began between the Wars. The first regular service was opened between Paris and London in 1919. In 1924 a company called _____ was formed. In 1935 another company _____ was formed which operated mainly in Europe. In 1940 two companies were merged to form the state-aided _____ . The Second World War had important effects on aircraft development, for example through the development of radar through the work of _____ while the importance of the jet engine, pioneered by _____ had been recognized. After 1945 air services were controlled by two public corporations which later were merged into _____ . The most important private company, after the collapse of _____ , is _____ .

light aircraft
aviation
Laker Airways
British Caledonian
Imperial Airways Ltd
Frank Whittle
Robert Watson-Watt
seaplanes
British Overseas Airways Corporation
British Airways
subsidy
Ministry of Aircraft Production
spitfire
Gatwick
Concorde

3 **Essay topic:** How has air travel affected the economic and social life of people since 1945?

26 Communications and the mass media

Important developments have taken place in the means of communication and the pace of change has accelerated in recent decades. A number of important inventions have occurred in the fields of telegraphy, the telephone, radio, cinema, television, communications satellites and the microcomputer. During the past century the newspapers have also undergone change. The communications 'revolution' has affected the lives of the whole population.

■ The telegraph

The sending of messages over long distances, in code, by means of electrical impulses is known as telegraphy. Apart from such early devices as the semaphore (signalling by means of levers to represent the alphabet) and the heliograph (signalling by means of a mirror to flash the sun's rays), the first apparatus to communicate over great distances was the telegraph. The earliest practicable instrument, invented by William Cooke and Charles Wheatstone, was patented in 1837.

Telegraphs were soon being used by the railway companies, and the first commercial telegraph line was set up between Paddington and West Drayton in 1839 (**A**). Telegraph links were also established between Britain and France in 1850 by means of a cable laid under the sea; and the first trans-Atlantic cable was laid in 1858. The telegraph came under the control of the Post Office in 1869.

■ The telephone

The telephone was invented in 1876 by Alexander Graham Bell, a British inventor who settled in the USA. In 1878, Bell demonstrated the telephone to Queen Victoria and, in 1879, telephone exchanges were opened in London, Liverpool and Manchester (**B**). In 1881, the Post Office was authorized by the Government to offer the public telephone as part of their services. In 1891, the first telephone cable was laid between England and France.

Under the Special Patronage of Her Majesty

And H. R. H. Prince Albert

GALVANIC AND MAGNETO

ELECTRIC TELEGRAPH,

GT. WESTERN RAILWAY.

The Public are respectfully informed that this interesting & most extraordinary Apparatus, by which upwards of 50 SIGNALS can be transmitted to a Distance of 280,000 MILES in ONE MINUTE,

May be seen in operation, daily, (Sundays excepted,) from 9 till 8, at the

Telegraph Office, Paddington,

AND TELEGRAPH COTTAGE, SLOUGH.

ADMISSION 1s.

" *This Exhibition is well worthy a visit from all who love to see the wonders of science.*"—MORNING POST.

Despatches instantaneously sent to and fro with the most confiding secrecy. Post Horses and Conveyances of every description may be ordered by the ELECTRIC TELEGRAPH, to be in readiness on the arrival of a Train, at either Paddington or Slough Station.

The Terms for sending a Despatch, ordering Post Horses, &c., only One Shilling.

N.B. Messengers in constant attendance, so that communications received by Telegraph, would be forwarded, if required, to any part of London, Windsor, Eton, &c.

THOMAS HOME, *Licensee.*

G. NURTON, Printer, 48, Church Street, Portman Market.

A *Advertisement for the Electric Telegraph*

Q (a) What evidence can you find of the following: that the electric telegraph had quickly made a favourable impression on the highest in the land?; that it became associated with other forms of rapid communication?; that it attracted newspaper and public attention (**A**)?

(b) How long would it take to transmit a message of 250 signals (**A**)?

(c) How were the messages forwarded on from the Telegraph Office (**A**)?

(d) How much did it cost to send a despatch by telegraph (**A**)?

B *A London Telephone Exchange in 1883*

The Postmaster General took over the National Telephone Company in 1912. For the first time, a unified telephone system was available throughout most of Britain.

Gradually, services improved and were extended. A '999' emergency telephone service was introduced in 1937. In 1958, the Subscriber Trunk Dialling system (STD) was begun and soon subscribers were able to dial direct to many parts of Britain. The International Subscriber Trunk Dialling system (ISD) was introduced in 1963 and it is now possible to make direct contact with most parts of the world by telephone or by telex.

■ The wireless

In 1896 Guglielmo Marconi, an Italian pioneer of wireless telegraphy, arrived in England. He conducted experiments in transmitting (sending) signals and, in 1901, succeeded in transmitting a signal across the Atlantic from Cornwall to Newfoundland. Although the first messages were in Morse Code (a signalling system invented by the American Samuel Morse) he was soon able to transmit voices and music.

The Post Office, the armed forces and the merchant navy recognized the possibilities of radio communication. The value of radio for shipping was highlighted in a number of dramatic incidents. In 1910, a radio message sent from the Captain of the ocean liner the 'Montrose' to Scotland Yard, led to the arrest of Dr Crippen who was wanted on a murder charge. In 1912, the famous liner 'Titanic' struck an iceberg and sank (**C**). Although more than 1000 of those on board died, hundreds more were saved following radio messages to other ships in the area.

How was the British Broadcasting Corporation (BBC) established?

People who owned wireless receiver sets had to be licensed by the Post Office. In 1922, a number of British wireless manufacturers formed the British Broadcasting Company and obtained permission from the Post Office to transmit regular programmes to those who had wireless receivers. The Government took broadcasting out of the control of the private wireless firms in 1926 when the British Broadcasting Company became, by royal charter, the British Broadcasting Corporation (BBC). News programmes were not to favour the government or any political party but had to be impartial. Under its first Director-General, John Reith, the BBC acquired a reputation for high-quality broadcasting.

As the production of wireless sets increased, their quality improved and the price fell. By the outbreak of the Second World War, the number of licence holders in Britain had increased to about 9 million.

How was the wireless used during the Second World War?

The major speeches of the Prime Minister, Winston Churchill, were heard on the wireless. Announcements and vital information could be broadcast without delay and BBC reporters covered the course of the war. The wireless was also a source of entertainment at a time of disruption and danger. The BBC broadcast programmes overseas. These broadcasts encouraged the belief that the war would end in victory for the Allies, and so kept up morale. On the other hand, the people of Britain were subjected to German wireless propaganda.

C "Those who had been saved, had been saved through one man – Mr. Marconi."
Extract from a speech by the Right Hon. Herbert Samuel, the Postmaster-General, on April 18th.

Q Look at cartoon **C**.
(a) Which sea disaster occurred in April 1912?
(b) What caused the disaster?
(c) Write out the captions in source **C**. Write two paragraphs, bringing out the most important points in the drawing.
(d) How was the call for help sent?
(e) Which ship answered the call?
(f) How had Marconi saved the lives of many people on the Titanic?
(g) Two figures are shown pointing at Marconi. Can you name either of them?

Broadcasting since the Second World War

Some developments have occurred in radio broadcasting since 1945. In particular, the transistor gradually replaced the large valve radios and prices fell. The number of broadcasting channels has increased, and local radio and commercial stations have been established. These developments have encouraged industries other than the manufacture and repair of radios. For example, a growing number of people have been employed in the production of records and cassettes.

■ The cinema

Photography and the cinema

The first photographic negative was produced by William Fox-Talbot in 1839. This invention marked the foundation of modern photography.

The appearance in the 1880s of the 'box' camera, invented by the American George Eastman, was another important breakthrough. More people owned cameras, and the 'snapshot' photograph of family and friends became common.

The beginnings of the cinema

Cinematography is the technique of making and showing motion pictures using a continuous strip of film to project a rapid succession of pictures on to a screen. These simple 'moving pictures' were first shown in public in Paris in 1895; and a short moving picture of the Derby horse race was shown in London in 1896.

The early moving films were silent although, usually, a musical background was provided by a pianist in the cinema. By 1914 London had more than 400 cinemas and most sizeable communities had at least one 'picture house'.

What was the Golden Age of cinema?

By the 1920s Hollywood, in California, USA, had become the capital of the film world and the silent cinema had created film stars such as Charlie Chaplin. In 1928 Walt Disney created Mickey Mouse, the first of his famous animated (moving) cartoon characters.

Despite its early beginnings, the British film industry was not well established and, in 1927, Parliament stated that the British cinema must show at least one British-made film for every five films shown. Most British films were short and these 'quota quickies' were not popular, thus the cinema in Britain continued to be dominated by American films.

The introduction of the 'talkies' transformed the cinema. The first successful feature film with sound was *'The Jazz Singer'* (1927). By the late 1930s, over half the population went to the 'pictures' at least once a week, and many new cinemas were built. However, the growth of the cinema led to a decline of some forms of live entertainment, particularly the music hall.

Decline and change since the 1950s

In 1946 there were about 4,700 cinemas in Britain with an audience of over 30 million people each week. By 1968 the number of cinemas had fallen to about 2,000 and weekly audiences had fallen to about 5 million. A number of factors have contributed to this decline, including alternative forms of leisure, but the most important single factor has been the popularity of television.

■ Television

The beginning of television

The first working television system was demonstrated in London, in 1926, by John Logie Baird. In 1935, Isaac Schoenberg and a team of British engineers developed an alternative system using the cathode ray tube. The first public television service in the world was started by the BBC at Alexandra Palace in London in 1936, using the new system.

Early television sets, which cost about £350, had only a nine-inch screen, and the pictures received were often poor. By 1939 there were only a few thousand television sets in use, serving an audience in and around London. With the outbreak of the Second World War the television service was suspended.

Television after the Second World War

Television broadcasting resumed in 1946. The number of sets in use in 1950 was about 3,000, and this increased significantly at the time of the coronation of Queen Elizabeth II (1953). By 1965 there were over 13 million licensed sets; and by the 1970s almost every household possessed at least one television.

The increasing popularity of television (**D**) contributed to its expansion and development. In 1955 the first commercial channel (ITV) was provided for the Independent Television Authority (later to become the Independent Broadcasting Authority); the BBC opened its second network (BBC 2) in 1964; and a second commercial channel (Channel 4) began in 1982. There was competition and rivalry between the publicly owned and financed BBC and the commercially based advertising channels of ITV, and in 1983 both ITV and BBC1 began 'breakfast television'.

Technical developments have included the introduction of colour and the development of video and the video recorder.

What have been the effects of television?

Television has patronized sport and made many sports more popular than before. It allows the general public to watch a variety of events, such as royal weddings and the proceedings of the House of Lords. As a means of communication, it provides up-to-date information through news programmes, and services such as Prestel and Ceefax. Educational opportunities have been increased, particularly through schools broadcasting and the Open University programmes. Experiments in shopping and banking via the computer-linked television screen are already being conducted. Such services will benefit the housebound. Television has helped to reduce the popularity of the cinema, while the number of people attending live events, such as football matches, has also declined in some areas. In some ways, television has taken over the role of newspapers, which have to compete with commercial television for advertising income.

D *Scene inside a modern TV studio*

Q (a) Identify the main features of a modern TV
   studio by linking the numbers in picture **D** with
   the correct descriptions in the chart.

Feature	Number
Mobile TV camera Sound microphone Studio lighting Studio audience	

(b) In what ways can the camera, sound and
   lighting equipment be moved easily?
(c) What are the advantages of this flexibility for
   'live' television?

■ **Communication satellites**

Scientists discovered that it was possible to
'bounce' telephone and television signals from
earth off a satellite in space to a receiving station
on earth thousands of kilometres away. The first
communications satellite, 'Telstar', was put into
orbit in 1962, and others have followed since.
Telstar permitted the transmission of the first
transatlantic television pictures. The present
global satellite system, INTELSAT (International Telecommunications Satellite Organization) assists in weather forecasting and has
made an important impact on the transmission
of news.

■ **The development of the electronic
computer**

A modern computer accepts information,
processes it according to a specified programme,
and then supplies the processed data. In the

early nineteenth century Charles Babbage pioneered a very primitive form of computer. Later, a system using punched cards was developed. By the early twentieth century, simple automatic calculating machines were coming into use.

The first electronic computers were made in the USA after the Second World War although British scientists also played a part in computer development. Countries such as the USA and Japan, have developed their electrical industries much more rapidly than Britain. Sir Clive Sinclair, a British electronics innovator, developed many new inventions but not all were commercially successful.

■ Newspapers

The early press

The first daily newspaper in the world, the *Daily Courant*, appeared in 1702. By the mid-eighteenth century local weekly newspapers were circulating in nearly thirty towns; and by 1815 more than 250 different newspapers were being published.

Between 1712 and 1855 newspapers had to pay a high stamp duty (a type of tax) to the Government and, as a result, the price of newspapers was high. This limited their circulation and prevented cheap newspapers from reaching the majority of the people.

Why was there a growing demand for newspapers in the later nineteenth century?

The stamp duty was ended in 1855 as were other taxes on paper and newsprint. As a result, the price of newspapers fell and circulation increased. Developments such as the electric telegraph and the railways improved the means by which news could be gathered and despatched. A number of news agencies which collected news (for example Reuters), were set up. The demand for newspapers also increased as one effect of the 1870 Education Act, which created a new reading public.

What is meant by the 'newspaper revolution'?

In the later nineteenth and early twentieth centuries, major technical changes in printing helped to reduce costs of newspaper production.

A rise in living standards enabled more people to purchase newspapers.

The new reading public found the existing newspapers dull and difficult to read, and it was recognized that there was a market for new kinds of popular magazines and newspapers.

The most famous of the early newspaper tycoons in Britain was Alfred Harmsworth, later to become Lord Northcliffe. He established the first national popular newspaper, the *Daily Mail*, in 1896. By 1900 the daily circulation was more than half a million. With such a large readership Harmsworth could afford to keep down the price of his newspaper to one old halfpenny (less than 1p). The *Daily Mail* set the standard for the 'popular' press of the twentieth century. The *Daily Express* was founded in 1900 by Arthur Pearson, and in 1904 Harmsworth started the *Daily Mirror*.

The press barons

The 1920s and 1930s saw fierce competition between the newspaper proprietors, many of whom were made lords. The 'Press Lords' or 'Press Barons' as they were sometimes known, included Alfred Harmsworth (Lord Northcliffe) and his brother Harold Harmsworth (Lord Rothermere) who had founded the *Sunday Pictorial* in 1915. The Canadian newspaper proprietor, William Aitken (Lord Beaverbrook), settled in England and controlled the *Daily Express*, the *Sunday Express* and the *Evening Standard*.

Since the 1950s, there has been a decline in readership and a fall in advertising revenue (income). Several popular newspapers have been forced to close down. In the 1980s rivalry has continued between a new generation of press proprietors such as Rupert Murdoch of the *Sun* (who also owns *The Times* and *The Sunday Times*) and Robert Maxwell of the *Daily Mirror*. Large money prizes have been offered by some newspapers to attract readers. The increasing use of a free press in some towns has also affected the sale of newspapers.

In 1986, the production of many national newspapers was revolutionized with the introduction of more advanced technology and new printing methods. Such changes met with opposition from the print workers who feared job losses.

QUESTIONS

A Multiple choice Choose the correct answer for each question and write it into your book.

1 On 1 January 1845 a message from Slough railway station led to the arrest of a murderer on his arrival at Paddington. To send the message the fastest means of communication was used, namely:
   (a) semaphore;
   (b) heliograph;
   (c) a horseback messenger;
   (d) the electric telegraph;
   (e) a mail coach.

2 Important inventions of recent times have included the telephone; aeroplane; sewing machine; and motor car. They share one feature in common. What is it:
   (a) they were developed in Britain with Government support;
   (b) they were invented in the period 1890–1914;
   (c) they were invented and developed outside Britain;
   (d) they were invented by foreigners working in Britain?

3 Marconi's early demonstrations of wireless communication were based on the scientific work of
   (a) William Cooke;
   (b) Alexander Graham Bell;
   (c) John Logie Baird;
   (d) Samuel Morse;
   (e) Charles Babbage?

4 The BBC first began broadcasting to the public in which of the following decades:
   (a) 1890–1900; (b) 1920–1930; (c) 1950–1960?

5 In which year did the BBC commence the regular transmission of television programmes from Alexandra Palace?
   (a) 1899; (b) 1922; (c) 1936; (d) 1953?

6 With which invention is John Logie Baird associated:
   (a) telegrams; (d) telephones;
   (b) wireless; (e) television;
   (c) 'talkie' films?

7 The ending of the stamp duty in 1855 meant which of the following:
   (a) newspaper readership became limited to the wealthy;
   (b) cheaper newspapers were possible;
   (c) many local newspapers went bankrupt;
   (d) a heavy tax was imposed on newspapers?

8 Lord Northcliffe was associated mainly with the growth of:
   (a) the telegraph; (d) the telephone;
   (b) the wireless; (e) television;
   (c) the popular press?

9 The first mass circulation newspaper was
   (a) *The Times*; (d) *Daily Mirror*;
   (b) *Daily Mail*; (e) *Sun*;
   (c) *Daily Telegraph*; (f) *Guardian*?

10 Place the following in correct chronological order:
   Marconi's wireless;
   Morse Code;
   Bell's telephone;
   Atlantic telegraph cable.

B Essay topics

Either

1 Use the following information as the basis for an essay on the growth of wireless and television as forms of communication and entertainment.

   1896 Arrival of Marconi in England
   1922 British Broadcasting Company set up
   1926 Formation of the BBC
   1936 First public television service at Alexandra Palace
   1955 Beginning of commercial television
   1968 Introduction of colour television

Or

2 Write an account of the development of radio and television. Comment on the changes these developments have brought about in social habits in the period after 1945 in the following areas:
   (a) attendance at other forms of entertainment, especially the theatre and the cinema;
   (b) family life;
   (c) the way in which people behave. What have been the good and bad effects of these changes?

27 Social reforms 1906-39

Important social reforms, passed by the Liberal Governments between 1906 and 1914 were intended to protect the sick, the old, and the unemployed. They established principles of state intervention and responsibility in social welfare, and provided the basis of what later became known as the Welfare State.

■ The need for social reform

What is a Welfare State?

A Welfare State may be defined as a state in which the community, acting through the government, provides a range of social services whose purpose is to guarantee to all the opportunity of a reasonable life. Under such a state, the care of those in need is a national duty. Benefits, such as sickness benefit and pensions, are regarded as a right.

Why was social reform needed?

1 In the 1890s, over the country as a whole, more than 40 per cent of the working class over 65 years of age were on poor relief.
2 Sickness and ill health, which affected the ability to work, still caused severe poverty on a large scale (**A** and **B**).
3 Unskilled workers with large families were often very poor, with the children suffering most.
4 Charles Booth, in *Life and Labour of the People in London* (1903), revealed something of the terrible conditions in the East End of London. Seebohm Rowntree, in *Poverty, a Study of Town Life* (1899) showed that in York about 30 per cent of the total population lived in terrible poverty.
5 In the early twentieth century there was an increase in the number of able-bodied unemployed applying for relief.

> **B** *From* My Autobiography *by Charlie Chaplin*
>
> When we entered the workhouse in 1895, my mother was shown to the women's ward and my brother and I went in another direction to the children's ward. Once a week we were allowed to meet. How well I remember that first visiting day: the shock of seeing mother enter the visiting room garbed in workhouse clothes. How forlorn and embarrassed she looked! In one week she had aged and grown thin . . . Sydney and I began to weep, which made mother weep and large tears began to run down her cheek.

Q (a) What evidence can you find of the poverty of this family (**A**)?
   (b) Using sources **A** and **B**, why might a family, however poor, be reluctant to enter the workhouse?
   (c) Why was Charlie Chaplin's mother embarrassed on seeing her children for the first time in the workhouse (**B**)?

A *A poor family in the East End of London about 1900*

C *Children waiting outside a hall for free dinners, 1912*

Q In what ways might this photograph **C** have been useful for reformers and politicians seeking to improve the condition of children? What improvements might they have recommended?

Pressure for reform

The pressure for reform came from leading writers such as G.B. Shaw, J. Galsworthy, and H. G. Wells who commented on social conditions in their works; from people involved in the field of public health and medicine; and from the Labour Representation Committee (which became the Labour Party in 1906).

The Royal Commission 1905–09

This was set up by the Conservative Government to inquire into the working of the Poor Law. It was a scientific investigation into the problems of poverty. The Commission made two Reports, both of which condemned the existing Poor Law. The Majority Report (the one agreed to by the majority of Commission members) was influenced by the ideas of the Charity Organization Society. In contrast, the Minority Report (agreed to by the minority of Commission members) accepted many of the views of the Fabian Socialists. This Minority Report was the basis for many of the Liberal reforms after 1906.

■ The Liberal reforms

The Liberal Governments 1906–14

The Liberal Party won a landslide election victory in 1906. Partly in response to the challenge offered by the rise of the Labour Party, they began a major programme of reform to deal with the social evils in Britain. One of the driving forces in the Liberal Party at this time was David Lloyd George. The Liberal reforms were concerned with those most in need: the children of the poor, the elderly, the sick, the low paid and the unemployed.

Children

Under an Act of 1906 the local education authorities were allowed to provide a service of free meals, out of the rates, in state schools (**C**). In 1907 free medical inspections were provided (**D**). Both measures helped to improve the health of working-class children. In 1908, an Act known as the Children's Charter made it illegal for children to do unsuitable work and protected them from some of the worst kinds of cruelty. The Liberal Government also intro-

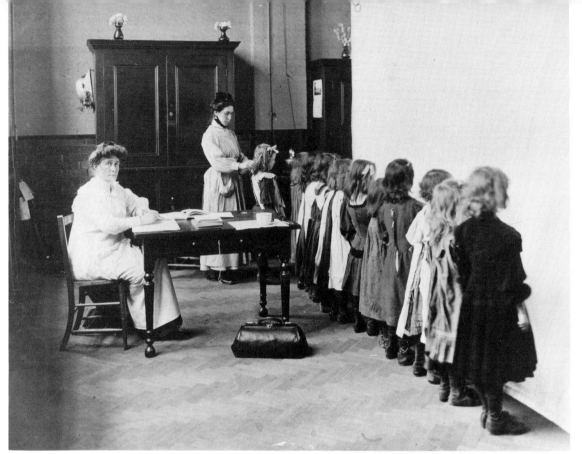

D

Q (a) What is taking place in photograph **D**?

(b) Where do you think it was taking place?

(c) What is the nurse looking for in the children's hair?

(d) What is the nurse writing at the table?

---

duced the probation service and a new system of borstal institutions, as an alternative to prisons for young offenders.

The elderly

Under an Act of 1908 Old Age Pensions of 5s (25p) per week for a single person and 7s 6d (38p) for a married couple were to be paid by the State to all people over 70 years of age who did not have any money of their own (**E** and **F**). Although the sum was very small, it was usually sufficient to ensure that the elderly could live with family or relatives without being a financial burden, thereby – in some cases – keeping the elderly out of the workhouse.

Working conditions and low wages

Under an Act of 1906, the right of workers to be paid a sum of money (known as *compensation*) for an injury received at work was extended to cover some occupational diseases (diseases brought about by the conditions in which people worked). In the same year the Merchant Shipping Act set out the minimum standards of food and accommodation for seamen on British ships. Other groups, such as shop assistants, were also given assistance or protection.

The Trade Boards Act of 1909 gave the Government power to set up Boards to inquire into any trade where wages were exceptionally low, and to fix minimum wages in 'sweated trades', where scandalous working conditions existed.

In 1912 there was a national coal strike and a Minimum Wage Act was passed to bring it to an end. Minimum wages were to be settled for each coal-mining district by special district boards with independent chairmen. By 1914 several other industries had minimum wages.

In 1909, Labour Exchanges were set up to provide unemployed workers with information about job vacancies. Within five years Labour Exchanges were filling over one million jobs annually.

THE NEW YEAR'S GIFT.

E *From a letter to* The Times *in 1908 about the Old Age Pensions Bill*

However the Ministers may attempt to hide it, we are in fact in the presence of the universal outdoor relief scheme divested of the restraining provisions of the present Poor Law. How can any prudent man contemplate such a situation without dismay? The strength of this kingdom has been its great reserve of wealth and the sturdy independent character of its people. The measure which is being pushed through the House of Commons with haste and acclaim will destroy both sources. It will extort the wealth from its possessors by unjust taxation. It will distribute it in small doles and will sap the character of the people by teaching them to rely, not on their own exertions, but on the State.

F *Old Age Pensions*

Q (a) What was 'outdoor relief' and 'the present Poor Law'? (See chapter 13.)
(b) List all the reasons set out by the writer to *The Times* against Old Age Pensions (**E**).

(c) What was the subject of cartoon **F** and when was it drawn? Do you think the cartoonist was in favour of the new scheme? Give reasons for your answer.

National Health Insurance, 1911

The Act made insurance against sickness compulsory for all people earning less than £150 per annum. Under the scheme, an employee paid contributions of 4d (2p) per week; the employer paid 3d (1½p) per week for each worker; and the State paid a subsidy of 2d (1p). David Lloyd George used the slogan '9 pence for 4 pence'.

From these insurance funds free medical attention and sick pay of 10s (50p) per week were provided. The new scheme was administered through friendly societies, trade unions and private insurance companies. Insured persons were put on a special list of doctors' patients, known as the 'panel'. For each 'panel patient' the doctors received a payment from the government.

Unemployment insurance, 1911

This was an experimental scheme which formed part of the 1911 National Insurance Act. The scheme was limited, at first, to seven industries, mainly engineering and building. Contributions were made by employees, employers and the State. Weekly benefits were fixed at 7s (35p) and at first benefit was restricted to fifteen weeks in any one year. By 1914 over two million workers were insured against unemployment.

The 'People's Budget'

In 1909 Lloyd George, the Chancellor of the Exchequer, had to find extra money to finance the building of battleships for the Royal Navy and to pay for Old Age Pensions. He was prepared to place extra taxation on the rich to benefit the poor. His budget of 1909 (the so-called 'People's Budget') was the most famous in British history (**G** and **I**). The proposals included graded and increased income tax and a 'supertax' on high incomes.

Lloyd George's budget was bitterly contested by the Conservative opposition. The budget was passed in the House of Commons but was rejected by the House of Lords. Parliament was dissolved and there was a General Election. The election was conducted on the issues of the budget and the power of the House of Lords.

THE PHILANTHROPIC HIGHWAYMAN
Mr. Lloyd-George. *"I'll make 'em pity the aged poor!"*

G

RICH FARE.

The Giant Lloyd-Gorgibuster: "FEE, FI, FO, FAT,
I SMELL THE BLOOD OF A PLUTOCRAT;
BE HE ALIVE OR BE HE DEAD,
I'LL GRIND HIS BONES TO MAKE MY BREAD."

H

I *From a speech by David Lloyd George, 30 July, 1909*

We are raising money to provide against the evils and the sufferings that follow from unemployment. We are raising money for the purposes of providing for the sick and the widows and the orphans. But there are some of our critics who say, 'The taxes themselves are unjust, unfair, unequal, oppressive'. Now are these taxes really so wicked? We are placing burdens on the broadest shoulders.

Sources **G** and **I** refer to the famous Budget of 1909.

Q (a) For what social welfare purposes was the Chancellor of the Exchequer, Lloyd George, raising money (sources **G** and **I**)?

(b) Why did some people criticize the Liberal Government's reforms (source **I**)?

(c) Who had the broadest shoulders to pay extra taxes, the rich or the poor (source **I**)?

(d) Copy out the captions on cartoons **G** and **H**.

(e) Who is represented as the central figure in sources **G** and **H**?

(f) To what sort of people might he appear as a highwayman or as a Welsh ogre?

(g) By robbing the rich and giving to the poor he might appear as the philanthropic (kindly) highwayman. Can you explain source **G**?

(h) In source **H** the empty plate represents the Chancellor's Treasury that must be filled. By what means does he propose to fill it (what is written on the club)? The rich man or 'plutocrat' is hiding. Can you explain source **H**?

(i) Which of the cartoons, **G** or **H**, is the more favourable to Lloyd George? Give reasons for your answer.

[J] *A Durham miner in the early 1930s, out of work*

[K] *Life on the dole*

The popular name for unemployment benefit since June 1919, when the *Daily Mail* first coined it, had been 'the dole' . . . The Press, with almost the sole exception of the *Daily Herald* and the Liberal newspapers, represented the unemployed as people too idle to seek work, and 'the dole' as a comfortable wage. The truth was that most working people had a strong aversion to public relief and at first would have preferred to work for less than the pittance that they drew in the form of unemployment benefit, if there had been work to do. But as unemployment increased, and the Government could do nothing to remedy it, there came to be 'distress areas' and all scruples against accepting Government money faded. The weekly payment was enough to keep the people alive but not enough to keep them in good physical condition to undertake any work that unexpectedly offered. The Means Test aroused fierce anger among the unemployed.

Q (a) Using the picture above and the extract (**K**) describe the attitude of the Durham miner towards life on the dole.

(b) Source **K** includes both short-term and long-term effects of unemployment. Give one example of each and explain the changing attitude of the unemployed to being out of work.

(c) Why, by the early 1930s, had some miners been continuously unemployed for many years?

In the election of 1910 the Liberals were returned to power, and the Conservatives accepted that the Liberal Government had popular support for the 'People's Budget'. In the following year, 1911, the Parliament Act was passed which greatly reduced the power of the House of Lords.

What was the importance of the Liberal Reforms 1906-14?

1 The desire for social reform indicated a profound change in public opinion.

2 It was accepted that the State should protect its citizens from extreme hardship in sickness, old age and unemployment.

3 The principle of redistributing wealth through graded taxation and social services had been established, although this had not been pressed very far by 1914.

■ Social reforms 1918-39

Why were attempts at reform limited in the inter-war years?

Unemployment was the most serious economic and social problem in the years between the two world wars (**J** and **K**). As social welfare was mainly funded by the taxes paid by those in work, the money to support welfare schemes was limited during periods of high unemployment because of the decrease in the number of workers paying taxes. This was, of course, the very time when money was needed, because there was an increase in the number of people requiring assistance. As a result, little progress was made in social reform.

The extension of unemployment insurance

In 1920 unemployment insurance was extended to cover practically all occupations except agriculture and domestic service. The scheme was designed to assist workers over short periods of unemployment and where the total number of those out of work was small. However, the scheme soon ran into severe financial difficulties due to the prolonged and high level of unemployment.

What was the 'Means Test'?

In 1931 an Act was passed which stated that the unemployment insurance fund was to be used only for the payment of limited, short-term benefits. The longer-term unemployed and those not covered by the scheme were to receive assistance only after a 'Means Test' had been carried out by the local authorities. The 'Means Test' took account of all sources of income for the family and, in some cases, benefit to an unemployed man might be reduced or refused all together. The test was resented by the working classes, and it was unpopular with the local authorities which had to administer it.

The Unemployment Act of 1934

This Act attempted to introduce administrative order into the muddle of unemployment relief, by distinguishing between unemployment insurance and unemployment assistance.

Unemployment insurance   An attempt was made to reconstruct unemployment insurance on a sound financial basis with benefits related to contributions.

Unemployment assistance   To help deal with the problem of long-term unemployment a special body – the Unemployment Assistance Board – was set up. This administered assistance to the unemployed – 'the dole' – and organized retraining schemes. However, it was unpopular because the Means Test was kept.

How were pensions extended?

In 1925 Old Age Pensions became payable at 65 years for men and at 60 years for women.

Widows were to receive pensions of 10s (50p) per week. Orphans at schools were provided with 7s 6d (37½p).

What measures were taken to protect the low paid?

Acts were passed to provide for minimum wages in agriculture and road haulage. Trade Boards to protect the low-paid were further extended to a number of industries in which workers' trade unions were weak.

The end of the old poor law

Although some categories of the destitute were no longer dependent upon the old poor law, its image was hated and feared by the working classes. The poor law remained the last resort for those who did not fit into any special category or whose relief from other sources was insufficient.

Under the Local Government Act of 1929, the Poor Law Unions and Boards of Guardians were abolished and the administration of the poor law was transferred to local authorities. The poor could now apply for outdoor relief to the Public Assistance Committees of the county and county borough councils.

What was the significance of the social reforms 1918-39?

1   In the period between the two World Wars, the number of people who were covered by health insurance almost doubled, but still only half of the population were in the scheme.
2   Unemployment became the main focus of debate in the years of depression.
3   There was a realization that trade conditions, and not individual character, were the main factors responsible for unemployment and poverty.
4   Public opinion recognized that the state had responsibilties towards those who were in distress through circumstances beyond their control.
5   There was an increasing tendency towards State intervention in social welfare.

QUESTIONS

1 Copy out and complete the following diagram using this chapter and pages 138–49 to help you.

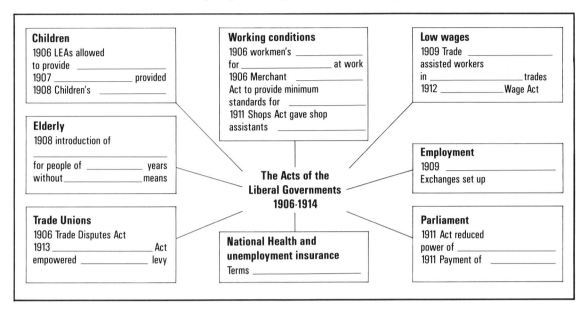

Children
1906 LEAs allowed
to provide _____
1907 _____ provided
1908 Children's _____

Working conditions
1906 workmen's _____
for _____ at work
1906 Merchant _____
Act to provide minimum
standards for _____
1911 Shops Act gave shop
assistants _____

Low wages
1909 Trade _____
assisted workers
in _____ trades
1912 _____ Wage Act

Elderly
1908 introduction of
_____
for people of _____ years
without _____ means

Trade Unions
1906 Trade Disputes Act
1913 _____ Act
empowered _____ levy

The Acts of the Liberal Governments 1906-1914

National Health and unemployment insurance
Terms _____

Employment
1909 _____
Exchanges set up

Parliament
1911 Act reduced
power of _____
1911 Payment of _____

2 (a) What was the most serious problem in the inter-war years?
(b) What factors caused this problem?
(c) How did some workers draw attention to their plight (see pages 129 and 144–7)?
(d) What was the 'Means Test'? Why was it hated by the poor and the unemployed?

3 (a) Which political party published this poster?
(b) Using the poster, can you explain Lloyd George's famous slogan '9 pence for 4 pence', intended to popularize the National Insurance Act of 1911?
(c) In which year was the 1911 scheme to be introduced?
(d) In your own words explain how the National Insurance Act provided aid from the State and the employer in an insurance scheme for the worker. What benefits was a worker to receive?
(e) State one benefit which a worker's wife would receive.

28 The Welfare State and nationalization

During the Second World War some people were thinking about the future and planning for when peace came. In the early 1940s the Government started to make plans for new social services in which William Beveridge, the great Liberal reformer, played a leading role. The Beveridge plan was revolutionary because it suggested that National Insurance should be extended to provide cover for all 'from the cradle to the grave'. After the Second World War the Labour Government embarked on a policy of 'nationalization' that is, bringing certain industries under state control. Today, there are growing criticisms of the Welfare State; and the Conservative Government have returned some nationalized industries to private enterprise.

■ The Welfare State

What was the Beveridge Report (1942) and what did it recommend?

This report, which was concerned with Social Insurance and Allied Services, was the work of a committee of which William Beveridge was the chairman. It investigated poverty and diagnosed its causes. It found that illness, unemployment and large families all affected the level of earnings and the amount of money spent. A model plan was drawn up and it was hoped that this 'Welfare State' would abolish what Beveridge called the five giants, namely 'want, disease, squalor, ignorance and illness' (**A**). It was hoped that a compulsory insurance scheme for everyone would guarantee a minimum income in times of unemployment or illness, or when people were too old to work. In addition, the insurance scheme was to provide funds for a national health service with free medical treatment for all. Family allowances were to be paid by the State, and there was to be an improvement in the quality of housing (**B**).

How was the Beveridge Report received?

Within a short time the plan had widespread popular support. Under the National Coalition Government steps were taken to set up a Ministry of National Insurance and, under the Children's Allowances Act, to pay Family Allowances for all children (except for the first child in each family).

Many of the recommendations made in the Report had long been Labour Party policy. Many Labour supporters believed that the welfare plans in the Report reflected socialist beliefs. In 1945, the Labour Party was elected to power with a massive majority. It was the first majority Labour Government in British history.

What measures were taken by the Labour Governments between 1945 and 1951 to improve the lives of the people?

Under the leadership of Clement Attlee, the Prime Minister, a number of important and highly controversial Acts were introduced.

National Insurance Act, 1946

Under this act, all workers (with the exception of the self-employed and married women, for whom the scheme was voluntary) were required to pay weekly national insurance contributions. The employer's contribution was paid by means of stamps on their employees' insurance cards. The money paid in was to go into a central fund and the Treasury was to add at least as much again from taxes.

In return for the payments, a system of benefits would be available during periods of unemployment or sickness. Old Age Pensions would be paid to women at the age of 60 and to men at the age of 65. Further benefits included Widows' Pensions, Death Grants to help in covering funeral expenses, and Maternity Grants which would be paid on the birth of a child. Special benefits and pensions were to be provided for people injured at work, under the National Insurance (Industrial Injuries) Act of 1946.

DAILY MIRROR, Wed., December 2, 1942.

Daily Mirror

DEC 2

No. 12,159   ONE PENNY
Registered at the G.P.O. as a Newspaper.

Allies separate
...is armies in

A MERICAN and French
forces were reported
last night to have driven a
...dge between the two Axis
...ies in North Africa—
...n Nehring, fighting to
...mel, at bay at El

...York stated that
...coast between
...a—where the
...by General
...ff.

Beveridge tells how to
BANISH WANT

Cradle to grave plan | All pay— all benefit

S IR WILLIAM BEVERIDGE'S Report, aimed at abolishing Want in Britain, is published today.

He calls his Plan for Social Security a revolution under which "every citizen willing to serve according to his powers has at all times an income sufficient to meet his responsibilities."

Here are his chief proposals:

All social insurance—unemployment, health, pensions— lumped into one weekly contribution for all citizens without income limit—from duke to dustman.

These payments, in the case of employees, would be:

Men 4s. 3d.   **Employer 3s. 3d.**
Women 3s. 6d.   **Employer 2s. 6d.**

Cradle to the grave benefits for all, including:

Free medical, dental, eyesight and hospital treatment;

Children's allowances of 8s. a week each, after the first child.

Increases in unemployment benefit (40s. for a couple) and abolition of the means test; industrial pension in place of workmen's compensation.

A charter for housewives, including marriage grant up to £10; maternity grant of £4 (and 36s. for 13 weeks for a paid worker); widow's benefit; separation and divorce provision; free domestic help in time of sickness.

Old age pensions rising to 40s. for a married couple on retirement.

Funeral grants up to £20.

To work the scheme a new Ministry of Social Security would open Security Offices within reach of every Citizen.

The 1d.-a-week-collected-at-the-door insurance schemes of the big companies would be taken over by the State.

Sir William says the Plan depends on a prosperous Britain, but claims that it can begin by July 1, 1944, if planning begins at once.

[See pages 4, 5 and 7]

...NS DEBATE BEFORE NEW YEAR

Govt. give hint of post-war planning

C HOOSING the eve of the publication of Sir William Beveridge's long-awaited report on Social Security, the Government yesterday gave the country its first indication of their own plans for post-war Britain.

These include the continuance of rationing for some time and control of industry (some industries being taken over as public corporations); the development of agriculture, forestry and public utilities like electricity.

The Government also announced the immediate setting up of a new Ministry of Town and Country Planning and the rejection of the Scott and Uthwatt Committees' proposals for placing main responsibility for planning in the hands of a permanent commission.

Victory First

Sir William Jowitt, Paymaster-General, answering a debate on reconstruction in the House of Commons, said:

"We must not allow ourselves to be distracted by talk of reconstruction from the stern task of securing victory.

"Talk of reconstruction is a mockery if the world is to remain hereafter under the constant fear of aggression."

Sir William referred to the Beveridge Report and said:

"The ideal of Social Security is one to which all thinking men and women can subscribe. We must survey his work as part of our reconstruction work as a whole."

A *Front page of the* Daily Mirror, *2 December 1942*

Q (a) When was the Beveridge Report published?

(b) What was the aim of the Report?

(c) At the time of publication what might be expected to fill the headlines of newspapers?

(d) How does the position of the Beveridge Report on the front page show that it was regarded as being very important?

(e) The editor has underlined certain phrases. Explain their importance.

(f) Is this newspaper primary or secondary evidence? Explain your answer.

RIGHT TURN

B

Q Look at cartoon **B**.

(a) What is the name of the bus and what is its destination?

(b) What does the bus represent?

(c) Explain why the bus is stuck in the mud on the road or 'way' along which it had been travelling.

(d) In which direction are *most* of the passengers and the bus driver looking?

(e) The bus driver represents the leader of the Labour Party at the time. Who was he?

(f) On the driver's uniform is the abbreviation 'Parlt'. What does that stand for?

(g) To what does the 'Beveridge Way' refer and how does it seem better than the existing road?

National Assistance Act, 1948

For persons not fully covered by the National Insurance benefits, further help was available to provide extra benefits for persons whose income was below a certain level, although payments were dependent on a 'means test'. It was anticipated that very few people would have to apply for National Assistance which, in effect, abolished the old poor law. However, accepting National Assistance meant drawing from a fund to which contributions had not been made. To some people, this looked like accepting charity and they preferred to do without. Inevitably, some people slipped through the social welfare 'net'. For example, in 1950 approximately two per cent of the British population remained below the poverty line.

National Health Service Act, 1946

This Act was largely the work of Aneurin Bevan, the Minister of Health. It sought to provide a free health service, with free medical, hospital, dental and optical treatment as a right. Most of Britain's hospitals were taken over by the State and run by regional hospital boards. In addition, the Act provided for a range of facilities run by the local authorities, including child welfare clinics and maternity care. One of the greatest difficulties facing Bevan was the suspicion of many doctors and dentists who feared loss of earnings and independence if they participated. Bevan persuaded the British Medical Association to join the scheme, on the understanding that the doctors could keep their private patients (**C** and **D**).

Private medicine

Private medicine continued to be practised and was both an alternative to, and complementary to, the National Health Service. Some doctors worked in the health service and in private practice. Hospitals continued to provide 'pay beds', that is, beds or places in hospital for patients who were willing to pay. Some people suggested that, at a time when waiting lists for treatment were growing, private patients were 'queue jumping'. Those who preferred private treatment could contribute to medical insurance schemes such as that offered by BUPA (British United Provident Association). In the 1970s and 1980s membership of such schemes increased.

The Health Service in practice

At first, under the new free system, there was a rush for treatment. The National Health Service cost much more than had originally been expected, and it has proved difficult to maintain (**E** and **F**). By 1951 the Labour Government had found it necessary to introduce charges for medical prescriptions. This was strongly opposed by Bevan, who resigned. Since that time, charges for medical, dental and optical treatment have increased. Shortage of money has also prevented all the necessary hospital building. A very important contribution to the service has been made by the many immigrant doctors and nurses without whom the system would have broken down.

"Just spots before the eyes. . . . Don't worry, we'll soon cure that!"

Q (a) What similarities can you see between cartoons **C** and **D**?

(b) The cartoon character who had the initials A.B. and was known as 'Ny', was Minister of Health. Who was he?

(c) Who are the people shown to be in need of and taking medicine? What do the initials M.D. stand for?

(d) What medicine are they being given (what can you see on the bottle and bowl)?

(e) Do the patients like the medicine? How do you know?

(f) What points of view do the cartoonists reveal in their drawings?

(g) Under what terms was the British Medical Association persuaded to join the new health scheme?

DOTHEBOYS HALL
"It still tastes awful."

E *From* An Autobiography *by H. Morrison*

While the Beveridge Report had provided a comprehensive idea of the cost involved in the Welfare State, the eventual dimensions of the Bill were much bigger than had ever been envisaged. The clash between the demands of the social services and of defence had been . . . the source of difficulties in the Labour governments since the war.

. . . the . . . historic crisis of spectacles and teeth . . . occurred . . . in the spring of 1951 . . . ministers had accepted the . . . defence budget, as indeed had Bevan. We all had regrets about this enormous bill, essential though we knew it to be. In the circumstances Gaitskell's insistence on a . . . cut in the Health Service . . . was economically understandable, especially as the health expenditure seemed out of control. This did not prevent Bevan indicating that there would be a showdown.

F *'All I ask is that you get it properly balanced'*

Q (a) What had the Beveridge Report underestimated (**E**)?

(b) Which part of the Welfare State proved to be very costly (**E**)?

(c) In what ways were members of the Labour Government divided after 1945 (**E**)?

(d) In cartoon **F**, the camel (the British State and economy) is being driven by Hugh Gaitskell, Chancellor of the Exchequer. What difficult task did Gaitskell face and how did he try to do it?

(e) For what other reasons might Gaitskell justify cuts in the Health Service?

(f) Why was Bevan particularly upset about the cuts in the Health Service and what was the outcome of the 'historic crisis of spectacles and teeth'?

(g) Was the author of source **E** involved in the events he described? Give reasons for your answer.

What criticisms have been made of the Welfare State?

A major criticism of the Welfare State is its cost. Opponents argue that taxation must remain high to pay for the system. The amounts paid out in social security benefits by the Department of Health and Social Security has greatly increased. This is partly due to a large number of elderly people; partly because of inflation; and partly because of high unemployment. Retirement pensions have cost much more than expected, and the amount paid out in unemployment benefits has increased greatly in recent years. At a time when there are growing demands from the elderly and the unemployed, the proportion of people paying taxes to support the system is declining.

Critics argue that the system is expensive to administer, and is complicated both for those claiming benefit and for those who operate it. It is also believed that the system reduces the incentive for people to work hard and save.

Some people argue that benefits in Britain are too low, and that they compare unfavourably with benefits paid in many countries in the European Economic Community (see Chapter 32). It is also pointed out that many people do not claim the benefits that are due to them.

A new inquiry

In April 1984 the Health and Social Security Minister, Norman Fowler, launched 'the most substantial examination of the social security system since the Beveridge Report 40 years ago'.

G *Cartoon by Gerald Scarfe from the* Sunday Times, *8 April 1984*

Q (a) Which two politicians are shown in cartoon **G**?

(b) What is represented by the building which they are thinking of knocking down?

(c) How does the cartoonist suggest that the existing 'building' is in need of urgent repairs?

(d) In what ways does the ageing population of Britain mean that the Welfare State faces a 'time bomb'?

■ Nationalization

What is nationalization?

The bringing of an industry or service under state control and public ownership is known as nationalization. Some services, for example the Post Office, have been under the control of the State from the start. Others, like broadcasting and the generation of electricity, were brought under state control in the inter-war years. The aircraft industry became a publicly-owned company in 1940, as the British Overseas Airways Corporation (BOAC).

Which industries and services have been nationalized since 1945?

After 1945 the Labour Government nationalized a number of key industries and services. Some industries were nationalized because they were 'essential' to the economy; others because they had a long history of poor management. Services and industries nationalized included the Bank of England (in 1946); coal, electricity and civil aviation (in 1947); railways, road transport and gas supply (in 1948); and the iron and steel industry (in 1949). By the end of its term of office (1945–51) the Government controlled about one-fifth of British industry (**H–I**).

The Conservative Party had opposed nationalization, but when returned to power in 1951, it did not de-nationalize any industries except iron and steel. The Labour Government re-nationalized iron and steel in 1967, and, between 1974 and 1979 it nationalized the shipbuilding and aerospace industries. It also established the British National Oil Corporation.

The Conservative Governments elected in 1979 and 1983 had strong views in favour of private enterprise and returned some public companies to private ownership, for example British Telecom in 1984.

Assisted and development areas

In the post-war period a number of areas such as Merseyside, South and North Wales, the North-East and the Glasgow region experienced severe industrial decline. By the 1970s the country had a number of development, or 'special' development areas, in which the Government encouraged firms to build factories and to provide jobs. Some aid was also received from the EEC (see Chapter 32).

H *Labour Party Policy Statement*

It is essential that the State should control the basic resources for the means of production and prosperity. This means state control or nationalization of essential industries.

I *From a speech by Ernest Bevin, 1945*

Now, why do we ask for public ownership? We want industry to serve the public and not just a few monopolies . . . I regard private monopolies, responsible to no one but themselves, as a danger to the state, a positive danger to the community . . . When a business becomes a monopoly or fails, owing to its structure, to provide a decent standard of life for its work-people, or to serve the public by providing goods or services at reasonable prices, then the Government ought to step in.

Q (a) In what ways does source **I** add to the information in source **H**?

(b) From source **I** give one *opinion* implied by the writer.

(c) What word is commonly used to show that an industry has been brought into public ownership?

(d) What is the meaning of the word 'monopoly'?

(e) Why did Bevin argue that monopolies were 'a positive danger to the community'?

QUESTIONS

1 Copy and complete the following passage by choosing (from the list below) the correct words or initials. (NB: there are more words than spaces)

In 1942 _____ had prepared a report on the social services and a model plan for the later _____ . In this he identified five basic freedoms which he believed all people should enjoy. These were freedom from _____ , _____ , _____ , _____ and _____ . To bring this about every adult would be involved in a compulsory _____ scheme. Before the end of the war, steps were already being taken to carry out some of the recommendations. For example in 1944 the Ministry of _____ was set up to plan some of the new measures.

With the end of the war it became the task of the _____ Government under _____ as Prime Minister to put the remainder of the report into practice. Two of the most important Acts were the National _____ Service Act of _____ and the National _____ Act of _____ . In looking after its citizens from the _____ to the grave, housing also played an important part. To provide temporary homes, large numbers of 'prefabs' were erected and New Towns such as Harlow were created.

After 1945 a number of important industries were _____ . These included _____ , _____ and _____ in 1947; and _____ , _____ and _____ in 1948. Among the services brought into public ownership was the _____ in 1946.

In 1985, after almost forty years and growing criticism of some features of the Welfare State and the public ownership of industries and services, the _____ Government launched a substantial examination of the _____ system. At the same time, some public enterprises were returned to _____ most notably _____ in 1984.

Aneurin Bevan	Welfare State	National Insurance	squalor	road transport
Clement Attlee	want	Labour	private ownership	electricity
Winston Churchill	British Telecom	Conservative	cradle	railways
Margaret Thatcher	nationalized	1948	social security	Beveridge Report
Sir William Beveridge	Bank of England	1946	civil aviation	disease
nationalization	illness	Assistance	gas supply	insurance
privatization	ignorance	Health	coal	

29 Education and the State

In the mid-nineteenth century the State played no direct role in the education of the nation's children. The elementary schools that existed were provided largely by the churches and the voluntary societies. Secondary schooling was almost entirely for the children of the wealthy at private and public schools. Today, the State requires that all children should receive both elementary and secondary schooling. Further years of study are permitted, at public cost, in further or higher education at technical colleges, polytechnics and universities.

■ Education before 1870

Schooling and the voluntary societies

The two voluntary religious societies, the National Society and the British and Foreign Schools Society provided schooling for some children of the working classes. The voluntary societies received a grant from the Government.

Ragged schools were sometimes provided in towns for the poorest children. In 1844 Lord Shaftesbury helped to form the Ragged School Union. By 1870 the Ragged School Union, using voluntary funds, ran 132 ragged schools with 25,000 pupils.

However, the rapid rise in population and the growth of towns made it impossible for the voluntary societies to provide schooling for all children.

The Newcastle Commission, 1858-61

This was set up to discover better ways for the government to support elementary schooling. The commission reported that only about 10 per cent of the children of the working classes received a satisfactory level of elementary schooling. Many children did not attend any school and few children attended regularly. Attendance rose and fell according to the weather and the seasonal demand for child labour. The wages earned by children were small but were often essential for the poorest families. Illness was also a cause of poor attendance. The Newcastle Commission recommended that the grants which the government paid to the voluntary societies' schools should depend on annual tests of each child by school inspectors.

What was the 'revised code'?

In 1862 Robert Lowe introduced a new system of awarding government grants to the voluntary societies' schools. Under this new system, or revised code, schools were to be inspected each year by one of Her Majesty's Inspectors (HMIs) and children were to be examined in the basic subjects of reading, writing and arithmetic (**A**). The amount of the grant was based on the number of children attending school regularly, and on their performance in the various tests. The system became known as 'payment by results'.

Teachers concentrated on those subjects which were being examined (reading, writing, arithmetic) and pupils were forced to learn by constant repetition (rote learning). Subjects for which grants were not paid were taught less in school. Thus the children of the working class received a limited education.

■ Education after 1870

The growing campaign to extend schooling

In 1867, an Act of Parliament enabled large numbers of town workers to vote for the first time and it was believed that voters should have some schooling. Changes in industry and trade and the expansion of the Civil Service required a better educated workforce. The voluntary schools could not provide sufficient places and pressure groups pointed out the shortcomings of the system in England as compared with rival industrial countries such as Germany, the USA and France.

W. E. Forster's Education Act of 1870

The 1870 Act was not designed to replace the existing voluntary school system but rather to provide schools where none had previously existed. In those districts where there were insufficient school places, School Boards were to

A WISE CHILD

Inspector. *"Suppose I lent your Father £100 in June, and he promised to pay me back £10 on the first of every month, How much would he owe me at the end of the year? Now think well before you answer."*
Pupil. *"£100, sir."*
Inspector. *"You're a very ignorant little girl. You don't know the most elementary rules of Arithmetic."*
Pupil. *"Ah, sir, but you don't know Father!"*

A *The school inspector's visit*

Q (a) How many pupils are being inspected?
(b) Who is the man with the top hat beside him?
(c) Why had he come to the school?
(d) Who is the man sitting at the desk?
(e) Why might he be anxious while the inspection took place?

be set up, with members elected by the ratepayers. The School Boards were to provide elementary schools for five- to ten-year-old children, which were to be built and maintained with money from the rates and from government grants. The 'board schools' could charge fees but poor children could attend without payment. Attendance was not compulsory throughout the country, but individual School Boards could insist that children in their districts attended. A 'conscience' clause in the 1870 Act allowed parents, on religious grounds, to withdraw their children from scripture lessons in board schools.

Elementary education in the School Board era

By 1900 there were about 2,500 School Boards in England and Wales which ran 5,700 schools. About two million children attended the board schools (**B**).

Q (a) In what ways are these classroom scenes in **A** and **B** different from your own classroom today? Make a list of the differences.
(b) Are there any similarities?
(c) Describe, using illustrations **A** and **B**, the sort of teaching and lessons which ordinary children would expect to receive at that time.

B *The new schoolroom*

Stimulated by the competition from the School Boards, the voluntary societies made great efforts to support their own schools. In 1870 there were about 8,800 schools in association with the various religious denominations (groups). By 1900 the number had increased to 14,500 schools with about 2½ million pupils. The voluntary schools obtained their money from church collections, fees and small government grants. The voluntary schools were less well equipped and funded than the board schools.

Improving school attendance

In the latter part of the nineteenth century a number of Acts were passed to improve school attendance. In 1876 (Sandon's Act) and 1880 (Mundella's Act) attendance at school was made compulsory up to the age of 10 years. In 1893 the school-leaving age was fixed at 11 years and was raised to 12 years in 1899. An Act of 1891 abolished fees for elementary education. The old 'payment by results' system was gradually relaxed, and was finally abandoned in 1898.

Secondary education

By the 1890s the improvements in elementary schooling led to a demand for more state- and rate-aided secondary schools. At a time of economic difficulty and trade rivalry, technical education in Britain had fallen behind that of other countries. In 1889 the Technical Instruction Act was passed which allowed the newly-created county councils and county borough councils to set up technical schools.

By the 1890s, some board schools were providing a higher form of education for able children who wanted to attain higher standards. More advanced subjects, for example science and French, were taught in special classes – or even, in some large towns, in separate Higher Grade schools (**C**). However, a law case in 1901 (the Cockerton Judgement) declared that it was illegal to use local rates for this purpose.

Many School Boards were too small or too poor to build Higher Grade or secondary schools. The Board of Education wanted to streamline educational administration and new laws were introduced in 1902 (**D**).

C *Report of Royal Commission (Bryce Commission) on Secondary Education (1895)*

Leeds Higher Grade School

This school is the most interesting in Leeds ... The building is divided into two halves, the one for boys and the other for girls, with a central double staircase which opens into long corridors separated from the class-rooms by glass partitions ... The classrooms which open from these corridors are large and airy, well-lighted, clean, and bright, and are perfectly equipped ... The school can be considered as consisting of two parts, the elementary school and the secondary school ... The children throughout the school pay a fee of ninepence a week, so that the lower part of the school is entirely fee-paying; but the upper part contains a large number of free scholars holding either board school scholarships, or the West Riding scholarships, or town council scholarships ... the Leeds Higher Grade School can claim to be a ... secondary school as it is keeping boys till they are quite as old as those in the ordinary grammar schools ... is passing them through the same examinations, is carrying off in competition with them the same scholarships ....

D *Speech of A. J. Balfour, 1902*

I do not blame the school boards because they have trespassed on the territories of secondary education. But they have exaggerated their capacity for dealing with secondary education. No mere addition of higher classes at the top of our schools will carry out the objects we have in view ... Our reform must establish one authority for education ... with power to provide for the training of teachers, and higher technical and secondary education.

Q (a) What evidence can you find that, through its Higher Grade School, the Leeds School Board was providing both elementary and secondary schooling (**C**)?

(b) What evidence can you find that the standard of education at the school was very good (**C**)?

(c) What was A. J. Balfour's attitude towards School Boards giving secondary schooling (**D**)?

■ Education after 1902

Balfour's Education Act, 1902

This Act abolished the School boards and made Local Education Authorities (LEAs) responsible for elementary and secondary education. Under the LEAs, which were run by the county and county borough councils, the former elementary board schools became county schools. The LEAs also took over the technical schools, colleges, and some teacher training colleges. They were given powers to build new secondary grammar schools and to administer existing grammar schools if requested to do so by the governors. Some children were therefore able to proceed from elementary school to a grammar school, either by winning a scholarship place, which meant they could attend free of charge, or by their parents paying fees.

The 1902 Act aided the voluntary schools, and the LEAs provided some of the funds which had previously been obtained from the Government. This greatly strengthened the Church schools but it angered the non-conformists who objected to any schools of a religious character being supported from the rates. The 1902 Act founded the system of education which lasted until 1944.

E *A class of 1908*

Q (a) What subject are the girls studying? How can you tell?
(b) Can you recognize and name any of the equipment being used?

Free places

An Act of 1907 stated that one-quarter of all places at the grammar schools supported by the rates were to be free places for children who had attended the State elementary schools. Working-class children had to compete for free places with the children from middle-class backgrounds whose parents had withdrawn them from private schools in the hope that, from the elementary school, they might secure a free place at grammar school.

The subjects taught to the older children at the grammar schools were usually those required for university entrance (**E**). Schools which provided more practical and vocational courses were built in some towns and these were known as central schools.

■ Education in the inter-war years

The 1918 Education Act

Under the terms of this Act the minimum school-leaving age was raised to 14 years. The Act promised that nursery schools would be set up for children of 3 years of age. Provision was also made for part-time education, in continuation schools, for children between 14 and 18 years of age. It was hoped that working teenagers would attend one or two days per week at such schools.

The proposals for nursery schools and continuation schools were not carried out because of the severe economic depression during this period.

The Hadow Report, 1926

This suggested two distinct stages of education; primary schooling, followed by a transfer to a secondary school at about the age of 11 years. It recommended secondary education for all children within two types of school, the grammar school and the modern school. Although these two kinds of school were supposed to be equally good, children were to take an examination at the age of 11 (known as the 11-plus) to decide which type of school they were to attend. Those who failed the examination would attend the secondary modern school.

The Spens Report, 1938

The Spens Report was concerned with secondary education and suggested that at the age of 11 years children should be selected by intelligence tests for secondary grammar, secondary modern or technical schools. It also suggested that the school-leaving age should be raised to 15 years and eventually to 16. The outbreak of the Second World War halted such plans.

■ Education after 1944

Butler's Education Act, 1944

Education was disrupted during the Second World War with the evacuation (**F, G, H**) of many children (sending them out of the large cities which might be bombed, to the countryside) and the shortages of resources, schools and teachers. At the same time, demands for a better system of education were growing.

The 1944 Education Act was largely the work of R. A. Butler (President of the Board of Education). The Act set out that the Local Education Authorities (LEAs) were to provide education in two stages: primary up to the age of 11 years; secondary education for all children over the age of 11. The LEAs were to provide free secondary schools according to the 'age, ability and aptitudes' of children.

The Act set up the tripartite (three-part) system of secondary education. Those pupils who passed the 11-plus examination were to attend the grammar school. Children who did not qualify for a grammar school place were to attend secondary modern schools. At a later age (13 years) children who did well at the secondary modern school might have the opportunity of a more practical education by going to a technical school. The school-leaving age was raised to 15 years.

The 1944 Act also made other changes. The LEAs were required to provide school meals and free milk, regular medical inspection, and special schools for handicapped children. To help the voluntary schools meet the costs of reorganization, they were asked to choose between controlled or state-aided status under which the LEAs paid many of their expenses. In return, all 'state' schools were to have a daily assembly or act of school worship. Fees were abolished in all state schools (except in some 'direct-grant' grammar schools which received financial support direct from the Government and not through the LEAs).

What were the effects of the 1944 Education Act?

By the early 1950s over 90 per cent of all pupils were in 'state' (LEA) schools, two per cent attended direct-grant grammar schools and about five per cent attended private schools. Critics argued that the 11-plus tests were unreliable and put pressure on the primary schools to get grammar school places for their pupils. Most 11-plus systems consisted of a test in English, arithmetic and intelligence to be taken in the last year of primary school. Reports showed that selection at the age of 11 was sometimes unfair and inaccurate (**I, J, K**).

The decision as to which type of school a child should attend was left to the LEAs, and

F *Children being evacuated from London. In the small cardboard boxes each one is carrying is a gas mask*

G *Oral evidence*

Many locals complained about their evacuees and called them dirty and bad-mannered.
I used to ask these people how they would like to be pushed out of their homes into a stranger's house miles away. Those evacuees were good children – they were genuine although some of them were a bit rough. The trouble was that some of the villagers didn't want to know that there was a war on.

H *Oral evidence*

The country people had to put up with a great deal. They took strange children into their homes. Some children were in rags. Some children were filthy. Some children were very naughty.

Q In what ways does the evidence in source **G** differ from that in source **H**? Can you suggest reasons for the differences?

problems could arise with borderline cases. There might also be difficulties when children from the same family had to attend different types of school.

Although, in theory, the secondary modern schools were to be as good as the grammar schools, in practice the secondary modern schools came to be regarded as second-rate. The number of working-class children in Britain was far greater than the number of middle-class children, yet a much higher percentage of the latter attended grammar schools.

Comprehensive schools

Dissatisfaction with the 11-plus and with the tripartite system were among the factors which led to the development of comprehensive schools. In the 1950s, and more particularly in the 1960s, there was a strong movement towards a comprehensive system of education, although the grammar schools continued to exist.

In 1965 the Labour Government issued a document compelling LEAs to announce what plans they had made to abolish the 11-plus exam and to introduce comprehensive schools. The development of comprehensive schooling became official Labour Party policy. Many LEAs went ahead with reorganization, particularly in periods when the Labour Party was in Government (1964–70; 1974–9).

In 1951 the General Certificate of Education was introduced and a system of 'O' and 'A' level examinations became available, mainly for the more able children in the last years of secondary school. In addition, in 1965, a new examination, the Certificate of Secondary Education, was introduced. Twenty years later a movement was underway for a new examination, the General

---

I The Crowther Report on Education between 15 and 18, *1959*

More and more people are coming to believe that it is wrong to label children for all time at 11. All over the country changes are being made that profoundly modify the previous pattern of education; and in certain areas the system is not being modified so much as being replaced by a different form of organization.

J *From the* Report on Admission to Grammar Schools *published for the National Foundation for Educational Research in England and Wales, 1964*

The 11-plus examination in its best form comes out as a highly reliable and remarkably valid instrument of prediction, considering what it is expected to do, but nevertheless the errors made can be fairly said to be not inconsiderable. Whether a 10 per cent error for the country at large, involving the apparent mis-allocation of about 60,000 children per annum, is to be regarded as reasonable or intolerable of course largely depends upon what particular values are regarded as most important.

Hospital beds for 11-plus

FROM OUR CORRESPONDENT
BIRMINGHAM, OCT. 29

Almost a third of the young patients being treated by a consultant psychiatrist at Birmingham Children's Hospital are suffering from emotional stress caused by worry over the 11-plus examination.

The consultant said today that the demand was so great for children needing psychiatric help in hospital that 30 beds were to be made available at the specialist Uffculme Clinic.

The strain of the examination was too much for some children. By the time a child was brought to him his emotional stress had reached an advanced stage.

Mr. Denis Howell, M.P. for Small Heath, Birmingham, and Parliamentary Under-Secretary to the Department of Education and Science, said: "It would be impossible to find more damaging evidence of the absurdity of the 11-plus, or any similar examination, than this."

K *From* The Times *30 October 1967*

Q (a) What have sources **I**, **J** and **K** in common?
  (b) Was the 11-plus examination at all reliable (source **J**)?
  (c) What was the likely scale of error by the early 1960s (source **J**)?
  (d) What stresses and strains were placed on children (and parents) by the 11-plus?

Certificate of Secondary Education (GCSE), to be taken by pupils at 16-plus in place of the older GCE and CSE examinations.

By the 1980s the country had a well-developed system of comprehensive schooling. Despite the changes, children from middle-class backgrounds continued to do better in terms of academic success than children from working-class families. At the same time, educational qualifications became increasingly important in terms of employment.

Further and higher education

The increasingly technical and scientific nature of modern industry and the complex nature of modern society requires a highly skilled and educated workforce. These changing demands have been largely met by the expansion of further and higher education.

Many of the older technical colleges became colleges of further education and, from the 1950s onwards, many Colleges of Advanced Technology (which later became Polytechnics) were established. Colleges of Higher Education, many of which developed from the old style teacher-training colleges, provided for a range of vocations including teaching, social work, and business and service occupations. The same period also saw a great expansion of University education, particularly in the 1960s when many new Universities were founded in the wake of the Robbins Report (1963). Twenty years later at a time of financial difficulties and falling school rolls the expansion of further and higher education was severely checked.

QUESTIONS

1 (a) Copy and complete this time chart based on the sketch map.

Date	Events	Information
1845	St. John's Church	Anglican Church
1890	St. John's School	Anglican School
	(to be completed)	

(b) What evidence suggests a rising population in the area in the 1890s?

(c) In the 1960s the two schools near Knighton Lane East were known as Secondary Modern Schools. Under which Act had they come into existence?

(d) These schools took only about 80 per cent of the children over 11 years of age. At which sort of schools (not shown on the map) would the remaining 20 per cent attend?

(e) What evidence suggests that there were also higher education institutions in the area?

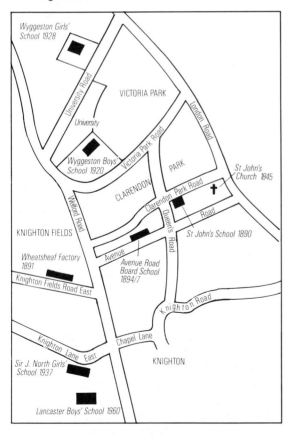

2

School Inspection	School Boards
Voluntary Schools	Increase in literacy
To educate new voters	Payment by results

(a) Choose *two* items from the above table, *one* of which was a *cause* and *one* a *result* of the Education Act of 1870. Write a few sentences on *each* explaining your choice.

(b) Add *one* item (not on the table) which was another important *cause* of the passing of the 1870 Education Act. Explain your choice.

(c) Add *one* item (not on the table) which was another important *result* of the 1870 Education Act. Explain your choice.

3 Complete each of the following sentences which deal with changes in Education since 1870.

The 1870 Act was the work of _____ and its main provision was to allow local rate payers to set up _____ .

The 1902 Act, known as the _____ Act ended the system set up in 1870 and placed primary and secondary education under the control of

_____ .

The 1918 Act raised the minimum school-leaving age to _____ .

In 1944 _____ was responsible for the Education Act which stated that secondary schooling was to be available according to '_____' of children.

In the 1960s attempts were made to provide more equality of opportunity in education by the introduction of _____ .

30 Medicine, public health and housing

In the mid-nineteenth century housing and living conditions were poor for many people and disease spread easily. The advance in medical knowledge, together with investigations into living conditions, showed that there was a link between housing, living conditions and disease. This knowledge and the occurrence of a number of epidemics led to demands for improvements in the field of public health. Although there have been major changes in these areas, progress in the provision of housing has been irregular. Changes in living standards in the twentieth century have brought many new health hazards.

■ Medical advances in the nineteenth century

How was hospital care improved?

A number of medical schools were founded, including Guy's Hospital in London. Better medical training for doctors, and advances in medical research, led to a greater understanding of disease and to better treatment for patients.

Standards of nursing and hospital conditions were greatly improved through the work of Florence Nightingale. She went to the Crimea to nurse the soldiers during the war. Her experiences made her determined to improve the standard of nursing for soldiers and for the public. She encouraged reforms in the Army Medical Service, and set up the first training school for nurses at St Thomas's Hospital in London.

What advances were made in surgery?

Anaesthetics   Until the mid-nineteenth century patients undergoing surgery often died from infection or the pain and shock of operations which were carried out while the patient was conscious. Sir Humphrey Davy found that nitrous oxide ('laughing gas') could make patients unconscious for a short time, thus helping to remove pain during operations. In 1838 Davy's assistant, Michael Faraday, discovered that the gas ether had similar effects. The breakthrough in anaesthetics came through the

work of James Simpson (**A**). Simpson, who was Professor of midwifery at Edinburgh University, used chloroform as a painkiller during childbirth. After Queen Victoria had been given chloroform during childbirth, the new anaesthetic became popular. Its use in surgery produced unconsciousness and inability to feel pain.

A *From a letter to James Simpson*

Before [your discovery] a patient preparing for an operation was like a condemned criminal preparing for an execution. He counted the days until the appointed day came. He counted the hours until the appointed hour came. He listened for the echo in the street of the surgeon's carriage. He watched for his pull at the door-bell; for his foot on the stair; for his step in the room; for the production of his dreaded instruments; for his few grave words and his last preparations before beginning. And then he surrendered his liberty and, revolting at the necessity, submitted to be held or bound, and helplessly gave himself up to the cruel knife.

Q (a) Why were operations greatly feared by patients?
(b) What evidence can you find that not all operations were carried out in a hospital?

Antiseptics   The use of antiseptics was pioneered by Joseph Lister, professor of surgery at Glasgow University (**B, C, D**). He was inspired by the work of the French chemist Louis Pasteur, who had discovered that disease was caused by bacteria. Lister realized that, in hospitals, open wounds were being infected by bacteria. He began to use carbolic acid as an antiseptic in the 1860s. The work of Simpson and Lister helped to reduce the number of patients, particularly those undergoing surgery, who died as a result of infection.

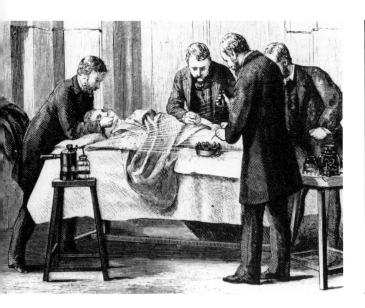

Memories of St Thomas's Hospital recalled by John Leeson in 1865

I entered as a first-year student at the newly erected St Thomas' Hospital. The building cost £600,000, a large sum of money for those days. But what was the result of all this expenditure? As far as surgery was concerned, practically nothing, for the old enemy septicaemia was as rife as ever. We students were allowed to go from the post-mortem room to attend midwifery cases. The ways of the operating surgeon seem almost incredible. An old sister, who had spent her life in the service of the Hospital once sadly said to me, 'I really think the surgeons do as much harm as they do good.'

B   *The use of Lister's carbolic spray*

D   *Figures relating to amputations by Lister*

Years	Total Cases	Recovered	Died
1864-66	35	19	16
1867-70	40	34	6

Q (a) What evidence can you find of the high death rate in surgical operations before the mid 1860s (sources **C** and **D**)?
(b) Suggest *two* reasons why so many patients died (source **C**).
(c) What evidence can you find that more patients survived operations after 1867 (source **D**)? Why do you think this was so?
(d) What is taking place in illustration **B**?
(e) What was the purpose of the carbolic spray which is standing on the stool?

What advances were made in medical treatment?

Vaccination Vaccination against smallpox had been developed by Edward Jenner in 1796. In the later nineteenth century Louis Pasteur developed vaccines against cholera, typhoid, typhus, plague and yellow fever. Vaccination helped to check the spread of these diseases.

Bacteriology Following the work of Pasteur and Lister, the German doctor, Robert Koch, showed that different bacteria caused different diseases. He identified the bacteria that caused tuberculosis (TB).

Chemo-therapy Paul Erlich was a German doctor who worked for a time under Koch. He identified chemicals that could be injected into patients (so-called 'magic bullets'). This process is called chemo-therapy and is used in the treatment of some cancers.

X-Rays The German physicist William Rontgen discovered X-rays in 1895. This development permitted the examination of the internal structure of the body by X-ray photograph. It revolutionized surgery and made diagnosis easier.

Radium This natural radioactive element was discovered by Pierre and Marie Curie in 1898. The X-rays from radium can kill living tissue and are used to treat cancer and tumours.

■ Medical advances in the twentieth century

What advances have been made in medicine?

Progress in vaccination has continued and a number of killer diseases, for example diphtheria, have been largely eliminated, as has polio. In the 1920s two Canadian scientists Frederick Banting and Charles Best, discovered the importance of insulin in the treatment of diabetes. The importance of vitamins came to be recognized. It was realized that a deficiency in vitamin C could lead to a condition called scurvy; and that a shortage of vitamin D could cause rickets. In 1929, Sir Alexander Fleming discovered the 'antibiotic' penicillin. Penicillin is an organic acid formed during the growth of common mould which can prevent the growth of certain bacteria. It was particularly useful during the Second World War, and other antibiotics have been developed since. Although many valuable drugs have been developed, some may occasionally cause serious side effects. One example is the use of thalidomide during pregnancy which led to the birth of deformed babies in the 1960s. Great improvements have been made in hospital conditions and standards of care, although some of the buildings are over 100 years old and new hospitals are needed.

Q (a) Identify some of the features of a modern operating theatre by linking the numbers in the photograph with the correct description in the chart (copy the chart into your book).

Feature	Number
Heart-lung machine	
Theatre lights	
Theatre sister	
The surgeon	
Surgical mask	
Surgical gown	
Close circuit TV camera	

(b) Compare the photograph **E** with illustration **B** on page 202. List as many differences in the pictures as you can. Are there any similarities?

(c) There were *many* reasons why the changes shown in the two illustrations took place. Can you list *some* of the reasons?

(d) Which of these reasons do you consider most important in explaining change, and why? What kinds of evidence would you use to test your explanation?

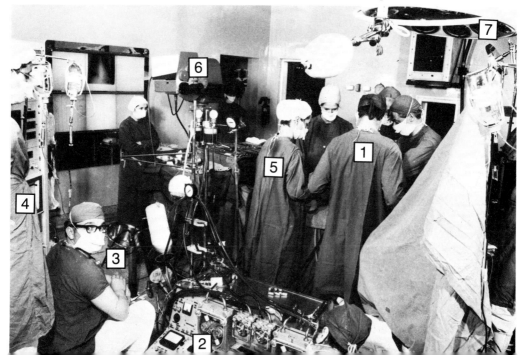

E *A modern heart operation*

What technical advances have been made?

The development and use of the electron microscope permits the observation of minute organisms and viruses which cause disease. Technical developments have assisted in the diagnosis and treatment of illnesses, and have enabled complicated and experimental surgery to be performed (**E**). The first heart transplant operation was carried out in 1967 by the South African doctor Christian Barnard. Transplants and 'spare-part' surgery involving other organs (kidneys, liver) have become common. Increasing use of the computer is made in the diagnosis of disease.

■ Public health

Informing public opinion

Dr John Simon, who was Medical Officer of Health to London, became adviser to the Government on public health matters in 1858. He fought an unceasing campaign for better houses, drains and water supplies. He also recommended the isolation and disinfection of infectious diseases. Simon produced annual reports on matters concerning public health which helped to educate public opinion of the need for reform.

Government attempts to improve public health

Greater medical knowledge of the causes of disease and attempts by people like John Simon to inform public opinion led to demands to improve public health. The outbreak of cholera in 1865–66 forced the Government to take action.

Sanitary Act, 1866

This Act compelled local authorities to provide sanitary inspection and to improve water supplies and the disposal of waste and sewage. Cholera did not return and other diseases of filth began to decline.

The use of iron pipes for carrying water enabled some towns to draw fresh water from great distances. However, few towns had their own water supplies and, as late as 1900, many houses had no direct link to a water supply.

Torrens Act, 1868

This Act permitted local councils to pay for the demolition of single houses, in an unsanitary state, which had been condemned as unfit by a Medical Officer of Health. Only a few councils took action (**F**).

F *Housing in a factory town*

Q (a) How was the court drained? What would the court be like in wet weather?
(b) Why did the court get little sunlight?
(c) How did the inhabitants obtain their water supplies?
(d) Where did people hang out their washing?
(e) How would waste be disposed of?
(f) What evidence can you find that living conditions were overcrowded in this court?
(g) Why was there a danger of disease as a result of conditions outside such houses?
(h) Why was there a danger of disease as a result of conditions inside such houses?
(i) Which diseases were likely to cause epidemics?

Local Government Board, 1871

A Royal Commission, set up in 1869 to investigate public health, reported that there was a need for good water supplies, proper drainage, healthy houses, clean streets and food inspectors. They advised that local public health boards required more guidance from central Government, and an Act of 1871 created a Local Government Board responsible for public health.

Public Health Act, 1875

This attempted to bring together all the Public Health Acts. The Act compelled local councils to appoint a Medical Officer and an Inspector of Nuisances (Sanitary Inspector). It allowed councils to build sewers, to improve street drainage, establish reservoirs, and to open public parks, swimming baths and public lavatories.

What are the 'diseases' of modern society?

Although there have been major changes and improvements in public health, modern society has it own 'diseases'. The number of road accidents has increased with the greater use of motorized traffic. Each year, many people in Britain die of the diseases (such as heart disease and cancer) associated with affluence (wealth), an unbalanced diet and cigarette smoking. The stress and strain of modern living has contributed to an increase in the numbers of people suffering from mental illness. There has also been an increase in alcoholism and drug addiction. The use of cannabis and heroin has particularly affected young people in recent years.

However, governments in Britain have come to recognize the benefits of a healthy nation, and have attempted to reduce the effects of living and working in modern society. Cigarette packets carry a 'Government Health Warning' and the Health Education Council seek to advise and inform on diet and other health matters. Regulations are enforced to limit the effects of pollution and to control the use of harmful or dangerous substances. Care is taken to protect workers from the harmful effects of radiation, radioactive materials and certain types of asbestos. Constant testing and vigilance is necessary in the use of pesticides and chemical fertilizers to prevent the pollution of food.

Thus, although many of the threats to public health have been removed by medical knowledge and better housing and living conditions, the twentieth century has produced its own health hazards.

Nevertheless earlier successes in health care have extended life expectancy and, in the 1980s, there are more elderly people than ever before, many of whom require specialized medical attention.

■ Housing the people

Private initiatives for housing

Although the provision of better housing was mainly the work of town councils, a number of private individuals also helped.

George Peabody Peabody was a wealthy American who settled in England. In the 1860s he set up the Peabody Trust to build homes (Peabody Buildings) for poor people in the Spitalfields district of London.

Octavia Hill Octavia Hill was shocked by the slums of London. She was influenced by the Christian Socialist movement and spent much of her life helping the poor, especially by housing schemes. She leased houses in Marylebone to poor families.

The industrialists Sir Titus Salt, a leading Yorkshire textile manufacturer, established a new model town for his workers at Saltaire. Housing of a high standard was provided together with a library, a park, a wash house and a social club (he refused to have a public house). William Hesketh Lever (later Lord Leverhulme), the leading British soap manufacturer, founded the garden village of Port Sunlight in Cheshire to house his factory workers. George Cadbury, the British manufacturer of cocoa and chocolate, established the garden village of Bournville for his workers. Bournville, a suburb of Birmingham, opened in 1900 and had 3000 houses.

Garden cities Ebenezer Howard, a British housing reformer, founded the Garden City Association in 1899. He argued for the building of small new towns that would have the benefits of both country and town life. Letchworth, founded in 1903, was the first British garden city. In 1919–20 Howard was active in the development of Welwyn Garden City.

Public initiatives for housing

The main initiatives for the provision of housing came from central government and local authorities.

The Artisans' Dwellings Act, 1875 Under this Act, powers were given to local councils to condemn properties, to clear slum areas within their boundaries, and to replace unsanitary dwellings with new housing. A few large towns made efforts to improve public health by slum clearance. Birmingham, under its mayor Joseph Chamberlain, also laid out parks and provided water and gas supplies. However, many towns did little and a Royal Commission on the Housing of the Working Class (1884–5) showed that bad housing was widespread.

Housing Act, 1890 This Act strengthened the earlier Housing Acts and encouraged local councils to embark on housing improvement schemes. Thousands of terrace houses were built in the new suburbs of towns. The building of back-to-back houses continued until 1909.

Housing developments 1918–39

During the First World War very few houses had been built. Under an Act of 1919 the Government offered a subsidy (money grant) for each house built by a local council for rent. Although the Government was forced to abandon the subsidies in the financial crisis of the early 1920s, it was the first time that the Government had been prepared to take direct action to encourage council house building. During the inter-war years a large number of housing estates were built by local councils and financed from rates and national taxes.

During the inter-war years there was a boom in private house building, particularly in the Midlands and the South-East where new industries and services were growing. Large numbers of semi-detached houses ('semis') were built in the suburbs of most towns and cities.

Why was there a serious housing problem in 1945?

During the Second World War no new houses were built. In addition, German air bombardments of towns and cities destroyed about 20 per cent of the houses in Britain. Thus, by 1945 the country faced a serious housing shortage.

How did the Government deal with the housing problem?

The Labour Governments (1945–51) encouraged the building of council houses to be rented out to tenants. Despite the shortage of basic raw materials, one and a quarter million houses were built during the six-year period.

Another feature of the post-war period was the building of a number of 'new towns' – for example, Harlow, Basildon and Aycliffe – under the New Towns Act of 1946 and the Town and Country Planning Act of 1947. The building of new towns had a slight effect upon the distribution of population in Britain.

A housing boom

In the 1950s and 1960s there was an expansion in house building. Slum clearance schemes were favoured, and the Conservative Minister of Housing, Harold Macmillan, increased the building rate to a peak of over 300,000 houses a year. The Conservatives encouraged the building of private houses for sale, and the number of private dwellings completed rose steadily.

Continuing housing problems

By the late 1970s there were about 21 million dwellings in Britain. Of these, 54 per cent were owner-occupied, 32 per cent were council houses and 14 per cent were privately rented dwellings. Modern styles of building such as tower blocks of flats have created social problems. In the 1980s some council houses were sold to tenants, as a result of Conservative policy to extend home ownership. A report published in 1985 showed that there was still a serious shortage of housing in Britain. Many thousands of people still live in overcrowded conditions and in houses classed as being 'unfit for human habitation', particularly in London and the larger cities and towns.

QUESTIONS

1 (a) Who was James Simpson and what contribution did he make to the development of anaesthetics?
   (b) What improvements were made in nursing from the 1860s?
   (c) With whom are the nursing improvements associated?
2 What changes were introduced by the Sanitary Act of 1866 and the Public Health Act of 1875?
3 What housing problems exist in Britain in the 1980s?

Year	Total Population	Birth rate	Death rate
1901	38·2 million	29	17
1911	42·1 m	25	15
1921	44·0 m	23	12·5
1931	46·0 m	16	12·5
1941	48·2 m	14	13·5
1951	50·6 m	16	12·5
1961	53·0 m	18	12
1971	55·7 m	16	11·5
1979	55·9 m	13	12

From Government Statistical Service

4 (a) Give the meaning of the terms 'birth rate' and 'death rate'.
   (b) State the Birth Rate in 1901.
   (c) State the Death Rate in 1979.
   (d) Why has the Birth Rate fallen during this period?
   (e) Why has the Death Rate fallen during this period?

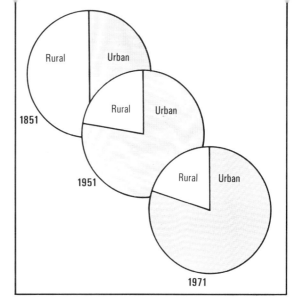

6 The diagram above shows the way in which the population of Britain has at various times been divided between those living in rural and those living urban areas.
   (a) Explain the terms 'rural' and 'urban'.
   (b) Why did the changes shown in the diagram take place?
   (c) What are the advantages and disadvantages of living in an urban community?
   (d) The 1981 census showed that many of the smaller towns of Britain have increased in population. Why have people and industry been attracted to these towns?
   (e) Why has the population of inner city areas decreased in recent years?

7 **Essay topic:**
Describe the main changes in public health and housing between 1860 and 1960 and show the main connections between health and housing.

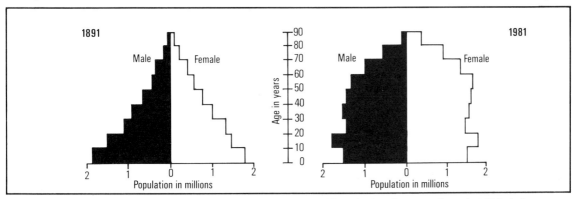

5 (a) The diagrams above are called population _____.
   (b) Which was the largest age group in 1891?
   (c) Which was the largest age group in 1981?
   (d) How many other differences can you find between the age structure of the population in 1891 and that of 1981?
   (e) How do the changes show that Britain has an 'ageing population'?
   (f) What are the kinds of problems that can arise from a country having an 'ageing population'?
   (g) How do you account for the differences in the age structure of the population between 1891 and 1981?

31 The struggle for women's rights

At the beginning of the nineteenth century women had very few rights. Male domination of the family and of society was upheld by the laws, the church and the state. The position of women in society gradually changed. This was due to a number of factors, not least to the determination of some women themselves. Progress in the twentieth century accelerated, with far-reaching implications for women of all social classes.

■ The Victorian family

The traditional view of the family
The Victorian family was the basic unit of society. The husband was the head of the family and, legally, when a woman married, all her property passed to her husband. The husband protected and provided for the family. His wife, children and any servants were subordinate to him (had less status than him and obeyed him). It was the duty of a married woman to bear and rear children, and to run the home.

Working-class women
Educational opportunities for the children of the working classes were very limited, although both boys and girls might attend an elementary school for a few years. Girls from working-class families often started work at a very early age, and domestic service was the most common form of paid employment (**A** and **B**). Other jobs for women were available in agriculture, in textile factories or in clothing workshops where they earned low wages.

Working-class women usually married in their late twenties. The wages of their husbands, if they were in work, were often low, and women found it a hard struggle to feed and keep the family together. Wherever possible, they tried to add to their husband's wages by working for a little extra money. Families were large and many women died before their family had grown up.

There were, however, differences within the working classes, and the wives and daughters of the skilled workers were in a better position than those of the unskilled groups.

A *A kitchen-maid's duties*

When I looked at this list I thought they had made a mistake. I thought it was for six people.

'Rise at five-thirty, come downstairs, clean the flues, light the fire, blacklead the grate, clean the fender and fire-irons, clean the brass on the front door, scrub the steps, clean the boots and shoes, lay the servants' breakfast. All this had to be done before eight o'clock.'

Q (a) In what ways was her life worse than that of a factory worker (see pages 18–23)?
(b) In what ways was her life better than that of a factory worker?

B *Kitchen staff of a big house*

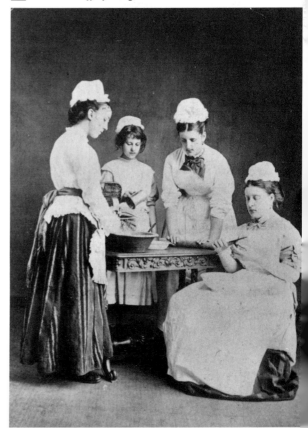

C *An evening at home in 1889*

Q (a) What does the picture suggest about the size of a Victorian family?

    (b) Using the information in picture **C** and the text, write a paragraph about the middle-class family.
Here are some topics you might like to mention: dress; the role of the various members in the family; occupations and responsibilities inside and outside the home.

Middle-class women

Middle-class women also had large families, but unlike working-class women, they were able to employ domestic servants to help in the home. Instructions on how to run a home could be found in household books, notably Isabella Beeton's *Book of Household Management*.

Although they lived comfortably, middle-class women were dependent on their fathers or husbands. Their behaviour was governed by a strict social code. Many middle-class girls were brought up at home and educated by their mothers or by poorly paid governesses. They were often taught that their main task was to marry or 'catch' a middle-class husband. An occupation for the unmarried daughter of a middle-class family might be as a governess, or a paid companion.

Changing patterns of family life

In the later nineteenth century, the idea of marriage as a form of companionship became fashionable, especially among the middle classes. With many women marrying at a later age, and contraception becoming acceptable, smaller families became more common. In general, smaller families, better living standards, and improvements in health all helped to improve the position of women.

The Married Women's Property Acts (1870, 1882) allowed wives to retain the property that was theirs when they got married.

■ Education and employment

How did changes in education improve the status of women?

In 1848 Queen's College, London was founded for the training of women teachers. A leading figure in promoting higher education for women was Emily Davies. In 1869 she founded Hitchin College which, in 1873, was moved to Cambridge as Girton College for lady students only. Other colleges were also founded for women at Cambridge (Newnham), and Oxford (Somerville, Lady Margaret Hall), although at first they did not permit women students to take degrees like the men. After 1878, London University allowed its female students to take degrees.

Important changes also took place in the education of girls. In 1850 Frances Mary Buss, an artist's daughter, founded the North London Collegiate School which aimed to provide an all-round education for girls. Some wealthy middle-class families sent their daughters to boarding schools, which were modelled on the Cheltenham College for Young Ladies founded by Dorothea Beale in 1858. The foundation of the Girls' Public Day School Trust in 1872 aimed to set up high quality secondary schools for girls. By 1900 more than one hundred secondary day schools for middle-class girls had been opened.

After the 1902 Education Act many more girls from the middle class, and a few from the working class, were attending grammar schools.

How did the changing nature of employment provide more opportunities for women?

Changes in shopping habits, in particular the growth of large department and chain stores, provided opportunities for a range of jobs from shop assistants to supervisors, principally for the working- and lower-middle-classes. Shop work often meant long hours and poor pay.

Typewriters and telephones played an important part in changing the employment position of women who had received some education. Office work was revolutionized and, between 1891 and 1911, the number of women working as clerks and telephone switchboard operators rose from 10,700 to 117,000.

More Government intervention in the economic and social life of the country increased the demand for civil servants, and many girls were prepared for Civil Service Examinations.

Another important occupation in which there were opportunities for women was that of school teacher. In the period of growing state education after 1870, the numbers of school teachers were greatly increased.

Florence Nightingale and the development of nursing

Florence Nightingale had grown up in a wealthy family and, against its wishes, managed to get some training as a nurse. At that time, nursing was regarded as a low kind of domestic work, and nurses were often portrayed as being ignorant and dirty. In 1854 the British Government permitted Florence Nightingale, together with a group of nurses to go to the Crimea to look after the wounded. Largely as a result of their endeavours, nursing became a respectable profession for women. In 1860 Florence Nightingale founded a nurses' training school at St Thomas's Hospital in London.

Women doctors

Elizabeth Garrett (later Anderson) started as a nurse at the Middlesex Hospital and, despite much hostility, she became the first woman doctor to practise in England (**D** and **E**). Later she helped to found a hospital in London where women were trained for medicine.

In 1876 an Act of Parliament allowed medical schools to admit women students.

■ Women and politics

What was the political position of women?

After 1834 all ratepayers and household heads – including, therefore, some spinsters and widows – had the right to vote in the elections for the local Poor Law Guardians. Following the 1870 Education Act, female ratepayers could vote and sit on the new School Boards. After 1888 women ratepayers were also allowed to vote in County Council and County Borough elections. However, women were not allowed to vote in Parliamentary elections. The Reform Acts of 1867 and 1884 had given the vote to the majority of men but not to women.

D *Suffragette poster*

E *From the 1871 Census Report*

They [women] are excluded wholly or in great part from the Church, the Law, and Medicine. Whether they should be rigidly excluded from these professions or be allowed on the principle of freedom of trade to compete with men, is one of the questions of the day.

Q (a) The two sources (**D** and **E**) were separated in time by about thirty years. In what ways did the employment opportunities for women in public life and the professions improve during those years?

(b) What point is being made in the poster (source **D**)?

(c) Do you think those who produced the poster were for or against improving the position of women? Give reasons for your answer.

Queen Victoria was strongly opposed to giving women the vote, which she regarded as a 'mad, wicked folly'. Many politicians, and members of the public, argued that involvement in politics was 'unfeminine'; and it was generally accepted that women were unable to make sensible judgements on political matters. Most MPs were determined to keep women out of national politics.

In the 1860s several groups were organized to campaign for 'Votes for Women'. They were supported by a number of highly educated men. To achieve their aims, women began to organize themselves on a national scale.

The 'Suffragists'

In 1897 Mrs Millicent Fawcett formed the National Union of Women's Suffrage Societies which sought to unite the various women's suffrage (voting) groups. Known as the 'Suffragists', they used various methods – meetings, petitions, persuasion, reasoned argument, legal propaganda and the threat of tax avoidance – to persuade Parliament to give women the same voting rights as men.

The Women's Social and Political Union (WSPU)

In 1903 Mrs Emmeline Pankhurst and her daughter Christabel broke away from the Suffragists to form the Women's Social and Political Union. The WSPU, which soon included Emmeline's second daughter, Sylvia, was prepared to take more violent action than its rival, the National Union. Although the WSPU, or Suffragettes, received support from the Lancashire women textile workers, many of their most active members were middle-class.

What methods did women use to gain the vote?

The suffragettes (WSPU) heckled (shouted and asked awkward questions) leading politicians at public meetings. When Winston Churchill addressed a meeting in Manchester in 1905, for example, he was interrupted by Christabel Pankhurst and Annie Kenney. The two suffragettes were roughly handled and thrown out of the meeting (**F** and **G**).

F *From the* Daily Mail *16 October 1905*

Miss Pankhurst and Miss Kenney, the two ladies whose zeal for women's suffrage led to their being ejected from a Liberal demonstration held in Manchester Free Trade Hall on Friday night, refused to pay the fines which were imposed on Saturday, when they were charged with disorderly behaviour, and are now in Strangeways Gaol.

The prosecution alleged that the two women went to the meeting with the intention of creating a disturbance, shouting and shrieking 'Treat us like men'. When the attendants turned them out they were however anxious to be treated like ladies. Miss Pankhurst was so angered that she spat in the face of a police superintendent, and an inspector, and the latter she struck twice in the mouth.

Q (a) Why did Christabel Pankhurst and Annie Kenney go to the Free Trade Hall in Manchester in October 1905 (source **F**)?

(b) Of what crime were they accused?

(c) Why were they sent to gaol?

(d) What evidence can you find which reveals the attitude of the *Daily Mail* towards the suffragettes (source **F**)?

(e) Is the attitude of the cartoonist similar or different (source **G**) to that of the newspaper (source **F**)? Give reasons for your answer.

(f) Which of the two women does the cartoonist regard as 'the sensible woman'?

(g) Who does he regard as 'the shrieking sister'?

(h) What do you think she is shrieking about?

(i) Why does 'the sensible woman' say that 'the shrieking sister is the 'worst enemy' of 'our cause'?

(j) What kinds of action did the suffragettes take to gain publicity for their cause?

Bernard Partridge

THE SHRIEKING SISTER

The sensible woman. *"You help our cause? Why, you're its worst enemy!"*

G *From* Punch *17 January 1906*

H *From* The Times *5 June 1913*

The Derby of 1913 will long remain memorable . . . .

The desperate act of the woman who rushed from the rails on to the course, as the horses swept round Tattenham Corner, apparently from some mad notion that she could spoil the race, will impress the general public . . . .

She did not interfere with the race, but she nearly killed a jockey as well as herself, and she brought down a valuable horse . . . .

A deed of this kind, we need hardly say, is not likely to increase the popularity of the cause with the public. Reckless fanaticism is not regarded by them as a qualification for the franchise [vote]. Persons who wantonly destroy property and endanger lives must be either desperately wicked, or entirely unbalanced.

J *From the* Daily Mail *5 June 1913*

Miss Davison is the hottest of all Suffragettes' 'Hot Bloods'. She is a BA of London University and joined the militants in 1906. Since then she has . . . hidden herself three times in the House of Commons . . . been imprisoned nine times . . . started a fire in the GPO . . . gained her freedom from prison by hunger striking three times.

I *From* My Own Story *by E. Pankhurst*

Emily Wilding Davison gave up her life for the women's cause by throwing herself in the path of the thing, next to property, held most sacred to Englishmen – sport . . . she rushed in the path of the galloping horses, and caught the bridle of the King's horse . . . the horse fell, throwing his jockey and crushing Davison in such a shocking fashion that she was carried from the course in a dying condition . . .

. . . so she threw herself at the King's horse, offering up her life as a petition to the King, praying for the release of suffering women throughout England and the world.

Q (a) Why would the Derby horse race of 1913 long be remembered (sources **H** and **I**)?
(b) For what reasons did *The Times* condemn the action of Emily Davison (source **H**)?
(c) Does source **I** support or contradict source **H**? Explain your answer.
(d) What had motivated Emily Davison, according to *The Times*?
(e) Why had Emily Davison been in the newspapers before (source **J**)?

The suffragettes organized large marches and rallies. They were arrested and imprisoned for various offences, some of which were relatively harmless, such as chaining themselves to the railings of Buckingham Palace and Downing Street. Later, they began to attack property; paintings in the National Gallery were slashed, and a window-smashing demonstration in Oxford Street, London, was organized. Some instances of arson (setting buildings on fire) also occurred. Politicians who opposed 'Votes for Women' were sometimes assaulted by the suffragettes.

In 1913 Emily Davison, a leading suffragette, drew attention to the women's cause by throwing herself under the king's horse which was running in the Derby at Epsom. Her death was the most dramatic event in the long suffragette campaign (**H–J**).

The struggle in Parliament

In 1907 and 1908, two Private Members' Bills failed to gain votes for women. The Liberal Government felt that women's suffrage would benefit the Opposition parties. Some Liberals who were in favour of the suffragettes opposed the growing use of violence.

Between 1912 and 1914 the bitterness between the suffragettes and the Government was at its height. When women were not included in new proposals to extend the vote the campaign became even more militant. This caused divisions within the ranks of the WSPU.

The suffragettes in prison

Many suffragettes were arrested and, when they refused to pay fines, they were sent to prison. To protest against their sentences, the more determined suffragette prisoners went on hunger strike. They were then forcibly fed (**K**), by a rubber tube forced down the prisoner's throat, through which liquid food could be poured into the stomach. This practice was both dangerous and painful, and there was a public outcry against forcible feeding (**L**).

In 1913, in order to deal with the hunger strikes, Parliament passed the so-called 'Cat and Mouse' Act. Under the terms of the Act, prisoners on hunger strike could be released and then, when recovered, be brought back to prison to complete their sentence. Opponents claimed that the Act could be compared to a cat cruelly playing with a mouse.

L *From a letter from Lord Stamfordham to the Home Secretary, 1913*

The King desires me to write to you on the question of 'forcible feeding'. His Majesty cannot help feeling that there is something shocking, if not absolutely cruel, in the operation to which these insensate women are subjected through their refusal to take the necessary nourishment. His Majesty concludes that Miss Pankhurst's description of what she endured when forcibly fed is more or less true. If so, her story will horrify people otherwise not in sympathy with the Militant Suffragettes. The King asks whether, in your 'Temporary Discharge of Prisoners Bill', it would not be possible to abolish forcible feeding.

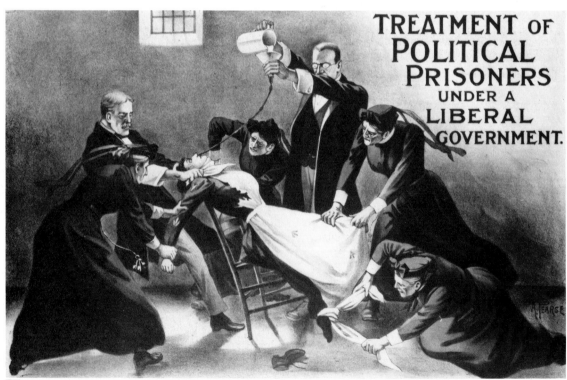

K *Suffragette poster*

Q (a) Who do you think published this poster? Was it (i) The Liberal Government; (ii) The Conservative Party or (iii) the Women's Social and Political Union? Give reasons for your answer.

(b) What is the 'torture' taking place and why is it being carried out?

(c) Why did the women regard themselves as 'political prisoners'?

M *Suffragette poster*

■ The changing role of women since 1914

What contribution was made by women during the First World War?

When war broke out in 1914, the suffragettes abandoned their campaign of violence. Emmeline and Christabel Pankhurst pledged the full support of the suffragettes to the war effort. During the war women filled many of the jobs vacated by men who had volunteered (or were later conscripted) for active service. Many women did jobs previously reserved only for men: some worked as drivers and conductresses on trains and buses; some worked on the land as farm labourers; others were employed in factories, and some made armaments (weapons) (**N**). Some women joined the special women's branches of the armed forces, or contributed to the war effort by serving as nurses.

N

Q (a) Why did King George V oppose 'forcible feeding' (source **L**)?

(b) What evidence can you find that he believed that forcible feeding might lead more people to sympathise with the extreme or 'Militant Suffragettes'?

(c) By what name was the 'Temporary Discharge of Prisoners Bill' more commonly known (sources **L** and **M**)?

(d) The 'mouse' in the cat's mouth is wearing a sash with the letters WSPU. What do the letters stand for and who does the 'mouse' represent?

Q (a) What do you think is being made and stored in this wartime factory (**N**)?

(b) Which people are carrying out the work?

(c) In what ways do you think it might be a heavy job and a responsible one?

The Representation of the People Act, 1918

Shortly before the end of the First World War, an Act was passed which gave the vote to all adult males over the age of 21 and to women over 30 who were householders or who were married to householders. Women were allowed to stand for Parliament and to become MPs. Christabel Pankhurst was defeated at the General Election of 1918 but, in the following year, Lady Nancy Astor was elected as MP for Plymouth.

How did the position of women change in the inter-war years?

In 1928 another Representation of the People Act was passed, which gave women the vote at 21 years of age. This meant that one of the main aims of both the suffragists and the suffragettes had been achieved.

As a result of the Sex Disqualification Removal Act (1919), women were able to hold public office and to enter the universities. Most (but not all) of the professions were opened up to women during this period. Employment opportunities for women also improved where new industries were developing. The growth of light engineering and electrical industries provided female employment, as did banking, commerce and a range of service activities. However, opportunities declined in the depressed regions on the old coalfields.

Family changes

Birth control within marriage became more acceptable, partly through the efforts of Marie Stopes who opened a special clinic in London in 1921. Smaller families became the norm for all classes and, because they had fewer children to bring up, many women were much healthier. Laws were passed which gave women more rights over property. The Matrimonial Causes Act (1923) allowed a wife to sue for divorce on the same grounds as a man.

The emancipation (setting free) of younger women could be seen in clothes, make-up, and in styles of entertainment. The 'flappers' (young, very fashionable girls) of the 1920s were strongly criticized by their elders.

Growing opportunities

The Second World War had significant effects on the range of jobs available for women. As in the First World War, women played a major part in the war effort.

After 1945 a number of Acts were passed which aimed to establish equal pay opportunities. For example, the Equal Pay Act (1969–70) stated that employers should pay women the same wage as men if they were doing a similar job. The Sex Discrimination Act (1975) made discrimination on the grounds of sex unlawful. The Equal Opportunities Commission was also set up to examine allegations of discrimination against women.

The expansion of opportunities for women were associated with continued technological change, the increasing use of electricity, and a revolution in labour-saving devices in the home, which helped to liberate married as well as single women (**O**). With smaller families, modern gadgets and easily prepared food, women could both go out to work and run a home.

O

Q (a) To what or whom is the woman in the cartoon speaking?

(b) How will the housework be done while she is out?

(c) Which domestic tasks are the pieces of equipment carrying out?

(d) How have modern gadgets assisted in expanding the opportunities for many women?

Equal opportunities?

1 The campaigns for women's rights were led, mainly, by middle-class women and it was to this class that the main benefits came.

2 Women have made great advances in education, employment, politics and within the family.

3 However, women have not yet achieved full equality of opportunity.

4 Up to the age of 16 girls do as well as boys at school, yet fewer girls continue to 'A' level and higher education.

5 The number of female MPs in 1945 was 24; in the 1983 General Election only 23 out of the 650 members returned were female.

6 Margaret Thatcher became Britain's first woman Prime Minister in 1979, but there have been very few female cabinet ministers.

QUESTIONS

1 Copy and complete the following passage by selecting the correct words from the list opposite. (NB: there are more words and dates than spaces to be filled.)

In 1903 _____ and her daughter _____ broke away from the _____ to form the _____ in order to fight for women's suffrage. In 1905 two suffragettes _____ and _____ were arrested for heckling at a political meeting held in _____ . The _____ government opposed the campaign which became more violent. In 1913 a leading suffragette _____ threw herself in front of the King's horse at the _____ and was killed. When arrested and imprisoned the _____ suffragettes refused to _____ . They were then _____ . To deal with the _____ the Government passed the _____ Act.

   When the First World War broke out the suffragettes _____ their campaign of violence and supported the war effort. In 1918 the _____ Act gave the vote to adult males over the age of _____ and to women over _____ who were householders or married to householders. In _____ women were allowed to vote at 21.

   After 1945 a number of Acts were passed which tried to provide equal opportunities, in particular the Equal _____ Act of 1969.

Christabel	1930
Emily Davison	1928
Lady Astor	drink
Sylvia Pankhurst	wear prison
Christabel Pankhurst	clothes
Emmeline Pankhurst	forcibly fed
National Union of Women's	hunger strikers
Suffrage Societies	Cat and Canary
W.S.P.U.	Cat and Mouse
moderate	intensified
militant	abandoned
Representation of the People	25
pay	21
Annie Kenney	30
Birmingham	35
Manchester	
Conservative	
Labour	
Liberal	
Grand National	
Derby	
eat	

2 **Essay topic:**
  How has the position of women in society improved in the twentieth century? Explain why these changes have taken place.

32 Britain and the European Economic Community

The foundation and growth of the European Economic Community (EEC) or Common Market has been one of the most significant developments of recent years. The history of the EEC has been marked by a number of controversies (disputes), not least the arguments over Britain's application for entry, and its membership.

■ The Community is formed

The first proposals

At the end of the Second World War, Europe was largely in ruins. Industry was almost at a standstill and there were many trade barriers between the countries. The British Prime Minister, Winston Churchill, called for the setting up of a 'United States of Europe' but the idea was not taken up at that time.

An important step in the close co-operation of the European countries was the European Recovery Programme which was established in 1948 as the Organization for European Economic Co-operation (OEEC). The OEEC was formed by the countries receiving economic aid from the USA under a plan known as Marshall Aid or the Marshall Plan, after George C. Marshall, the American Secretary of State.

The European Coal and Steel Community, 1952

France, Germany, Italy, Belgium, Netherlands and Luxemburg joined together under the Treaty of Paris to form the European Coal and Steel Community (ECSC). The ECSC was set up to control production and prices of coal, iron and steel, and to make these industries more efficient. The six countries established a 'Common Market' in which coal, iron and steel could be sold to consumers in the Community without any trade barriers.

The experiment proved successful. Between them the six countries had a market of 170 million consumers and the products covered by the agreement accounted for 25 per cent of their total trade. Output increased and the six countries decided to unite even more closely.

The Treaty of Rome, 1957

The Treaty of Rome, signed by France, Germany, Italy, Belgium, Netherlands and Luxemburg, formally set up the European Economic Community or Common Market. Members of the EEC were to work together to expand trade and the production of all products; to reduce competition within the Common Market; to agree on the purchase of each other's products; to fix targets for agricultural products and prices; and to co-operate on transport regulations, investment, working conditions and social services. To achieve their aims, the six countries agreed to abolish tariffs among themselves and to set up a customs union. In addition, a common tariff was to be imposed on trade with countries outside the European Economic Community.

To share the high costs of atomic energy development for peaceful uses, the six countries also united in the European Atomic Energy Community (Euratom).

Why did Britain not join the EEC in 1957?

In the 1950s Britain proposed setting up a customs union with a wide 'free trade area' which did not impose external tariffs. This proposal was rejected. Britain was therefore concerned that EEC membership might affect its trade with the Commonwealth. Britain also wanted to exclude trade in agricultural products from any agreements.

Britain started negotiations with a number of Western European countries which eventually led to the formation of the European Free Trade Area (EFTA) in 1960. Unlike the EEC, the countries in EFTA only intended to co-operate in the trading of certain products (**A** and **B**).

Changing British attitudes

When it was seen that the EEC was prospering, Britain's attitude began to change. In addition,

Q (a) The stamps shown in source **A** were issued to commemorate the setting up of EFTA. What do the letters EFTA stand for?

(b) In what ways does the design of source **A** show the purpose of EFTA?

(c) Source **A** shows the flags of the seven original member countries, and one later associate member. Identify the flags marked 1–8 (the map will help you) then copy and complete the chart below.

Flag number	Country	Flag design (to be drawn)
1	United Kingdom	
2	(to be	completed)

the issue of Commonwealth trade declined in importance as more and more countries became independent of Britain. Britain therefore decided to apply for membership.

■ Britain's application for membership

Britain's attempts to join the EEC

In 1960, and again in 1967, Britain applied for membership of the EEC. Although five of the six countries agreed, the Government of France under President De Gaulle vetoed (rejected) the proposals. Many Europeans, particularly in France, believed that **Britain was too dependent on the USA** and were not convinced that the British people were totally in favour of member-ship. In 1969 there was a change of political leadership in France and the new Government was willing to consider Britain's case for membership of the Common Market more favourably.

QUESTIONS

Use these photo-fit illustrations to help explain the four cartoons.

Charles
De Gaulle

Konrad
Adenauer

Harold
Macmillan

Harold
Wilson

Edward
Heath

Roy
Jenkins

1 Cartoon I: Britain's application 1960–1;
Scene: The Directors' Office of the EEC Club

(a) Who are the two EEC leaders (directors) and which countries do they represent?

(b) What evidence can you find that the EEC 'club' is doing well?

(c) Which British politician is holding the football?

(d) Why has he come to see the directors of the EEC club?

(e) Does the British politician look hopeful of joining the EEC club?

(f) British public opinion was not all in favour of the application to join the EEC. How does the cartoonist show that the British politician may have difficulty in transferring to the EEC club?

(g) Which other country is shown looking on? What kind of football did that country play?

"AH, I HEAR YOU WANT TO JOIN OUR CLUB AND PLAY FOR EUROPE. AFTER ALL . . ."

I *From the* Evening Standard, *4 May 1961*

J *From* Punch, *1962*

2 Cartoon J: Britain is refused entry;
Scene: From an old fairy tale

(a) Which fairy tale is the cartoon based on?

(b) Which parts are played by President de Gaulle of France and Chancellor Adenauer of West Germany?

(c) Who is holding the Common Market ticket?

(d) Why has the cartoonist shown them as 'the ugly sisters'?

(e) What part is being played by the British politician, and who is he?

(f) Who is preventing him going to the 'Common Market Ball'?

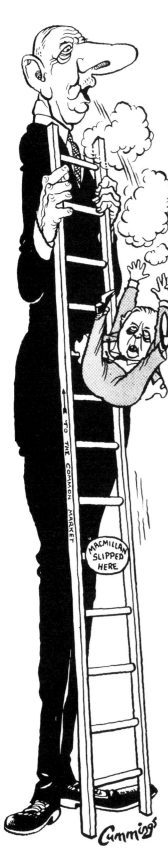

3 Cartoon K: Britain's attempt to join the EEC in 1967
(a) Which EEC leader is holding the ladder?
(b) Where does the ladder lead?
(c) Which British politician had fallen off the ladder in the early 1960s?
(d) Which British politician climbed higher up the ladder in 1967? Why did he fall off?

K *From the* Daily Express, *1967*

4 Cartoon L: Britain joins the EEC;
Scene: A marriage
(a) Between which two parties has a marriage been arranged?
(b) What is the 'bride' dressed in, and which country does she represent?
(c) Is she eager or reluctant to join with 'Mr Europe'?
(d) Which two British politicians are dressed as the bride's parents?
(e) Where is the marriage shown to be taking place?
(f) Can you explain why those inside 'Church of St. Parliament' were divided between the bride's friends (those reluctant to join) and the bridegroom's friends (those who favoured Britain's entry)?

L *From the* Daily Express, *1971*

"My dear! One doesn't marry for LOVE! One makes a GOOD marriage arranged by one's parents who know best!"

What were the arguments against Britain's entry into the EEC?

Some opponents of membership argued that Britain would lose some of its independence. It was argued that Britain should rely on its connections with the Commonwealth rather than go into Europe. It was also felt that Common Market membership would weaken Britain's special relationship with the USA.

Some industrialists were worried about the likely increase in competition both from within and outside the Common Market. It was argued that the Common Agricultural Policy of the EEC would restrict what could be produced by British farmers. British farming was generally believed to be more efficient than that of the Common Market countries so that entry would mean Britain subsidising inefficient European agriculture. In addition, Britain imported cheap food such as butter and dairy products from New Zealand, wheat and grain from Australia and Canada, and sugar from the West Indies. However, membership of the Common Market would mean the imposition of external tariffs in trade with non-member countries, which could lead to higher food prices in Britain. Each year Britain would also be required to pay a considerable sum of money to the Common Market budget.

What were the arguments in favour of Britain's entry to the EEC?

Supporters of Britain's application for entry to the EEC pointed out that Commonwealth trade with Britain was growing only very slowly. In contrast, Britain's trade with the Common Market, and with EFTA, was growing rapidly. Nor would the special Anglo-American relationship be damaged, for the USA wanted Britain to play a full role in a strong western Europe.

Many British manufacturers expected to benefit from a larger market, particularly those who conducted their businesses efficiently and could compete effectively. Therefore, although food prices might increase, Britain would be able to afford the rises because the wages of an expanding industrial workforce would be higher. In addition, it was argued that British workers would have greater opportunities to look for work in the Common Market countries.

■ British membership of the EEC

Britain joins the EEC

In 1972, Britain left EFTA and, together with Ireland and Denmark, joined the EEC. There was still some opposition in Britain both to joining the Common Market and to the terms of entry.

Britain achieved membership of the EEC during the term of office of Edward Heath, the Conservative Prime Minister. When the Labour Government was returned to office in 1974 it promised to improve the terms agreed on entry, and to consult the whole of the British people on whether or not to continue membership. When re-negotiations were completed in 1975 it was decided to hold a referendum (a ballot in which voters are asked to answer 'yes' or 'no' to a specific question) in which 67 per cent of those who voted were in favour of Britain remaining in the Common Market.

Problems of Britain and the EEC in the 1970s and 1980s

Controversy continued after Britain's entry, for example over the amount that Britain should contribute to the Common Market budget. The policies and practices of the Common Agricultural Policy also caused concern on the grounds that it encouraged inefficient farming; that it kept food prices high; and that it led to the creation of large farming surpluses, like the so-called 'butter mountain' and 'wine lake'.

Unfortunately, Britain joined the Common Market shortly before the occurrence of severe economic setbacks. These were partly due to the international oil crisis and, for a period of time, the oil and energy crisis posed a threat to the very existence of the EEC.

A changing market

Although the Common Market has built up a framework of institutions, the hopes of the founder members for closer political union of the member countries, have not been realized. Nevertheless, the character of the Common Market has changed with the addition of new members, most recently Greece, Portugal and Spain.

Index